AGGRESSIVE FICTIONS

AGGRESSIVE FICTIONS

Reading the Contemporary American Novel

KATHRYN HUME

CORNELL UNIVERSITY PRESS
ITHACA AND LONDON

First published 2012 by Cornell University Press
Printed in the United States of America

Library of Congress Cataloging-in-Publication Data

Hume, Kathryn, 1945–
    Aggressive fictions : reading the contemporary American novel / Kathryn Hume.
        p. cm.
    Includes bibliographical references and index.
    ISBN 978-0-8014-5001-3 (cloth : alk. paper)
    1. Aggressiveness in literature.   2. American fiction—20th century—History and criticism.   3. American fiction—21st century—History and criticism.   4. Aversion in literature.   I. Title.
    PS374.A38H86   2012
    813'.5409—dc23   2011022561

Cornell University Press strives to use environmentally responsible suppliers and materials to the fullest extent possible in the publishing of its books. Such materials include vegetable-based, low-VOC inks and acid-free papers that are recycled, totally chlorine-free, or partly composed of nonwood fibers. For further information, visit our website at www.cornellpress.cornell.edu.

Cloth printing   10 9 8 7 6 5 4 3 2 1

For Robert D. Hume

Contents

PREFACE

Anyone who has read much serious American fiction published since around 1970 has surely struggled with novels that seem designed *not* to give readers pleasure. Not only do writers scream in your ear, but they do the mental equivalent of pissing on your shoes, holding a knife to your throat, or spouting nuclear physics at you as well. A surprising amount of the fiction makes readers feel attacked or abused by an author who seems hostile. Why would authors write such aggressively off-putting novels when all evidence points to the fact that the reading public is increasingly enticed away by the visual media now available 24/7? Furthermore, why risk alienating middle-class readers, who constitute most of the book-buying public?

And what about us, the readers? Why do we read novels that make us feel so unwelcome? Are we conditioned by our predominant religious heritage to think that if something is unpleasant and accusatory, it must somehow be good for us? Or is it that we as readers enjoy rejecting that heritage and embracing what we are told is bad for us? In short, what are the rewards for persisting with a book we find so difficult to enjoy, and is there a way to make the unpleasantness worth the effort?

This book is exploratory. It grows out of these questions, which I have asked myself many, many times. Frankly, I have no grand models for answering them. High theory has its own answers for the why of narrative fragmentation, the rejection of meaning, the destruction of genre, and the reduction of characters to non-psychological, non-unified conventions. If fiction is to be read by other than academics, however, it needs to offer something of value to intelligent but nonprofessional readers who come with expectations based on more conventional fiction. Those readers need tactics for approaching unfriendly novels, and so do students in the classroom. This book pursues these questions and tactics.

Here are some of the kinds of attacks that we may encounter when reading what I like to call "user-unfriendly fiction." William S. Burroughs famously cut typescript pages up the middle and taped pieces together randomly; this let him project paranoia very effectively, but it also left the reader feeling that meaning lies under the surface, just beyond one's grasp. Bret Easton Ellis and Brian Evenson depict gruesome dismemberments, while Samuel R. Delany vividly describes chewing and swallowing a fresh human turd. Or take a different kind of attack. Ruth L. Ozeki, in an attractive-seeming novel full of both pleasurable humor and instructional data, leads us carefully through her argument that American agribusiness meat endangers all who produce or eat it, and then drops these intractable social, ecological, and economic problems on our plates without suggesting any hope for a solution. On one level we may enjoy the book, and yet we may also end up wishing we had not read it. Some authors—most notably Mark Leyner and Ishmael Reed—glory in the rapid multiplication of events, giving us the sensation of speeding. This form of narrative denies readers explanations and connectives and leaves them floundering because they cannot quite stitch things together. Instead of multiplying events, Mark Z. Danielewski multiplies levels of narrative and conjoins these to a physically impossible house until our usual ability to identify what is fictively true fails us. As if these were not obstacles enough for the reader, some writers (think of Cormac McCarthy and Chuck Palahniuk) exhibit despair about our future, which only adds gloom to our discomfort.

Aggressive fiction of this sort is not the only serious literature one finds in bookstores. The novels I discussed in my earlier book *American Dream,*

American Nightmare: Fiction since 1960 were written to persuade as many readers as possible that they should rethink their complacent assumptions about the United States. Communication is critical to persuasion, so most of the novels were traditional—not necessarily realist, but they tended to be character-oriented, and they mostly concerned the suffering and experience of people-like characters. Leslie Marmon Silko's *Ceremony* might please the non–Native American reader with elements of the supernatural, but overall, readers are drawn to sympathize with Tayo as a person, feel outraged when his cattle are stolen, and rejoice in his grounding himself in tribal life and its realities. Readers were expected to learn through sympathy and shared human feelings. While the authors were angry at America, they mostly still believed that something better might be achieved. T. Coraghessan Boyle's *World's End,* Saul Bellow's *Dean's December,* William Kennedy's Albany series, Richard Brautigan's *Sombrero Fallout,* and Carolyn Chute's *The Beans of Egypt, Maine* all show much that is very wrong with American society, but they retain some sense of awe at the immense energy and potential of the country, or at the very least, they still believe in people and the right of the oppressed to something better. These writers may have been sick at heart and uncertain how to bring about improvements, but most of them seemed to feel that improvement was still possible. Most of the novels covered in this book are more hostile to America, or to capitalism, or to Western civilization. Moreover, the writers do not seem to value direct communication and careful persuasion, leaving their readers to do much of the interpretive work on their own.

I come to this book as a professional amateur. I trained as a medievalist and slid into contemporary fiction by way of fascination with Calvino and Pynchon. I approached what I read with the untutored joy possible when one has not taken courses in something, when one has not had official narratives imposed on one's responses. While the later twentieth and early twenty-first centuries offer much fiction that I can enjoy unreservedly, their major figures kept challenging me with books that I did not relish reading. But I wasn't willing to give up so easily. At first I could not imagine why anyone would read Burroughs or Kathy Acker, but I worked at it until I got some inkling of their attractions and rewards. While I must confess that I gravitate to the more orderly mythical and metaphysical elements in fiction, I continue to probe the disorderly, resistant, and chaotic. I want to understand the appeal.

My way into this fiction might have been smoother had I been more of a moviegoer. A friend of mine insists that all the techniques I discuss in this book appear in film, usually somewhat before they appear in fiction, and that seems plausible. To take an example, the quick cutting associated with 1960s directors like Sam Peckinpah undoubtedly influenced, directly or indirectly, the flash-flash-flash effects of Ishmael Reed and Mark Leyner (as did channel surfing and animated cartoons). Given the speed with which contemporary films reach a global audience, one can only assume that many of the destabilizing techniques found in recent movies made their way very quickly into fiction.

I recognize that the phenomenon I am describing here is not necessarily original to America, nor is it limited to America. The robust avant-garde and surrealist tradition in France and various Latin American countries encouraged ready acceptance of estranging elements. Use of such techniques by American writers, however, is especially interesting to me because it goes against the literary mainstream. It is intriguing to consider why this is so. Our Puritan tradition must surely be part of the answer. Consider the outrage when *American Psycho* was published in 1991. Another culprit is certainly our worship of practicality and efficiency. Fiction that strays too far from "real life" seems impractical—impracticality being one of the grounds on which we commonly disparage fantasy. Many different kinds of books could be written on the phenomenon of user-unfriendly fiction, but mine focuses on American novels because, frankly, I am fascinated by these novels and the ways in which they attack America, American readers, and American mindsets.

Because I am dealing not with a genre but rather with a broad array of books that feature highly varied forms of challenge to reader comfort, I offer many partial answers to the questions I have raised here. Unfriendliness toward readers takes numerous forms; so do the reasons why readers persist in buying and reading these books. Some of the reasons are more or less traditional: expanding personal horizons, reconsidering norms and values, rethinking familiar history we learned in the classroom. Other, less traditional reasons can also be found. Reader response theory tells us that we gain pleasure from learning to appreciate something that is initially baffling to us, or that we feel good about increasing our literary competence. There is also a moral element. Even when characters repel us, their defects may permit us to enjoy a pleasant sense of superiority.

In the chapters that follow I argue for what I take to be to be an underrecognized aesthetic. When we read such books, we are being pushed to submit and surrender to author and text, to accept the experience and not try to control the text or impose our own meaning and values on it. The message may even be that we should not expect meaning. This can take different forms. Acker, Burroughs, Evenson, Donald Antrim, and Danielewski all leave us feeling that no reasonably secure interpretation is possible. Andrea Dworkin and William Kotzwinkle, in contrast, refuse us any leeway in interpretation. We must either swallow their argument or put down the book dissatisfied, for we are given no freedom to rethink their evidence. Both approaches are anti-hermeneutic, and this aesthetic encourages a kind of reader masochism. I raise the possibility that we are meant to find pleasure in this surrender of the impulse to control and conquer the text through our own mental engagement with it. Opening ourselves to a work has always involved some element of surrender, but to a surprising degree much recent fiction seems to demand that we submit unconditionally. But should we?

ACKNOWLEDGMENTS

A version of chapter 1, on narrative speed, appeared in somewhat different form as "Narrative Speed in Contemporary Fiction," *Narrative* 13.2 (2005): 105–24, with a follow-up, "Speed, Rhythm, Movement: A Dialogue on K. Hume's Article 'Narrative Speed,'" with Jan Baetens, *Narrative* 14.3 (2006): 349–55. Copyright (2005) The Ohio State University. Reproduced with permission.

My gratitude to David Cowart, Jeffrey Gonzalez, Brian McHale, Ashley Marshall, Sean Moiles, and Linda Woodbridge for reading all or part of this book in manuscript. Peter Potter, editor in chief at Cornell University Press, was exceptionally helpful in identifying places where I could improve my argument. My thanks, as always, to Robert D. Hume, for reading the manuscript many times, and for helping me rethink my stances.

INTRODUCTION

The Author-Reader Contract

Wordsworth could startle his readers by writing about a leech-gatherer; how could such a person or activity qualify for aesthetic appreciation? Faulkner trampled even more forcefully on reader expectations when *The Sound and the Fury* commenced with an idiot's version of events. Both works are now canonical. The same conversion will happen for many of the novels discussed in this book, but they resist being naturalized into tradition. They not only attack the literary expectations specific to their time but also break a very old contract between reader and author, and do so in ways that demand new motives for reading.

Horace opined that poetry, and by extension all fiction, is properly *dulce* (entertaining) and *utile* (useful, informative), and his formulation has stood the test of two millennia.[1] Why should we spend our free time reading if we get neither pleasure nor useful information or insight? Other elements that help a work fit into the literary tradition are its relative emphases on action, character, or idea (elements identified by Aristotle). Genre, likewise, makes a new work assimilable. Action or interesting characters offer entertainment, while idea introduces us to new ways of thinking. Genre sanctions particular twists and turns of plot. Expectations adhere to each genre, and gratifying those expectations is one of the ways that fiction gives us a sense of meaning.

For a surprising number of recent American novels, this long-standing author-reader contract has been broken. Modernist fiction ostensibly rejected that author-reader relationship, yet initial bafflement or indignation caused by Joyce, Faulkner, and others faded because our readerly drive to solve puzzles succeeded. In general, if not always in each particular work, what initially seemed like jagged pieces proved to fit into a relatively coherent and therefore satisfying picture. The authors of the more aggressive novels considered here not only refuse to give us a coherent picture but also tend to abandon the generic patterns of plot and closure, and thus deny us relief and enjoyment.

Why should we keep reading when novelists strive to undermine our values, push gross unpleasantness in our face, omit connectives and explanations that would help us understand, reduce characters to placeholders, and fail to come to any resolution? These authors presumably know that they endanger their chances of attracting any readership beyond a coterie of like-minded fans, so what alternative inducements are they offering a larger audience to keep reading? Let's look at it from the audience perspective: If reading is not to be pure misery, what can readers do to make themselves more receptive?

Before we look at a range of recent novels that have abrogated the traditional contract, consider briefly the Horatian basis of that relationship. His sweetness refers to the elements in the reading experience that give pleasure. Pleasure mostly involves reinforcing values that make us feel good about ourselves. Entertainment is another word used for what gives pleasure, but entertainment tends to be passive, even escapist. Entertainment helps us formulate wishes and gratify them vicariously. Pleasure includes that gratification, but it can also involve active participation from the readers. Pleasure derives from the mental activities of the reader while reading, from plot- or content-oriented features, from overall aesthetics, and from the engaging side of instruction, as opposed to straight preaching.

Pleasure deriving from active reading takes at least two forms. One comes from readers exercising their skills of interpretation, and feeling that they have been successful with a particular work. This kind of pleasure can be aesthetic and psychological. Peter J. Rabinowitz sees both in the process by which the actual reader adapts enough to the text to become more like the author's posited reader.[2] Susan L. Feagin argues that pleasure comes from exercising one's ability to *appreciate* the text.[3] Responding appropriately to a work of art is not something that everyone has the ability to do for every aesthetic creation. When a novel leaves us cold, it may have failed us, but we may also have failed to open ourselves in the right fashion. We feel good about ourselves when we do appreciate something, particularly when what it offers is neither easy to like nor obvious. The challenge posed by fiction that undermines our assumptions can repay highly skilled readers with pleasure, but that reward may be out of reach for much of the reading public. Lisa Zunshine and Norman N. Holland feel that we derive pleasure from psychological sources. Zunshine argues that we read because we are always testing and exercising our "theory of mind" as we mentally analyze and predict characters' behavior.[4] Holland posits that our interpretations reflect our own individual mental patterns, and that we find pleasure in unconsciously imposing our inner template on an artistic work and then "discovering" our pattern in something external to us.[5]

Deriving even these pleasures from fiction does require some compatibility between that fiction and reader expectations. Understanding the mentality of characters works better for fiction that has characters than it does for fragmented foci with changing names and genders. The pleasure of impressing our mental pattern on a text is available only if we like the novel enough to read it through and think that we understand the text well enough to identify pattern.

Pleasure and enjoyment also come from plot- and content-oriented features—action and character and how they are deployed according to generic conventions. At a simple human level, we enjoy the success and happiness of sympathetic characters—the traditional happy ending in which lovers marry and family members or friends are reunited. Unless they are dismissive Marxists or feminists, most readers enjoy the ending of Jane Austen's *Pride and Prejudice*. Similarly, we can feel good about the "rightness" of an action or end, even if it seems tragic: *In the Time of the Butterflies* tells how three of the four Mirabal sisters die martyrs to the Trujillo dictatorship, but we nonetheless enjoy their story as Julia Alvarez tells it. We can be pleased by the moral rightness of an outcome: the Odyssean return of Francis Phelan in William Kennedy's *Ironweed* signals that he has done penance enough. Whether Francis dies in the last mystic passage or lives on does not matter. He has reached such peace in his life as he can. Genre and experience let us anticipate certain kinds of endings, and when we get an appropriate outcome, we feel gratified.

Frank Kermode describes plots as *ticks* that demand *tocks,* and with a suitable tock to resolve the plot, we feel a release of tensions.[6] Jonathan Lethem achieves such a resolution for his *Motherless Brooklyn;* his narrator, who suffers from Tourette's syndrome, solves the mystery (as is appropriate to the genre), preserves the limo-and-detective company, and frees it from ties to organized crime, all the while engaging in situations that embody the hero monomyth. A variant on this teleological pleasure comes when the ending pleases us in a more philosophical fashion: a reader's wish to live a more eco-sensitive life can be stimulated by reading Ernest Callenbach's *Ecotopia Emerging.* The pleasures of seeing how this lower-tech world might be achieved in real life differ from enjoying "They lived happily ever after," if only because the density of data and ideas differs from happy feelings that come from simple identification. Much utopian writing would fit into this category. Let these suffice to exemplify kinds of pleasurable endings; many more kinds exist.[7]

At least two instruction-related features give us a means of feeling pleasure. One is confirmation of some idea, belief, or ideology that we hold dear. A Christian will feel good about an ending that confirms faith or about a plot that details the struggle to lead a religious life in our secular society, as evidenced by the followings of C. S. Lewis and Marilynne Robinson. We may also feel exhilarated if the book introduces us to some new idea or philosophy or process that seems worth exploring or adopting. I have no idea how scientifically plausible Kim Stanley Robinson's Mars trilogy may be, but as a template for trying to colonize another planet in this solar system, it offers tremendous food for political thought. Varied and attractive though these and other literary pleasures may be, few such rewards are found in this unfriendly strain of recent fiction.

Instruction seems to me less varied and more obvious. The book can launch an overtly political, ethical, or philosophical argument, or showcase a debate on such subjects. Here we come to Aristotle's plot that exists to present thought or idea. Thomas Mann's *Magic Mountain,* Doris Lessing's *Canopus in Argos* series, and Saul Bellow's *The Dean's December* come to mind as exemplary. Bellow questions the nature of evil as it manifests itself from the trenches of World War I to Chicago's ghetto conditions for African American inhabitants; he also probes the pattern of oppression in a communist country, trying to see whether capitalism or communism seems morally preferable from the perspective of those who are oppressed. As when reading utopian and dystopian literature, which is always idea-centered, readers must possess a high tolerance for discussion (or preaching). Unless they are completely unwilling to listen to the sermon, they may enjoy the ideas. Other ways of seeing pleasure in instruction relate to kinds of pleasure mentioned earlier: gratification at moral rightness, enjoyment of a new argument. The more one feels converted by a book to its intellectual position, the more pleasure one is likely derive from its instruction, since conversion makes one feel superior to one's past self.

Much of our pleasure and instruction come from plot and from our tendency to identify with characters. Identification is a crude concept, but Susan Feagin has parsed it elaborately and convincingly into such elements as mental simulation, sympathy, and empathy. In discussing the grotesque, Leonard Cassuto points to the hardwired human tendency to anthropomorphize anything remotely human, and that applies to characters, even when very thinly constructed.[8] Raymond Federman speaks of such non-rounded characters as "word-beings" and approvingly mentions Italo Calvino's Qfwfq, a being without fixed body or location in space or time.[9] Some word-beings never engage us, but however fantastic Qfwfq may be, we can sympathize (or feel impatient) because he mostly broadcasts simple, even childish longings for various manifestations of the female in the universe. He is an emotional being, and we respond to expression of recognizable feelings. Our mental reactions to what even nonrealistic characters do may only weakly simulate what we would feel toward actual people, but that simulation is enough to trigger some kind of emotional response.

Both the elements of fiction that produce a sense of pleasure and the channels through which they work continued to function into the modernist period, but they lost favor with writers. *Ulysses* and *The Sound and the Fury* struck early readers as very aggressive and unfriendly. To begin with, those books seemed to lack the obvious rewards for reading, though in retrospect we can see that they still offer character and some sense of an ending. The feeling of being attacked by authors hostile to reader desires eventually lessened as readers learned to cope with the new complexities. Understanding Benjy's section in light of later information gives our minds the kind of pleasurable workout that Lisa Zunshine attributes to the finish of a detective story, and as Brian McHale notes, "the detective story is the epistemological genre *par excellence*,"[10] and epistemology is the dominant of modernism, even as ontology characterizes postmodernism.

Postmodern fragmentation is more difficult to piece together. We may enjoy picking at the puzzles embedded in *Gravity's Rainbow,* but its pieces truly do not all go together; some bits contradict others. That novel does teach us about corners of history we may not have known about, so we can enjoy the instruction because we feel better about ourselves for mastering such arcana. We are even less likely to feel that a novel by Kathy Acker or William S. Burroughs can be explained down to the last detail or fitted into a recognizable plot sequence. We can enjoy trying to identify what "paradigms for understanding reality" these authors offer us, but are unlikely to emerge feeling that we have made any such text truly our own.[11]

With the experimentalism of the 1950s, 1960s, and 1970s, and to some extent with postmodern fiction in general, many authors ceased to foreground either plot or character. Some experimentalists were actively hostile to traditional elements. John Hawkes declared that "the true enemies of the novel were plot, character, setting, and theme."[12] Raymond Federman and Ronald Sukenick seem equally eager to cancel the author-reader contract by jettisoning plot and character on essentially moral grounds. Sukenick claims that "reality doesn't exist, time doesn't exist, personality doesn't exist,"[13] so to pretend that they do for the sake of a story or a neat ending betrays life. In *Critifiction,* Federman says that "reality is but a fraudulent verbal network" and what will replace character is not a "man or a woman of a certain moment, it will be the language of humanity. Totally free, arbitrary, and disengaged, uncommitted to the affairs of the outside world to the same extent as the fictitious discourse in which it will exist, this creature will participate in the fiction only as a grammatical being (in some cases devoid of a pronominal referent)."[14] Well, philosophically, reality, time, and personality indeed may not exist. Richard Powers's *The Echo Maker* is devoted to abolishing personality or self as an entity. Nonetheless, I am reminded of the faith healer of Deal. "He said that though pain isn't real,/when I sit on a pin/and it punctures my skin,/I don't like what I fancy I feel." In theory, we may not be entities, but under most circumstances we feel that we are. The number of readers who will wander happily in Federman's theoretical world for the sake of arbitrary and uncommitted language is small. In fairness to Powers, he also shows us how strong our drive is to create a coherent self and world, no matter how fragmented either of them may have become through accident or disaster.

Do these books embody the experimentalism of the 1960s as a trickle-down effect? Yes, some experimental breakthroughs do gradually get co-opted, adapted, and subsumed into mainstream and even popular literature. My sense, however, is that political despair aimed at America is important for motivating this drive to bewilder and nauseate the reader. The estranging techniques abet this attack on reader sensibilities. For many of these writers, that despair is self-damaging; they almost certainly know that attacking readers' values and repelling the audience will turn those readers off and make them reject the book. Such writers cannot refrain from attack, though, because middle-class readers are part of the problem as they see it. The growth of the underclass, ecological degradation, our inhumanity to other humans on racial and gender grounds, or our inhumanity to animals: these problems degrade not only this country but the world and its possible future as well. For such writers, silence or friendly entertainment is not an option. Somehow these writers have faith enough in fiction to put their energy into producing it (rather, say, than film), yet they often must feel as if they were sawing off the limb they sit on. This self-damaging impulse is one of the puzzling but intriguing issues that arise when one tries to respond to the novels.

What remains after plot and character disappear, and with them the intellectual pleasures identified by Feagin and Zunshine as well as obvious story-listening pleasure? Idea remains. Furthermore, in these novels that fall somewhere between the traditional and the radically experimental, we find that something else remaining that is not exactly covered by conventional assumptions. Emotion remains. Emotion can be projected and manipulated by characters so nondeveloped that one would not expect them to exert much pull on readers. Kathy Acker can destroy conventional character, yet her word-beings can and do emit pain, outrage, and anger at high intensity. Robert Coover can give us fifty or more characters in *John's Wife,* none such that we might wish to identify with them and very few who garner sympathy. Perhaps because of this lack of fellow feeling, he can provoke disgust at their endless patterned interactions, their bondage to their past and to the structures of a small town. Both expressing and provoking emotion remain possible.

No matter how strange the content of some novels, any book is likely to find some readers who happily batten on it. An author may please one group (say, an ethnic, racial, gender-oriented, political, or religious group) while outraging or repelling mainstream readers who do not happen to belong to that group. The fiction I discuss will seem unfriendly and difficult to assimilate for many readers, at least on first reading. It often batters us with material we do not wish to face. The response it demands is also unusual. Instead of striving to master the text, our more effective tactic is to surrender to it. We should open ourselves to the emotions, and eventually, after full exposure, we should think our way through its ideas. We are not to impose our own standards, at least at the beginning; we should experience rather than recoil or force a preexisting framework on such aggressive fiction.

Since I shall be talking a lot about "aggressive" fiction and "attacking the reader," I should define what I mean by these words. Aggressive fiction tramples reader sensibilities, offends and upsets willfully and deliberately. The authors discussed may partly address themselves to a coterie audience of kindred spirits who revel in the subject matter and stylistic extremism. Most writers, though, also hope their novels will be read by a wider public, many of whose members will be upset by this sort of fiction. Given the profile of those who buy books or read them in the university, that group is mostly middle class. To talk about attacking readers is shorthand for attacking their society's economic structure, their class beliefs, lifestyle, philosophy, and literary expectations. Attack has the effect of *making ordinarily competent readers wish to stop reading*. By ordinarily competent, I mean people who do read nonformulaic fiction for pleasure. The term "attack" might also be applied to the element that *makes those who did read a book wish they had not*. They regret the emotional aftermath, and feel unpleasantly haunted by the images and information they ingested. They may acknowledge the information to be true, but admit they would be more comfortable if they had never stumbled across this exposition of the full enormity of the problem, be it the frantic pace of computerized life, gruesome slaughters present and past, or the unsavory but probably irreversible practices of American food production. Some of these writers long for revolution but know historically that most revolutions just transfer power to other hands and create new tyrannies. We are at a tipping point, culturally speaking, but see no action that is feasible and could be counted on to produce genuine improvements. Writers who feel this evidently wish to force others to share their anguish.

An author's trying to destroy reader comfort may result in the reader's feeling five basic emotions: frustration, revulsion, irritation, discomfiture, and anxiety. Aggressive fiction aims both to upset the reader's beliefs and to disturb that reader's comfortable confidence in the reading process. Whereas conventional fiction reinforces cultural norms, this fiction tends to consider those norms evil or idiotic and works to undercut the reader complacence that rests on those common beliefs.

An author who attacks may do so with varying levels of seriousness. For some writers, half of their mission is performative, and they revel in producing fireworks as well as in arousing discomfort. Some make their attack satiric, which gives the reader a chance to identify with the author's position rather than absorb the attack personally. Some focus on more literary issues of textuality, others on political or spiritual issues. Some go for the jugular and mean to make the reader squirm; these mostly work from a position of moral righteousness and have no respect for the middle-class values of the readers. They genuinely want revolution.

When faced with an aggressive novel, a reader may wish to stop reading for many reasons. The text seems too difficult and returns too little reward for the effort involved, as can happen with fast narrative speed or formally avant-garde fictions. The reader does not like the feeling of being unable to follow the text and hence of having lost control of it. The subject matter may cause unease or distress at mental or physical levels. Listening to complaint can be supremely irritating, and if the complaint consists of a long exposé of some cultural practice (such as the treatment of lab animals) or political stance (capitalism), this will be felt as an attack on reader belief if the reader has preferred to accept the practice rather than acknowledge its debatable morality and try to break free from it. Even if readers agree with the excoriation, they may wince a bit because they know they have no plans to change their lifestyles or even to go out and demonstrate against the use of lab animals, and they have no idea where or how to protest the nature of corporate power. Grotesque bodies undermine our comfort at very primitive psychological levels by rousing irrational fears of contagion. Grotesque situations, with their combination of horror and laughter, cause a contradictory and indecorous combination of emotions that upsets us by its feeling wrong or inappropriate. Vivid descriptions of rape, dismemberment, and torture can upset us through fear and even nausea. Even if only mildly successful, attacking our assumptions about the nature of reality destroys our assurance in everyday transactions and thus provokes anxiety. While the author's coterie audience may cheer at every exposure of evil capitalist practice and welcome all depictions of unpleasantness and pain, most readers cherish their own comfort of mind and body, and do not automatically welcome more anxiety into their lives.

Since most contemporary fiction that is not purely traditional tends to feel aggressive, I could have identified the kinds of attack in any number of ways. Of the five I have chosen, two have an intellectual bent, while three are more emotional. Since intellectual distress is also an emotion, however, these are not absolute distinctions. The first, what I call *narrative speed,* is characterized by technique, and I would call it intellectual in that it undermines our ability to interpret. Writers creating this effect of speed do so by cutting connective tissue, motives, explanations, and descriptions, all the material that provides substance and subtlety to traditional fiction and explains the logic behind plot. What they do technically can be more complex than that, but in simple terms, they deliberately feed us inadequate information for our interpretive techniques to work. Their action whizzes by seemingly too fast for us to catch the detail. Speed is by no means completely negative; it also provides an emotional rush, and cultural logic suggests that younger readers will respond more positively, given that speed characterizes some of their pleasures—rap, music mixing, and channel surfing, not to mention drug rushes. Overall, though, speed often produces insecurity for readers who wish to understand, and it undermines the pleasures normally derived from mastering a traditional text. Authors who work in this vein include Ishmael Reed, Mark Leyner, and William S. Burroughs.

The next three modes of challenging reader assumptions work with intensifying strength on reader emotions and even on physical, gut reactions. The exemplifying fictions exhibit *complaint, the grotesque,* and *extreme sex and violence.* With increasing strength, these force unpleasantness at us. Through their manipulation of our emotions, they also push us to think through the issues generating those emotions. Among the authors who complain, Philip Roth and Andrea Dworkin raise cultural and gender issues, while Ruth Ozeki calls attention to the treatment of animals. Grotesquerie makes us flinch as boundaries we rely on disappear, and all our ways of defining what it means to be human seem to dissolve or rot away, leaving us unprotected against a threatening other, whether that be the deformed, the female, the animal, or the supernatural. Katherine Dunn, Chuck Palahniuk, Gerald Vizenor, and James Morrow supply some of my examples. The extremities of violence and exploitive sex often overlap with the grotesque, but for purposes of argument, I focus on the violence in Samuel Delany, Brian Evenson, and Bret Easton Ellis, among others. While these authors differ in the degree to which they use plot or character, they all rely heavily on emotions and ideas.

The final mode of undermining reader comfort returns, at least initially, to the conceptual and intellectual. This is the strategy of destabilizing our ontological certainties. Because Brian McHale has made that famous as a hallmark of postmodernism,[15] a great many books might be considered, but I have chosen examples that represent extreme cases by Mark Salzman, Mark Danielewski, and Thomas Pynchon. The books try to disturb us intellectually, and that naturally has an emotional effect.

Given the unpleasantness of some of these novels, or the novelists' despair of finding resolutions, or even just their manic glee in their own performance at the expense of reader comfort, I argue that we need to try to understand what rewards they offer that replace pleasure and instruction. Many fine books have been written about contemporary American fiction, but all that I have seen assume a sophisticated reader—an academic critic, a theorist, or an experimental writer.

Like me, Alan Wilde concentrates on the fiction that lies between the most traditional and the most experimental (or in his terms, the most reflexive). Listen, though, to how he talks about readers in *Middle Grounds:* "To be sure, this community of empathetic readers is no longer, if it ever was, naive. It includes, after all, not only readers of nineteenth-century fiction but those self-conscious, provoked, and battered readers of Cervantes, Scarron, Sterne, and Diderot—not to mention Borges, Cortázar, and the small armies of meta- and surfictionists doing battle once again with realism and its still hardy assumptions."[16] Perhaps he has given up all hope that anyone will read this fiction except academic readers, and sufficiently few English department readers know Scarron or Cortázar that one can really limit his reader pool to members of comparative literature departments. Reading of this sort resembles the sciences, something to be practiced only by licensed professionals in laboratory spaces. Other sophisticated, theoretically oriented commentators on America's experimental scene similarly assume highly trained readers. Gordon E. Slethaug supplies us with detailed analysis of chaos theory and systems theory, those being necessary in his analysis to understand, let alone appreciate, a good deal of experimental American fiction.[17] Critics including James Annesley, Elizabeth Young and Graham Caveney, John Johnston, and Fredric Jameson all assume considerable knowledge of and agreement with Marxist theories of late capitalism, and to that economic state they link the strange and estranging qualities of the fiction.[18] Marcel Cornis-Pope and Marc Chénetier have written extremely complex and imposing books on recent fiction.[19] Cornis-Pope finds deep authorial concern with changing the relationship between history and fiction, such that the fiction presents the local and particular, not grand narratives. Chénetier notes the explosion of genres and sees the novel itself dying and being replaced by fiction, a distinction that is useful to critics but probably means more to them than to most readers. His assumed reader is equipped to deal with avant-garde originality.

Many critics and experimental writers wish to open readers' minds to the falsities of and damaging political assumptions behind realist literature. That reason for violating traditional patterns may be justifiable, but it runs the risk of simply alienating readers and causing them to put down books exhibiting such antirealist assumptions. After all, such disgruntled readers can always turn to visual media; because actors are people, they produce an imitation of "real" life that provides something to hold to even if the film plot becomes chaotic. Federman may sarcastically say that readability is "what is instantly and clearly recognizable, and thus orients us, within ourselves and outside of ourselves, in the 'reality' of the world…and therefore gives us comfort— *the pleasure of easy recognition*." His calling unreadability "the agony of unrecognition" is not particularly sympathetic to the reader who is thus lost.[20] He cherishes Roland Barthes's distinction: the text of pleasure is the readable one; the text of bliss is the one that discomfits the reader on all levels, the experimental text. What provokes bliss in a Roland Barthes may not win many converts among the less sophisticated. Robert Alter put the problem well when he said, "We seem now, however, to run some danger of being directed by the theorists to read in a way that real readers, on land or sea, have never read. If one insists on seeing all novels as congeries of semiotic systems intricately functioning in a pure state of self-referentiality, one loses the fine edge of responsiveness to the urgent human predicaments that novels seek to articulate."[21]

One way to approach difficult texts is to call them experimental and figure that a few will succeed through some hard-to-define virtue that catches readerly attention. Jean-François Lyotard says that "if a work is strong (and we don't really know what we are saying by this) it will produce people to whom it is destined. It will elicit its own addressees."[22] Though undoubtedly true, that approach and attitude do little to broaden the audience or let in readers who are curious but not naturally attuned to whatever the inner strength may be. This problem of readability and of enjoyability is where I want to focus. I am evidently not the natural audience for such unfriendly fictions, but I would like to be able to read them with some confidence. Only after considerable struggle have I found some of these texts enjoyable. I wish to see what authors are doing that might draw readers. What hooks do they use to pull us in a desired direction, given the common reduction of characters to Federman's felicitously named "word-beings"? Why do we persist in reading if their endings rarely give us the relief of resolution, the plot-driven pleasure of expectations gratified? How can we best open ourselves to fiction that repels us? Professional readers may continue to derive their pleasures from their skill at appreciating a new aesthetic, and most critical books to date on recent nontraditional fiction assume the pleasures of professional reading. The value of the new rarely seems to be questioned. Why, though, should more ordinary readers keep reading? What is in this for them? Why should they submit to being mauled? And if they wish to read and understand, what tactics will help them approach a reader-unfriendly novel?

1

Narrative Speed in Contemporary Fiction

Many contemporary novels subject their readers to a breathless sense that the events are hurtling by too fast for real understanding. Scenes and focal figures change quickly, and helpful transitions are missing. The resultant feeling of excessive rapidity is what I mean by narrative speed, and for many readers, this speed produces frustration and serious discomfiture. This effect occurs so frequently in contemporary fiction, and its mechanics are so readily grasped, that it seems a good place to start investigating fiction that denies readers their expected comforts. The immediate lesson to be learned? Relax. Give up the assumption that you must control a text. Then, perhaps, you can enjoy it.

Why has speed become a commonplace in fiction? What effects do authors seek by using it? Why do they refuse to supply the connections and transitions that would help their readers? These questions confront readers of numerous recent novels, and they invite us to ask how one might best understand speed as a narrative technique and as a factor that makes readers feel rebuffed or even attacked. Narrative theory to date seems to offer relatively little insight into these problems. Critics have so far theorized pace (fast or slow) in just four basic fashions: (1) prose portrayal of physical speed; (2) narrative retardation; (3) the amount of story time covered per page; and (4) fictional reflections of cultural speed.

Critical concern with *portraying physical speed* focuses on the modernist fascination with the sensation of speed and how to represent it in painting, sculpture, and writing. This is only marginally relevant to the kind of frantic narrative I am trying to analyze, because narrative speed does not necessarily increase as one describes physical speed, though the two sometimes coincide. Thomas De Quincey's prose, for example, actually slows down as he attempts to catalog the sensations of fear provoked by a speeding mail coach. One significant connection between mechanical speed and prose speed has been helpfully analyzed by Stephen Kern.[1] In exploring the speed-up mechanisms of the modernist era—bicycle, telegraph, telephone, car, and film—he notes that reporters wired stories to their newspapers. He attributes to this practice the paring away of unnecessary words, the "telegraphic" style that gains recognition in the writing of Ernest Hemingway.[2]

A second way to theorize narrative pace—*retardation*—was propounded by Viktor Shklovsky. His approach was conditioned by his viewing folktales as growing from a kernel that could be rendered in a sentence or two. For them to become stories demanded ways of delaying. Likewise, many novels could be summarized in a paragraph. Shklovsky focuses on techniques for slowing down, and gives no thought to speeding up. Hence, for him, stories always consist of a string of delaying devices. He analyzes retarding techniques such as defamiliarization,[3] repetitious structures, and the framing of tales within tales. Even characters can function as delaying devices: Conan Doyle's Dr. Watson, he avers, exists "to retard the action" (104). Shklovsky's famous image of art slowing our automatic visual processing to make us see the stoniness of a stone puts retardation at the heart of his aesthetic.

Structuralist desire to make literary study a science is what generates the third approach, namely, *quantifying literary speed*. Gérard Genette tried to describe narrative speed in numeric terms so that texts could be compared mathematically. He conceives of speed primarily as a ratio between the time span covered in the novel and the number of pages allotted to it, so that Proust's volumes contain passages that cover variously one minute of social action to a page all the way to one century to a page.[4] Genette's *Narrative Discourse Revisited* reuses this measure of speed and notes that *Eugénie Grandet* averages ninety days per page, while Proust averages five and a half days.[5] Being able to derive a number this way is useful for the traditional fiction that concerns Genette, but it does not explain the contemporary phenomenon. Robert Coover achieves the effect of upsetting speed in the three-hundred-plus-page *Gerald's Party,* which covers roughly a dozen hours, or very approximately two and a half minutes' action per page. The novel is very slow in Genette's terms, but not in readers' experience of the text.[6]

The fourth approach to speed almost passes as a given for many current texts. Critics simply postulate correlations between narrative speed and *contemporary cultural speed*.[7] Speed notoriously characterizes our culture.[8] We acknowledge the multiplicity of images streaming ceaselessly past our eyes; we converse about the velocity with which technology changes basic ways of handling everyday life. The faster one's computer, the faster one's Internet connection, the better. The sensation of speed is provided by many uppers in the recreational pharmacopoeia: amphetamines (nicknamed "speed") in the 1960s, cocaine in the 1970s, crack in the 1980s, and methamphetamines in the 1990s. Speed figures as an element in TV cartoons, in film editing, in jazz, and in rap performance. Many novels have been said to embody such cultural acceleration, whether as realistic representation, as Jamesonian hysterical exhilaration, as anxiety about such headlong movement, or as a prose equivalent to wheels spinning on ice, resulting in the stasis of going nowhere fast. Most if not all of the texts I discuss here do reflect cultural speed in some fashion, but as I argue, reflecting it is not all that they do. Narrative speed has many uses, and one is to play with reader anxiety, deliberately provoking it in order to point to some greater cause for anxiety and stress.

So what, more precisely, is narrative speed? The effect I focus on is a sense of *the narrative accelerating beyond some safe comprehension-limit.* This phrasing equates safety and comprehension. The prose whizzes by us, and we suffer from the sense that it flashes along too rapidly for us to grasp the logic or keep track of what is happening. Reading slowly and carefully does not solve our problem: certain explanatory elements simply do not exist. While knowing the end will make a second reading feel less threatening, we are still unable to reduce most such narratives to conventional logic.

To map the ways that speed is functioning, we need both to identify the main techniques that produce the effect and to study the evident authorial goals fostered by such narrative rapidity. In the first section I discuss three techniques for producing the effect of narrative speed: *multiplying elements, subtracting expected material,* and *rendering actions fantastic.* While the techniques are separable in theory, they almost never function alone, so the exemplary texts cannot be neatly divided into three groups. After discussing technique, I consider the kind of effect encouraged by the speed: satire, mystery, protest, exaltation, revolution. Despite their pacing, the novels discussed have relatively little in common. One might link William S. Burroughs's *Ticket That Exploded,* Mark Leyner's *My Cousin, My Gastroenterologist,* and Darius James's *Negrophobia* for their drug-like rush, but the similarities are not profound. Po Bronson's *Bombardiers,* Robert Coover's *John's Wife,* Douglas Coupland's *Microserfs,* Ishmael Reed's *Terrible Twos* and *Terrible Threes,* and Fran Ross's *Oreo* will seem even more dissimilar. The closest they come to common ground is their targeting of some oppression or institution or system of order, social or mental.

Insofar as all these speeding texts result in attacks on some form of authority, the politics of narrative speed seems to be radical or at any rate rebellious, with the authors being the rebels. Insofar as the author is attacking us as readers, though, and deliberately inducing anxieties, we feel oppressed and are the ones trying to escape or dissipate the effect of the attack upon us. Paul Virilio shows that the various sorts of physical speed he analyzes can serve the purposes either of hegemonic powers or of revolution; revolution may be movement but can be met by police pursuit at higher speed.[9] Narrative speed similarly serves both escape and control functions—but with an interesting modification. The speed effect operates best during one's first reading but loses its ability to bother us as much on subsequent readings. The politics of using narrative speed are thus relatively ephemeral. In addition to seeing how narrative speed is generated, we need also to look at its politics and their implications.

Speed through Multiplication: *The Terrible Twos, The Terrible Threes, John's Wife, Bombardiers, Oreo*

Multiplying units—be they characters, plot elements, episodes, newsbytes, or events—creates the effect of narrative rapidity, especially if little information is given about each. We see this multiplying impulse in Ishmael Reed's novels *The Terrible Twos* and *The Terrible Threes.* Reed creates the effect of careening along by firing at us a plethora of names, topics, and temporarily focalizing characters. Sometimes each paragraph coalesces about a new character, and readers desperately wonder if this character is a one-off, or should be remembered as a key to what the plot might be. In the first few pages of *The Terrible Twos,* we get volcanoes, wolves in Greece, the American president wearing extravagantly expensive clothes (prices all given), Ebenezer Scrooge, three newspapers commenting on the president, Mrs. Charlotte Ford, 7.8 million unemployed people, including four who freeze to death during inaugural week. Santa Claus appears in many guises, from a Santa doll in Dolly Parton's cleavage to a Santa robot. We get members of Truth Tabernacle Church deciding that Christmas is the work of the devil and hanging Santa in effigy, Percy Ross (the Jewish Santa Claus), Steven Jones (an assistant professor at Ohio State University, who says Santa is a sexist fertility symbol), a poll that says 75 percent of American women are sexually dissatisfied, Professor James Deetz commenting on the food actually served at the original Thanksgiving (eels), and the Thanksgiving Day parade in New York, watched by two department store magnates, Herman and George Schneider.[10] These items and considerably more tumble out in the space of five pages. Sentence by sentence we get no impression of speed, but five pages' worth will tire us out.

In an interview with John O'Brien, published in 1974, Reed says, "I've watched television all my life, and I think my way of editing, the speed I bring to my books, the way the plot moves, is based upon some of the television shows and cartoons I've seen."[11] Reed's narrative structure works like channel surfing, which of course combines multiplication and subtraction. We get momentary fragments of scenes or even whole scenes if we're intrigued by what we see, and as we cycle through the channels, we can add to our knowledge of what is happening on any one of them, but we lose the connected form of the various narratives. His is a many-channel system, so anxiety accrues simply through our fear that we will forget something important. We ignore TV shows of no interest, but if we are traditional readers, we are less cavalier with novelistic story lines, and continue to assume that all parts of a novel are somehow useful. Reed makes us feel that we are not in control, that we cannot organize the chaos. In the long run, he brings the many threads of story more or less together, but his plot, such as it is, offers no real-world consistency. One character in *The Terrible Twos* goes from being a blackmailing broadcast executive to a born-again follower of a corrupt evangelist; in *The Terrible Threes,* that same person turns out to be an extraterrestrial whose orders were to encourage nuclear war to fumigate Earth for extraterrestrial occupation, but who has fallen in love with humans instead of carrying out his mission. One can relax and enjoy this, but one pays the price: giving up expectations and forgoing the rewards of expectations gratified. That means that the ending can give little sense of resolution. The author had better wish to leave readers dangling, unsatisfied.

In a narrative characterized by speed, slowing down the pace naturally focuses our attention. The central scenes in *The Terrible Twos* use Dickens's "Christmas Carol" as its "classical myth" and reworks Scrooge's visions as various ghostly figures of power who lament the moments when they had a chance to improve the world but chose wrongly and spread long-lasting evil. Truman reviews his decision to drop the bomb; Ike, his to have Lumumba assassinated; Nelson Rockefeller, his to bed his girlfriend rather than answer the phone when Attica prisoners rioted. That irresponsibility produced carnage. Rockefeller, chained to demons dressed as his victims, reminisces:

> I loved this glory more than I loved my children. It made me hard....I felt the testes shoring up within. I felt like I could squirt it from here to across the continent. I called my friend and told her to meet me. I loved that woman. Southern girl. She used to call me her old billy goat. She'd give me golden showers and other techniques she was so good at.... The phone rang. I let it ring. I was having a good time. I was feeling no pain. And so when the phone kept ringing I took out the plug. The next morning they told me. They said they'd been trying to reach me all night. The fuckers had gone into the jail and killed over thirty people. The fuckers were only supposed to kill a few to show those people in the Southwest how tough I was. How I wasn't just a stupid rich boy with café society connections, but how I could really get the job done. (128)

Such self-contained visions, detailed in part because they need to persuade us that the speaker regrets what he did, make the general speediness all the more noticeable by contrast.

Robert Coover's novel *John's Wife* uses all three techniques: multiplication, subtraction, and intruding the fantastic upon the realistic. At the outset, Coover rather ostentatiously overwhelms us with multiplication.

He gives us so many characters that we struggle mightily to retain detail about any individual. John, Floyd, Gordon, Ellsworth, Otis, Kevin, Nerd, Rex, Pastor Lenny, Fish and Turtle (two teens), Alf, Trevor, Waldo, Stu, Mitch, Barnaby, Maynard, Snuffy, Dutch, Oxford and his three sons (Harvard, Yale, and Cornell), Bruce, Daddy Duwayne, and Mikey turn up in the first few pages, and those are just the men and boys. The women are equally numerous: Floyd's wife, Edna; Gordon's senile mother; Waldo's wife, Lorraine; Gordon's wife, Pauline; Trevor's wife, Marge; Lenny's wife, Beatrice; Maynard's wife, Veronica; Columbia (daughter of Oxford); Cornell's wife, Gretchen; Kate, the town librarian (and Oxford's wife); John's daughter Clarissa; Marie-Claire; Opal (mother of John and wife of Mitch); Stu's wife, Daphne; Barnaby's wife, Audrey; Jennifer; Harriet; and Nevada, to name the main ones. And of course we also have John's wife, never given a name, often invisible, sexually coveted by the men in their various fashions, known and mostly liked by all the women. Call it fifty characters that we must keep straight. The most remarkable thing is that for the most part we succeed if we try. We stumble and say, "Is she the one suffering from clairaudience or the one haunted by the abortion?" but we usually figure it out, though the fact that we are always struggling makes us feel that they come on too fast and too many.

Multiplication also characterizes Coover's handling of topics. One woman wonders, "Why couldn't life be spread out like memory was, with past and present all interwoven and dissolving into one another, so you could drift from story to story whenever the mood struck."[12] Something like that is how Coover orchestrates his material. A topic—it might be love—will emerge, and most of the characters will show their concept of love: that it exists or doesn't, that it is dangerous or silly. Furthermore, they do so in a fashion that interweaves them with half a dozen other characters. We see how they lose their virginity, for instance: most of the women of his generation lose it to John, the fairy-tale "hero" ("Once, there was a man named John. John had money, family, power, good health, high regard, many friends" [7]). Coover swirls back and forth over topics, giving us cross-sectional pictures of this town. Memory gives us John's generation in high school, in college as frat rats and sorority sisters, buoyant with youth if nothing else; we also see them later as lushes and hags and semi-failures, as voyeurs and parents and town council members, as wheelers and dealers and backstabbers.

The technique of multiplication creates a different effect in Po Bronson's *Bombardiers*.[13] This novel is set in the financial world, where the characters mostly sell junk bonds and mortgages. The sellers are all given unreasonable quotas: sell $20 million, sell $50 million worth of some very scummy financial instruments, often to savings and loans already in trouble, on the theory that the government will bail them out. The salesmen in *Bombardiers* despise their products, which makes their lives and tensions worse. A newcomer projects authority with this gabble:

> With industry, companies had inventory and long-term labor contracts and product loyalty, all of which kept those companies stable. But nobody inventories information, and they don't manufacture it, and consumers don't have any more loyalty. It's the Third Law of Information Economics: Knowledge has no shelf life. Market share can vanish in a single day. All of this leads to greater volatility. You have to think of how to profit from up *and* down. (42)

At a neighboring desk we soon hear, "It's the Third Law of Information Economics: Knowledge has no shelf life—you have to eat it off the vine. You have to learn to profit from volatility" (42). Further along this becomes, "Nobody carries inventory anymore. Knowledge is on the vine. That's the Third Law of Information Economics. It's a long-term trend, and you've got to get on board" (43). Each spiel is shorter, less detailed, faster, and more nonsensical.

Sid Geeder, the focal figure, *hates* selling what he knows to be worthless, but he values his reputation as the "mortgage king" of the office, so he manages to meet totally unreasonable quotas. Sid excels at the bamboozling double-talk, and holds himself together with the thought that he can cash out of his company shares in a few more months, despite the evidence that people are frequently fired just before they can do so, no matter how good they may be, and despite the evidence that he might well be fired for failing to make a quota, no matter how insanely high that had been set. He cannot win but refuses to see that. Instead, he leads his life at the hectic pace suggested by the snippets of phone calls and sales pitches that bombard us.

"It was a filthy profession, but the money was addicting, and one addiction led to another, and they were all going to hell" (3). This same line begins the last chapter, except that the later phrasing is "they had all gone to hell" (304). The addictive nature of the behavior is clear and will tie in with other drug-rush narrative speeds. One of the sellers actually does do drugs, using a different drug each day so he does not become addicted to any particular one. Others can be addicted to the reputation of being a tough woman in a man's world, or to the reputation of meeting higher quotas than anyone else in the company, or be so addicted to coffee as nearly to die of caffeine poisoning. When they break down or burn out, the symptoms vary: one develops a walleye that won't focus, another develops itching teeth, and one stutters when he tries to say any number, although non-numbers come out clearly.

Drug addiction changes the user's perceptions of time, speeding it up during the rush, slowing down to nothing while waiting for the fix. In the frantic life of *Bombardiers,* we do not see many longueurs, which intensifies our sense of overall speed. Almost everything is rush, but with no ecstasy in the high, just scrabbling urgency. In one three-page sequence (298–300), a man collapses because his asthma inhaler has been emptied by an angry colleague (and he is nearly killed by an accountant doing CPR on him). Another smashes his Quotron screen, and because all the other screens are linked to a single cable, all of them go out, bringing sales effectively to a halt. Flying glass from the screen slightly cuts someone, who has hysterics over the blood. Those trying to sell scream when their screens go blank. Indeed, Sid shrieks that he's blind, since being unable to see quotes essentially blinds him. High tension, multi-event scenes like this are commonplace.

Bronson contextualizes these brokers as just parts of a much larger machine. We see how its units multiply:

> The information economy was a Ponzi scheme spiraling out of control. The investment bankers got rich slaving away, so they called in their tax accountants, who got so rich filing government forms that they called their investment bankers back for advice about where to invest their surging wealth. The investment bankers were also miserable, so they called their therapists.... They worked so hard they neglected their families, so many of which ended up in divorce. They called their divorce lawyers. The lawyers worked even harder than the investment bankers and suffered physical maladies that the doctors charged them ridiculous fees to attempt to cure. The doctors, worried about being sued by the lawyers, called their insurance brokers for malpractice coverage. The engineers built computer systems that helped all of them speed up this cycle so they could call and bill at a faster pace. (66)

The passage goes on to politicians, and eventually back to accountants and investment bankers. Not only do individuals become addicted to the demands, but the whole system is addicted to its own surges of power as well and cannot survive without them.

Let me offer a final example of multiplication from Fran Ross's *Oreo.* Like John Edgar Wideman in *Hurry Home* and William Melvin Kelley in *Dunsfords Travels Everywheres,* Ross is an African American experimentalist demonstrating skill at playing the Joyce game. Like *Ulysses, Oreo* is based on classical myth, the story of Theseus, so all the encounters (once Oreo starts her quest) refer to Theseus's rather obscure adventures on his way to Athens and from there to Crete and back. This gives Ross a large number of plot elements, which, since even well-read readers are unlikely to recognize them, means that we find many episodes that do not seem to link to one another particularly logically. Not only do seemingly unconnected plot elements pile up, but also multiplication is seen in registers of voice. Oreo (Christine Schwartz), daughter of an aspiring Jewish actor and an African American woman, speaks all the tongues of those around her: Yiddish, southern "mush mouth," the French of gourmet menus, mathematical equations, the clotted prose of agronomic economics, the language of dirty jokes and heavy breathers, the arcana of the *OED*, sometimes mingling several on the same page.[14] Like the narrator of Paul Beatty's *White Boy Shuffle,* she can do anything from many different cultural registers exceedingly and zestfully well. Multiplying these elements, however, does not make Oreo believable as a person; rather, it ultimately tells us that we should not try to read her in any realistic fashion, so we lack that particular reading pleasure.

Speed through Subtraction: *Oreo, Microserfs, John's Wife*

Subtraction almost always works in tandem with multiplication. If you multiply events but connect them logically, the speed effect will be minimal. The narrative is more likely to seem overly long. To get speed, we need to feel that we are missing out on meaningful transitions and links. Ross's presentation of Oreo subtracts such links. Oreo's omnicompetence produces a kind of speed because her performative displays so lack supporting detail that we cannot connect these skills realistically with a single person. We can shrug and say that she must be brilliant, or give up representational assumptions and remember that she is not a "person." We lose our sense of control because of what is missing.

One way for a writer to achieve speed, therefore, is to cut out the Barthesian effects of the real,[15] the narrative material a traditional reader expects to provide what John Gardner's Grendel calls "a gluey whine of connectedness."[16] When the details that stabilize fictional "reality" are absent, those trained in conventional literature feel that absence as an artifact of speeding along too fast. Ross ostentatiously calls attention to cutting such detail. "There is no weather per se in this book. Passing reference is made to weather in a few instances. Assume whatever season you like throughout. Summer makes the most sense in a book of this length. That way, pages do not have to be used up describing people taking off and putting on overcoats."[17] Given that Oreo sleeps in a park one night and wears a white dress, we can assume summer weather, at least for the quest sequence, but we are not otherwise given accounts of the weather that would supply detail to make the text feel realistic.

Oreo's travels by bus and subway become frenetic not because she travels fast but because we follow her mind as it leaps from one fantasy to the next without significant linkages. She wonders about the funk quotient of the Jets versus the Knicks: Is football smellier than basketball (105)? She fast-cuts to imagining a female fan running onto the field during the Super Bowl and being eaten by the players in a strange ritual subsequently denied by all concerned. She finds herself on a bus full of "crazy ladies" (107), and we hear some of their comments. She reads headlines from tabloids and fastidiously recoils at the use of "tots" and "mom" in a story about infanticide (110). A few pages later she decides that a redheaded boy has midget blood, although he is of normal height, and when she meets his parents, she finds them indeed to be midgets—midgets, moreover, who talk in rhyme (115). Thus the unlikely or irrational or magic realist detail can also add to our sense of haste if it is not developed to the point of seeming logically appropriate to a generic framework. We are left panting for connections, for some kind of logic to hold this together. The effect works for conventionally trained readers, but it would obviously not work the same way for someone with no sense of what we call realistic fiction or for someone trained in speedy forms of popular entertainment.

The Canadian writer Douglas Coupland makes *Microserfs* seem speedy through subtraction. His target is the lives of those who work for Microsoft (or any Silicon Valley industry). He follows several semi-interchangeable people working at Microsoft who decide to split off and form their own company. One shorthand, speed-inducing technique is to characterize each person through *Jeopardy!* categories. One, for instance, would use FOR-TRAN, Pascal, ADA (defense contracting code), LISP, Neil Peart (drummer for Rush), Hugo and Nebula Award winners, and Sir Lancelot.[18] The others are similarly computer-oriented and lacking in outside interests. We watch these geeks tying themselves in knots over possible implications of taking a shortcut across the lawn, being flamed by Bill Gates, or wondering how much it will affect them if the project they work on turns out to be a loser. Such trivia would not in itself make this a speed novel were the characters themselves not so thin, their lives so lacking in connective tissue. Because they do lack depth, we watch many slight variations on their daily lives, such as the *Jeopardy!* categories, and have trouble distinguishing one from another, which forces us to flounder for logic and meaning. The sense of speed also comes from the characters' always feeling behind, feeling that they need to do more, stay later, push themselves harder, write more code, and worry about shipping dates. They don't feel they can sustain serious relationships with anyone because Microsoft consumes their lives.

Coupland thinks in terms of cartoons, which make quick jumps from one state to another rather than giving us logical development. One character, Dan, says, "And then, I thought about us...these children who fell down life's cartoon holes...dreamless children, alive but not living—we emerged on the other side of the cartoon holes fully awake and discovered we were whole" (371; ellipses in the original). In a realistic novel, the action covered would be this change from nerd and geek dissatisfactions to an elective extended family. Dan does not articulate that process, nor do we see much of it; cartoonlike, his friends fall down a hole and emerge as part of a family, feeling better about themselves and life.

Speed through Rendering Fantastic: *John's Wife,* *Negrophobia, The Ticket That Exploded,* *My Cousin, My Gastroenterologist*

Turning consensus reality into phantasmagoria is the third technique for creating narrative speed that I find in transgressive fiction. Fantasy of many sorts can exist without affecting narrative pace. What makes such departures from reality relevant here is the creation of puzzling anomalies for which no explanation is given. Without any logic supplied—a subtractive technique—we feel that we must have missed something, or that we are too dense to see a symbolic meaning and should go back and read again. Doing so will not help us, though. This simple puzzle effect leading to speed can be seen in Coover's *John's Wife*. Pauline grows to giantess size in a few days, and adds breathless haste to her other problems by being driven about town in a van, screeching around corners and skidding, the pace necessary to keep rumor from catching up with her and Cornell and to let them find or steal enough food to keep her from starving. We never know why she grows or how large she becomes. Statements that she can kick a car as if it were a football are called rumors, but we do see her pick a man up in one hand as if he were a doll (381), and bullets merely sting her (387). The mob has to kill her by burning down the woods around her. In another fantastic sequence, a young man nicknamed Turtle has been missing for several months. He is literally reborn, in his adolescent size and shape, from the monstrously large belly of the preacher's wife (333). Her own, normal-sized baby pops out after this teenager, almost unnoticed. Even Turtle's amniotically wet clothes come out after him. While Turtle is in this second womb, we experience a variety of his ecstatic experiences that seem part orgasmic and part cosmogonic, as if we were witnessing the big bang or a nova.

When we try to put such phantasmic events into some sort of meaningful perspective, we find that we cannot. We sense that John's wife's becoming invisible bears some relationship to Pauline's becoming all too visible; the women are each other's opposites, and they mysteriously blend on a film by the photographer Gordon. John's wife was evidently the only one of her set to be a virgin at her wedding, while Pauline had inducted most of her male cohort into sexual joys. In her sexual connectedness, Pauline is like John himself, though Pauline's promiscuity grows out of grotesque sexual abuse in childhood from Daddy Duwayne. Practically all the town's men have slept with the one woman but covet the other. Only when Pauline is burned as a monster can the local society cast out its shadow-scapegoat and return to a semblance of normality. Why does John's wife again become visible at Pauline's death? What are we to see in Bruce's sadism, hitherto unmanifested? Were those or the rather active aborted fetus that haunts one of the women the only mysteries, we could cobble together explanations, but what price Turtle's being reborn? and from that mother? What is served by that departure from consensus reality?

The phantasmagoria we cannot explain, the relative shortness of scenes, the lack of clear transitions from one to the next, the repeated scenes of physical speed, and above all the sheer number of plot units and people: all these leave us feeling disoriented. Clearly we are not supposed to be able to put everything neatly into a framework; the town itself is, on the surface, such a framework, and we are all too aware that the frame belies the darker shadows beneath the surface. Were we just to say that kinky sexualities lurk beneath respectable surfaces, this would be unsurprising and of no great interest. More intriguing is the sense that the book reflects tensions between order and disorder, the latter not being chaos so much as an active force for anti-order, something trying to overthrow the accepted way of doing things. While middle-class readers ordinarily opt for order, they may feel uneasy about that choice for this book, given the unattractive nature of the social interactions we watch. Moreover, disorder is not shown to produce much that is attractive either.[19]

When confronted with texts that challenge us by cutting out connective narrative tissue, we mostly rely on our rational faculties to try to put the narrative fragments together in some meaningful fashion. The phantasmagoric works that model drug experience make that futile.[20] They attack rationality itself. Burroughs is famous for having used every drug and combination of drugs invented by humanity, and while I am not arguing that any particular text of his was written under chemical influence, he does in literary terms create a narrative fragmenting of consciousness that suggests drug experience. By contrast, Mark Leyner leads a drug-free life, according to William Grimes.[21] Nonetheless, the characters in his novel *My Cousin, My Gastroenterologist*[22] mention using marijuana (35), snorting cocaine (44), and being on Methedrine suppositories (49). They use drug words frequently: one is "habitually abusing an illegal growth hormone" and has "overdosed" on television (3–4). Leyner's blurb writers note the meth-like rush of his writing. Whether the drugs are literal or merely a model for the literary technique, they lie behind the speed effects in Darius James's *Negrophobia* and Burroughs's *The Ticket That Exploded,* as well as Leyner's *My Cousin, My Gastroenterologist.*

James, Burroughs, and Leyner all challenge reality, though in a manner that creates confusion rather than Coover's sense of mystery. James's

Negrophobia, for instance, uses many of the subtractive and multiplying techniques but pushes us much further into the realm of the phantasmagoric. In such a world, we have no way of supplying connections. Not only are they missing but we cannot deduce them from generic convention. Or as Ronald A. T. Judy puts it in his article "Irony and the Asymptotes of the Hyperbola," "*Negrophobia* is about order, about the presence or absence of order ... about what order means, how it is apprehended." He goes on: "The idea that linguistic order implies meaning—that a narrative is the sign of purposive reality—is a principal casualty of *Negrophobia.* The narrative of *Negrophobia* provides no clear perspective, no point of view from which it can be determined when one reality collides or slips into another."[23] In this satiric farrago, a white girl called Bubbles Brazil is punished for her racist attitudes through Vodoun and the transdermal application of belladonna by her family's black maid. We realize that what she experiences may have no relationship to an external reality, but we are never sure of any episode's reality status because all of this is a phantasmagoria of white fears and stereotypes regarding black people, all of them being made angry fun of.

What we are to make of Bubbles is further confused by her preference for talking jive, dropping into rap verse, and seeming very like many of the shadowy black figures she feels threatened by, such as the roller derby girls who menace her in a restroom. Naturally, readers do not have uniform responses or assumptions. For most African American readers, Bubbles's exaggerated fears of blacks are presumably funny as well as deeply disgusting, and punishing her for them seems only fair. Some white readers will feel threatened by black attacks on whites. Religious readers, black or white, might be offended by some of the jokes. How does a pious Black Muslim feel about "Min. Louis Farrakhan's 'Ambrosia of Islam' Do-for-Self Designer Chocolates '*Allah eats 'em! And you will too!*'"[24] These prove to be "frog-faced fudge figurines ... [bearing] the likeness of the Honorable Elijah Muhammad. He clutches candy genitalia in tiny fudge fists. Spurts of white chocolate fleck his thighs" (3). Even those of other faiths might be made uncomfortable by that comic-grotesque portrayal of a religious leader, and we know that while an African American writer may just be able to get away with this, no white writer could thus treat a black leader or Allah.

James emphasizes his techniques for cutting narrative connectivity by setting up the entire novel as a film script. He describes the images he wants, and adds some commentary as continuity. Film expects viewers to handle jumps, and in this novel we leap from scene to scene, the transition signaled only by the instructions as to what the camera will show. The scene will be an interior—a cave one time, a church the next. In the cave Bubbles is surrounded by licorice men, doughboys, and flaming tar babies, their actions reminiscent of a Broadway chorus line. In the church, H. Rap Remus preaches the craziness of the "Whyte Man" and upholds Idi Amin, not Haile Selassie, as the "*living incarnation of God on Earth*" (77). Bubbles is at first accepted by them because her skin is covered with paint from a paint factory scene (signifying on Ellison's *Invisible Man*). When her baptism washes off the paint, however, she vomits up huge worms in a very Burroughsian sequence and manages to run away. She next finds herself in a series of movie theaters, and what happens on screen or between her and other viewers supplies the next action sequences. How she gets to more than one theater or why is not explained.

Bubbles as embodier of white prejudices and fears is not the only target. Her equivalent at the social level is the world of Walt Disney. A "honkie-mutant crowd" roars "*Heil Mickey* CHRIST!" (106), and we see a new crucifixion. "Mickey Christ hangs by his inflated white-gloved hands on a neon-lit cross with his owlish Walter Kean eyes staring sadly at the sky." Meanwhile, "a YARMULKED BIRD peeps under Mickey's loincloth" and says with a thick Yiddish accent, "Circumsize [*sic*]? What's to circumsize?" (107). Without warning, we then find ourselves in Sleeping Beauty's castle, and a giant snot-pouring nose snails its way in. "With a mighty sneeze, the GODZILLA-SIZED PROBOSCIS erupts like a lava-spewing volcano, slathering the streets in a thick carpet of mucus. Brown boulder-sized boogers tumble down the street, crushing panicked pedestrians" (108–9). This gleeful, childish grotesquerie seems somewhat Burroughsian, but it is also reminiscent of Pynchon's sequence concerning a giant adenoid.[25]

So what does this fantasia accomplish? Disney's sexless world is undercut, as is the Disney empire's maintaining those traditional white, sexless values. That neutered world produces the sexual fantasies projected by whites on blacks. If whites were in better touch with their own bodily urges and less repressed by their cultural patterns, such projections might not have encouraged lynching. We see an effect of white repression in the fantasies that burgeon in Bubbles's mind. They well up uncontrollably, one following fast upon the next. In a blurb on the cover, George Trow points out that James's "subject is the big one: slavery; his questions are the big ones: who is slave to what?" Bubbles in her helpless mental whirl is very much enslaved by her fears, her fantasies, and the manipulations of her family's servant, and part of what builds that mental world is the combination of subtraction and the fantastic.

Subtracting so much that we get choppy fragments can produce a phantasmic effect. We see this, for instance in Burroughs's novel (or is it a collection of stories?) *The Ticket That Exploded*. He makes no pretense of telling even as much story as Ishmael Reed does. Burroughs talks about his cut-up technique, the splicing of tapes or films in order to produce the merging of two people (by intercutting sounds such as heartbeats) or to produce physiological effects by intercutting body sounds with those of a riot.[26] He elsewhere talks about cutting and pasting manuscripts so they become interwoven from tiny units of text. Part of what he plays on is the idea of subliminal conditioning, the theory that one frame per second in a film showing a bottle of Coca-Cola, though not consciously registered by viewers, would make them thirsty for Coke.

Burroughs gives us cut-up effects, which rely on multiplying, subtracting, and rendering fantastic, in the chapter called "Do You Love Me?" Lines from old-fashioned popular songs, some of them heterosexual love songs, are interspersed with the sexual imagery Burroughs uses for homosexual orgasms. For a conventional reader who recognizes the songs' words, those fragments define the foreground of the passage, while the more enigmatic references to Burroughs's sexuality form the subliminal disturber. "Jelly jelly jelly shifting color orgasm back home—Scratching shower of sperm that made cover of the board books—It's a long way to Tipperary—soft luminous spurts to my blue heaven—Pieces of cloud drifted through all the tunes from blue—Exploded in cosmic laughter of cable cars.... Me?—Oh, darling, i love you in constant motion—i love you i do" (45). If not alluding to homosexual love, then the subliminals include images of wandering in alleys, of skin seen through an open shirt, plus instructions to take an audio tape and splice it with other sounds. We get the subliminals that belong to the real sex world of Burroughs, while the banal songs supply much of the foreground: "A Bicycle Built for Two," "Bye Bye Blackbird," "Tipperary," "Waltzing Matilda," "If You Were the Only Girl in the World," "Red River Valley," "The Sheik of Araby," "When the Saints Go Marching In," and "Rock Around the Clock." Throughout is a third theme, basically statements such as "I love you" or questions "whether you love me," *demands* for love, for acknowledgment of love. Burroughs associates such demands for demonstrativeness and exclusivity with heterosexual love and women, and treats everything heterosexual as viral in origin, a horrible disease.

The snippets of heterosexual love songs bombard us with their assertions of implicit slavery to the woman. Breaking through this oppressive layer are flashes of Burroughs's alternative world at the almost subliminal level. That alternative offers a release from maddening banality. His next chapter speaks about the "Other Half," a "separate organism attached to your nervous system on an air line of words" (49), which he treats as female, possibly as a wife. His way of escaping the other half is to splice tapes: "Splice your body sounds in with air hammers. Blast jolt vibrate the 'Other Half' right out into the street" (50). For Burroughs, the authority being revolted against is female, and drugs help break down all the systems of order which arise from those female demands that life be regulated.

Burroughs uses his cut-up effect either to evict an unwanted part of the self or to join the true self to another, friendly male self. The intercut material speeds by too quickly to be controlled, which he hopes will dissolve ties or create more satisfactory mergers. Insofar as he writes for an audience other than himself, he probably wishes to have something like that effect on readers, making material flash by but influencing them with the many repeated phrases, the subliminals, the vivid images. Because these come at us quickly, we can do little to process and control them consciously.

Mark Leyner ratchets up the effect of speed in *My Cousin, My Gastroenterologist*. Whereas Burroughs's chapters often have some kind of core fantasy, Leyner's chapters (or are they stories?) seem even further removed from ordinary narrative. Burroughs's use and reuse of particular characters, such as the Nova Police, produce passages with the same general tone. Leyner repeats his material far less often, and seems more zany, less limited in situation and tone, and hence less predictable. He cites animated cartoons as one of his models: "Anything could happen and inevitably did and at dizzying speeds. A character could drive a hot rod to Mars and back, pull into a diner on the highway, sing a duet with his fried chicken leg, and then become the king of the Eskimos—in five seconds! Wonderful!"[27] Leyner has, of course, been interpreted as reflecting the speed of his era. Larry McCaffery makes this point: "With *My Cousin* Leyner had invented a new form of 'realism' perfectly suited to the postmodern Electronic Age. The 'experimental' features of his work are in fact 'natural' reflections of the frantic pace of mass media (and of MTV and rock music particularly)."[28] We have to enjoy being surprised when we read Leyner's *My Cousin, My Gastroenterologist,* because we can derive no generic expectations from his riffs, and although I have read it three times, I cannot say what it is "about." William Grimes unequivocally calls it a collection of stories rather than a novel; Leyner himself claims the opposite.[29] Neither one nor the other by most standards, it has much the same wandering pattern and shifting focal figures, unified only by the general choppiness and speed that characterize Burroughs's book.

In the first chapter, for instance, the narrator is driving to Las Vegas (echoes of *Fear and Loathing in Las Vegas*), and has swerved to avoid running over crusty scabs scratched from the heads of passengers in the convertible ahead of him. He follows signs for "FOIE GRAS AND HARICOTS VERTS NEXT EXIT" (3). At the roadside eatery he orders primordial soup ("ammonia and methane mixed"), but then leaves because he dislikes the atmosphere and tries another eatery, where the Japanese waitress slices wafers of gallium arsenide crystal and serves them with soy and wasabi. Later he finds himself in a bar, where a cyborg "walks in and whips out a 35-lb. phallus made of corrosion-resistant nickel-base alloy and he begins to stroke it sullenly....It can ejaculate herbicides, sulfuric acid, tar glue, you name it" (5). The narrator mentions some of the drugs he is on—steroids, growth hormone—and he gets high on Sinutab. When he sees a woman he fancies in a bar, he cracks "an ampule of mating pheromone" (6) and drinks methyl isocyanate (of Bhopal disaster fame) on the rocks. She falls for him, but they are declared genetically identical, and such incest is forbidden, so he brings out a device that fragments genes in cells, and he scrambles their chromosomes. But then we segue into a fantasy of his being born a chicken bouillon cube, his growing up a weakling until he started to work out and took hormones and steroids, and now at the sight of him "the mightiest oaks blanch and tremble" and birds shit from fear (8). Because the actions are arbitrary and nonsensical, and because no explanations are given, the result is speed as well as phantasmagoria.

Some of these images do recur, for example, the gigantic sexualized robot, whose bulging anatomy parallels the narrator's steroid-enhanced musculature. Mostly what we get, though, is a random-seeming exposure to fantasies derived from popular culture. Flashing by us are filmic robots; the narrator striding into the forest ("my whistle is like an earsplitting fife being played by a lunatic with a bloody bandage around his head," he says [8], referring to Archibald Willard's painting *The Spirit of '76*); knowledge of sushi and computer chips; jokes based on Elvis Presley's "Jailhouse Rock"; colonic irrigation clinics (the gastroenterological motif); and a beauty salon parody of military maneuvers.

Some of the cultural allusions are more academic: reference to an Israeli semiotics journal (44), a T. S. Eliot takeoff ("salesmen come and go, murmuring 'jerry lewis est mort'" [70]), and reference to Dino de Laurentiis's film of "The Love Song of J. Alfred Prufrock," in which "the huge metal robotic women who come and go talking of Michelangelo collapsed— crushing the aging Oscar winners" (103). Someone's skin is "as translucent as the tissue-thin page of a norton anthology" (109). Sometimes he plays semiotic games: pronounce the "th" in Thailand as a voiceless dental fricative, and what evolves is "all restaurants in thighland offer ballet parking lanky black youths in fuchsia tutus glissading into automobiles and gracefully backing into rows" (36).

Some of the registers are more mythological or spoof mythology. "This father's nose is so big that if you took each of his nose hairs, tied them together, and put a hook on the end, you could stand on the moon and fish in lake michigan" (111), though this may also parody Barthelme's *The Dead Father* or some trickster myth behind Barthelme's scenario.[30] Some passages are definitely Burroughsian in their physical grotesquerie. Also mentioned along the way are various drugs that might have some bearing on this vision of the world: Methedrine suppositories, cocaine, quaaludes, and crack.

The Methedrine passage illustrates one kind of speed by cramming in lots of productive activity:

As I iron a pair of tennis shorts I dictate a haiku into the tape recorder and then dash off to snake a clogged drain in the bathroom sink and then do three minutes on the speedbag before making an origami praying mantis and then reading an article in *High Fidelity* magazine as I stir the coq au vin...cleaning the venetian blinds, defrosting the freezer, translating *The Ring of the Nibelung* into Black English, gluing a model aircraft carrier together for my little son. I'm writing to my congressman, doing push-ups, changing a light bulb as I floss my teeth and feed my fish with one hand, balance my checkbook with the other and scratch my borzoi's silky stomach with my big toe. (49)

That, though accelerated to the maximum, is in fact easier to follow and rationalize than other parts of the novel. This meth-suppository-enhanced passage is merely filled with more activities than one could actually carry out at once. Leyner's usual style produces the effects of going too fast because we cannot understand the often fantastic actions and stitch them together into a coherent whole.

Multiplying, subtracting, and rendering fantastic, then, are three techniques used to generate rapid narrative pace in contemporary fiction. In some ways they cannot be separated, since multiplying without subtraction just produces long narratives, subtracting without multiplying would produce very short narratives, and rendering the fictive world fantastic relies both on adding puzzling elements and on removing any explanation. Magic realism results from combining subtraction with the fantastic, but this need not result in speed, as anyone reading Salman Rushdie's *Midnight's Children* or *The Ground beneath Her Feet* can testify. Simply noting techniques, though, is not enough to make sense of narrative speed or answer why it seems so common in contemporary fiction. We need to consider what authorial aims these techniques satisfy, the effect on readers, and the politics of their deployment.

The Aims and Effects of Narrative Speed

Speed produces a range of effects varying from irritation and bewilderment to exhilaration. Because these are audience responses, a single novel may produce any of the possible effects, depending on the outlook of the reader. In simplest terms, the negatives typify a first (though not necessarily a final) reaction of conventional readers, while younger readers attuned to popular culture rather than novels are more likely to find the speed acceptable or even attractive. Further variations in response stem from whether the novel resembles a satire in attacking some portion of its world, or whether the reader's own mind is targeted.

I hesitate to call any of these novels satires in a traditional sense, because they show no signs of expecting reform; they project no high moral norm (Burroughs, Leyner). Some do seem diffusedly satiric, and show humor, wit, and anger. Fran Ross, celebrating a young girl's superlative performance, is to some extent targeting male aspects of society, black or white, though particularly white. Reed invites our contempt for governmental and legal sources of oppression. His focal figure, Nance Saturday, had done well in law school but dropped out once he realized that "there's no law in this country. Only power and class—" (*Twos* 27). James blisteringly makes fun of the web of unconscious white fantasies and fears that continue to poison racial relations in America. The nightmare side of those fears produces the fantasias of genitals, mutilations, Burroughsian metamorphoses, and many situations of threat, disgust, and distaste. The daytime side, just as sickening, produces African Americans tamed and whitened, co-opted, stolen from, or Disneyfied. Bronson and Coupland savage the world of business and its inhuman efficiency ethic. Burroughs turns the blowtorch of his mind against bourgeois values; these he associates with female values, which he sees as a terrible virus that has infected humanity.

The attitudes of Coover and Leyner are harder to discern. Coover to some extent invites us to disparage heartland American small-town society, but he also plays against generic expectations, as, for instance, when he introduces John as a fairy-tale hero. Leyner seems more celebratory than critical, but the world of his characters is a yuppie Me Generation world, and it does not emerge as particularly attractive, what with cocktails made of poisons and food made from computer chips. As in Coover's fiction, any restraints we can sense in the world of Leyner (and of Burroughs) must be broken if we are to be free or enjoy ourselves. Not for Leyner or Burroughs the careful pondering of Saul Bellow's Albert Corde in *The Dean's December,* who feels that some restraints are necessary for civil society and tries to figure out which ones matter.[31] The speed vision is more romantic or anarchic, and perhaps also a more infantile concept of bliss in its self-centeredness. Bellow remains concerned with society as a whole, while Burroughs and Leyner exalt the individual and the pursuit of enjoyment. In that sense they are consumers, not producers.[32] The practicalities of making a living do not intrude on their plots. This makes their fictional worlds singularly privileged, though they might claim that the privilege was matched by their risks in exploring the further limits of the mind and pushing conventional readers far beyond where many would wish to go.

Readers susceptible to the euphoric effect are likely to be young and probably non-mainstream in some fashion. Part of what this audience would enjoy is these authors' display of superior flash in contrast to plodding, middle-class norms. Authors such as Reed, James, Ross, Coupland, Bronson, and Leyner revel in their knowledge of popular cultural references, black and white. They deliberately juggle these in a way that commands admiration. The effect of speed has always been one tool for separating an "us" from a "them." One often talks as fast as one can in jive, or in Cockney in London, or in pig Latin and other transposition and deformation languages among children, or in Verlan in French. Whitey or the powers of law and order or the squares or parents will never understand. Such a "we" may be minority in identity, or can even just be those who see themselves as radical, rebellious, and young. One learns to deal more comfortably with speed from rap, standup comedy, and *South Park* than from grand opera or Victorian novels. Leyner clearly expects an audience with this taste, and assumes that exposure to his speed is a purely enjoyable experience. Far from seeing his work as assaulting the reader, he claims to see it as "so dense with pleasure, so unrelentingly enjoyable, so packed with event" that the reader cannot skip over any of it.[33] Everything wordy and boring has been excised. Anyone who has taught novels by Burroughs, Leyner, or Kathy Acker will remember that most of the students seem puzzled and even offended, but a few will glow with approval and feel that at last they have found someone who speaks to them. Writing for this audience only, however, would be preaching to the choir; they are not the ones in need of being troubled or shaken by the politics of such speed. Hence the necessity of reaching a larger and less compatible audience.

Speed rewards the hip reader, and anyone not perfectly attuned to the idiom suffers the assault. Some readers will persist and get a feel for the rhythm—and, indeed, second readings rarely feel as speedy—in which case the reader wins some protection from the attack and to a degree accepts new standards. That first reading, though, produces in the targeted reader a sense of disorientation, an inability to understand all that happens because it rushes by too quickly to be pinned down.

The most immediate effect of narrative speed upon resisting readers is bewilderment. That sensation makes most readers feel more vulnerable to any source of force within the narrative, whether authority against which the speed is being used or the power of the author. One feels smaller in regard to the nexuses of political power in Reed, to Microsoft or capitalist enterprise in Coupland and Bronson. Bewilderment also serves the ends of those writers who wish us to ask why one should be mistreated for being female or black or homosexual (Ross, Burroughs).

Narrative speed, when used to produce drug-like effects, pushes us beyond bewilderment to a sense that we have lost control. Our lives are held together by the ordering systems we generate, and aggressive speed pushes us to experience life without such systems, a situation resembling some forms of insanity. The ideology of producing this effect is paradox-ridden. Being unconstructed by the discourses of others makes one remarkably free; but without the power or impulse to form one's own systems, one is likely to be passive, helpless, and vulnerable to others who are more organized. One can withdraw so far into oneself that society ceases to be meaningful, in which case the value of freedom is questionable. We see this much more fundamental kind of attack in Burroughs and Leyner. We see a more modified form in James, who seems at first to produce this state of asocial liberty; one point to Bubbles's mind trip, though, is to expose her to her own prejudices so she can learn to be a more worthy member of society. Reform hovers in the background as a possibility, even if it seems very secondary compared to the pleasures of scaring and punishing her.

Readers of nontraditional fiction subject themselves to the experience of vulnerability and loss of control for a variety of reasons. We may temporarily enjoy being lost in a funhouse, and bewilderment can supply that frisson of being disoriented while not posing so much threat as to drive us away from the book. Or we may enjoy a book that seems to outsmart us, that takes us beyond our usual relationship with reading matter. We may welcome a new experience or the sense of transgressing social boundaries. Even the most logical and controlled readers may enjoy vicarious fragmentation of mind; such readers might not risk drugs in real life, but may be curious. We may read the text to fight with it. We may try to impose our sense of an appropriate order, even if in the end we fail; the text is in that case a challenge or test to us. We may read because we do not like being bettered (or battered) by a book, and refusing to be cowed is our answer to the assault. We may be carried along by humor or zest. Normally we attempt to control a book, but if it defeats us soundly, we may find pleasure in submission to its ways, even a kind of masochistic pleasure.[34]

Those most alienated from the values of their culture may truly enjoy all radical fracturing of order, all attempts to smash and destroy assumptions, expectations, and rules. The radical destructiveness that upsets one reader may exhilarate another. Such violence in literature, however, is a far cry from acting it out in real life. In this sense the politics of speed is limited to a temporary effect. Not only does it tend to attenuate upon a second reading, but also it does not have much immediate effect outside of literature. Randy Schroeder argues, regarding Burroughs's *Naked Lunch*, that it "tries to leap beyond social and representational structures into new, chaotic, energetic life.... But because it fails to critique its social object, because it has no ethic, it unwittingly finds new ways to engage in old conversations. *Naked Lunch* demonstrates that it is not always enough to simply overturn narrative structures." He goes on later to argue that "A shift in narrative strategy does not guarantee a shift in how we think of and negotiate power."[35]

I suggested at the outset that speed in these novels does not just reflect or complain about cultural speed, though it does do that. Rather, narrative rapidity usually points to something beyond cultural speed as its target. What I sense as the targets are ultimately stable structures in society and in consciousness. The target is rationality, our desire for order and our usual means of making sense of confusion. This attack is most obvious in the visions modeled on drug speed. Where these authors differ from the humdrum bourgeois attitude is in enjoying and encouraging the breakdown of control and logic. Kathy Acker shares this viewpoint: in *Empire of the Senseless,* she screams: "GET RID OF MEANING. YOUR MIND IS A NIGHTMARE THAT HAS BEEN EATING YOU: NOW EAT YOUR MIND."[36] Clearly we are supposed to enjoy casting off inner restraints and going with the flow, and cover blurbs on these novels suggest that some readers do. Although drugs are not part of their technique, Coover, Ross, and Reed also enjoy breaking social constraints.

The emotions ultimately produced by speed are a critical attitude toward the world and a sense of personal exaltation, often combined. Speed frequently correlates to literary high spirits. Ross, Reed, and James certainly seem to value speed for its lightness, and lightness as antidote to the ponderous burdens of the white middle-class power structure. Leyner and

Burroughs are high on their own novelty, their visionary departures from consensus reality, their rejection of old-fashioned writing. Because their worlds are least structured, they risk the most in terms of readers closing the book, but they offer the most to readers capable of feeling their ecstasy. They try hardest to push the reader beyond some kind of edge, shake the reader loose from comfort and tradition. All of these writers chance something to put the reader in that place beyond the edge, an edge that has little to do with any sense of cultural velocity and its anxieties. These authors have found that only by speeding can one outrun and outstrip constricting tradition and norms. Since the mental distress and confusion wear thin on second reading, the politics of this kind of speed must be seen in terms of long-term effects. No single work will change readers' outlooks, but the accumulation over time of authors and texts like these create familiarity, even comfort, with the unstructured world.

Modalities of Complaint

As we try to come closer to being ideal readers of novels characterized by narrative speed, we learn to relax, to stop wanting to be in control. We attempt to open ourselves to the exhilaration of the rush. When we read complaints, that tactic will not work, because complaint does not produce exhilaration. We need other reasons to open ourselves to these irritating narratives. Understanding why a complaint makes us so uncomfortable can reduce our negative response. Other reasons for trying to accept these novels include the self-interest that would help us learn from warnings and the practice of our social skills. Not only do we serve the role of friend, who by listening helps keep the social fabric from tearing; we are even in the position of manning a hotline, learning to understand and perhaps, eventually, applying what we have learned by helping others.

Complaint as a genre was popular from classical through Renaissance times. It sometimes projected distress stemming from love: seduced and abandoned women complained about men, while betrayed men criticized their fickle lady loves. Outraged moralists such as Juvenal, Donne, and Marston complained about people in many professions. The love complaints in particular were primarily aesthetic, and were enjoyed for their artistry. Novels exhibiting these attitudes and stances, however, are not recognized as contributing to a tradition, and they enjoy no such popularity. Authors who project this kind of vision arouse resentment and irritation rather than admiration, in part because the modern version makes readers feel attacked. Readers of Ariadne's lament in Ovid's *Heroides* are not personally blamed for her plight, but in modern complaints, we the readers are held at least indirectly responsible, and are being asked to change something in ourselves or in the world. Our making that change would be costly to our comfort or income or way of living. Unlike the less satiric classical and Renaissance predecessors, modern complaints are designed to make the reader uncomfortable by means of content and tone. This chapter concerns both how they assault the reader and what inducements they offer to continue reading despite the unpleasantness. It also explores how we can open ourselves to material we find unpalatable, and what we might gain from doing so.

The novels create a voice, and they pitch that voice to an implied reader who colludes in or ignores the injustices of the world. Pitching the voice, in the sense of tuning it to a particular frequency, says something important about the modern form; readers who resist novelistic complaints usually characterize that voice as high-pitched, whiny, and even hysterical.[1] Adrenaline does make the voice rise, and somehow the words chosen for such spates of criticism suggest such a rise in pitch, even though they are just marks on a page. As illustration of that shrill tone used for complaint, let me invoke the movement in Mussorgsky's *Pictures at an Exhibition* called "Samuel Goldenburg and Schmuyle" or "Two Polish Jews, Rich and Poor." The composer gives us two voices, the rich Samuel Goldenburg, complacent, harrumphing and pontificating in low registers, while nattering at our ears in a mosquito-like whine is a pesky muted trumpet, obviously complaining. Many complaint novels treat readers as if they were comfortably off, self-satisfied, and likely to pontificate. The complainer's voice in fiction need not be the author's own, even when apparently autobiographical material intrudes, as it does in Andrea Dworkin's *Mercy* or Kathy Acker's *Don Quixote*. Occasionally in satiric works that voice may argue the very opposite of what the author evidently believes, as in William Kotzwinkle's *Doctor Rat*. The tonal quality is also inflected by the pace and intensity of bombardment as well as by what is said. Such a voice in its extreme form admits of no exceptions, and will seem unfair or at least lacking judiciousness. These qualities can irritate readers to the point where they stop reading. Even readers who agree with the complaining voice can be put off by a violent presentation of the argument. These novels embodying complaint basically stage an author-reader confrontation, which makes them useful for studying the abrogation of the author-reader contract.

Complaint is often self-centered or at any rate convinced that the author's view is the only ethically possible one. If not focused on the injustices suffered by the narrator or focalizing figure, then it may concern the physical plight of or the injustices done to other people, or the treatment of animals or the ecosphere. Some novels see the unfair sufferings of the self as representative of a larger problem and so combine the two orientations; in *The Color Purple,* Alice Walker rages at black men's treatment of black women, but she opens the target field to include anger at white treatment of all African Americans. Other-centered complaint—on behalf of animals, for instance—is often expressed in ways that we label satiric.

In addition to the self-oriented versus other-oriented division among complaints, we find some kinds of complaint to be influenced by gender, or at least by the patterns of dominance and submission often associated with gender division. A sociolinguistic study of "complaint stories" characterizes them as a female-to-female social interaction; they rarely appear in male-to-male exchanges, at least in Anglo-Western-Christian patterns.[2] Within that cultural context, the feminine world is the subordinate sphere, and within that realm, complaint stories let a woman blow off steam and encourage other women to offer sympathy. Within the dominant sphere, a man does not expose his weaknesses and failures to others lest he lose prestige and power, so he does not complain to his friends. Historically in Western literature, the complaining voice is usually female (even if authored by men), but as we shall see, Jewish tradition offers us male voices of complaint: David of the psalms, for instance, and Alex Portnoy in *Portnoy's Complaint.* So does Old English poetry. Thus the gender-inflected expectations of modern readers help explain why recent complaints disturb some readers so severely; upsetting a reader's sense of gender and hierarchy is a sure way to destroy readerly comfort.

If depriving us of comfort is one element of attack, another is demanding that we do something, that we change or that we change the world we live in. This too we find in contemporary complaint. Personal miseries may be beyond our immediate range of action. Granted, the parents of Alex Portnoy or of Kathy Acker's persona are fictional; even were they not, the fact that they did not treat their offspring as those children wished cannot be changed by us or anyone. We are, though, challenged to recognize our complicity in the social values that produced those parental attitudes. Larger social ills, though not very yielding to individual action, nevertheless cannot be fixed unless many individuals decide to make changes in their lives. Complaints hammer upon that obligation. Nothing will happen if people are too lazy to take action. Readers are asked to make sacrifices: their health might benefit from reducing the mass use of antibiotics and hormones on cattle, but they would also have to accept a steep rise in the price of beef.

Various elements that play a part in the complaint tradition emerge at different times in its development. From Jeremiah's Lamentations in the Hebrew Scriptures, we get a male accusatory and lamenting voice (other-directed) and the female voice of Jerusalem as widow lamenting her own degradation (self-directed). David's voice in some psalms (e.g., 69) is self-oriented and self-abasing, a pattern that avoids damaging his status only because the Lord is so immeasurably above him.[3] Immensely influential were the dolorous cries of Ovid's abandoned women; these were long popular in the European tradition, translated by schoolboys up through the eighteenth century. The Old English "Wanderer" and "Seafarer" cry out against the loss of one's lord and one's place in the lord's hall. These last voices, whether representing a secular or a spiritual warrior persona, avoid humiliation in admitting these losses because the complaints are voiced in a vacuum, with no implied audience except (probably) God. Throughout the Middle Ages, many professions (friars, pardoners), nonprofessional groups (women, social upstarts), abuses (avarice, lechery), and general themes (the evils of the present times) were the objects of political and social complaints.[4] Medieval lyrics from all over Europe show male lovers complaining about a woman's having rejected them. We also find dissatisfactions expressed in a female voice (though often written by men) that tell of male sexual perfidy and subsequent female suffering. The Elizabethan era enjoyed a flowering of male-authored, female-voiced complaints, and John Kerrigan anthologizes the tradition as background for analyzing Shakespeare's "A Lover's Complaint."[5]

All of those forms are relatively short, most of them poems of a few hundred lines at most. When novels in the nineteenth century used elements of the complaint modality to tackle social ills, they intermingled their social critique with story and personality. Dickens's *Hard Times,* for instance, gives us the warm family life of the circus and the tensions of the Gradgrind family as well as the complaint over the hardships of factory workers. Dilution helps sustain reader interest in the face of prolonged criticism and soften the aggressiveness that might make readers wish to stop reading.

For the purposes of this chapter, I define complaint as the *relentless articulation of discontent,* usually characterized by *strong emotive elements.* For some purposes, theorizers may wish to differentiate between complaint and satire. I am not trying to elaborate on that distinction but rather see many satires as part of a larger complaint mode of thinking; they too project a vision designed to upset the reader. One of my examples, *Doctor Rat,* is certainly satiric. Whatever the generic label, I am concerned with authorial persistence and emotional temperature; in the most aggressive complaints, these result in a whining or hysterical tone.

That complaint can be felt as an attack on the reader is illustrated by what happened when I assigned Kathy Acker's *Don Quixote* in a graduate seminar. One older male student arrived fuming: "What the hell right does she have to complain in this fashion? What's so bad about her life? Why do I have to listen to all this whining?" He did read the whole book rather than throwing it aside, and because he was intelligent, he wrote his seminar paper on Acker so he could try to figure out why she made him so angry. His response, though, illustrates the danger of writing in this vein: quick rejection from those who value positive attitudes and dislike victim stances. Possibly, too, his hackles were raised by having to insert himself into what he unconsciously felt to be a female interactional pattern.[6] Nonetheless, some writers express themselves in this mode, despite its potential for alienating any but the most radical or empathetic audience. Evidently nothing else seems direct and honest enough to address the problems that concern them.

Novelistic complaint is an urgent form. Writers feel certain wrongs and crave changes that would right them. The underlying subtext for such complaint runs as follows: "This abuse is horrible, disgusting, disgraceful. They/We do this and that to me/to other people/to animals/to the ecosphere. This is unjust and unfair. If they/we continue, readers too may suffer, or the world as we know it may come to an end. Therefore, you readers should pitch in and help/join the revolution." The tone of the cry will be one thing if the victims are like the narrator in class, race, or culture, as is usually the case with Kathy Acker. That tone will be something else if the victims differ from the narrator, in which case the narrator may have problems justifying speaking for the oppressed and may be accused of condescension or appropriation. Tone will again differ if the victims are not human—animals being the main alternative.

This chapter considers works by seven authors. They represent male and female voices, self-centered and other-centered lamentations, and speakers from a variety of subordinate positions. *Portnoy's Complaint* (1969) makes a good starting point. Its very title stakes a claim to this mode of expression. Moreover, that novel made numerous readers angry. Philip Roth's family was deeply affronted, as were other Jews, over Portnoy's exhibitionistic, ever-present sexuality, and gentile readers often found it an uncomfortable read because of his emotionality.[7] A couple of Kathy Acker novels offer interesting female parallels, albeit with different gender and political agendas. In all of her novels, one or more voices are nearly identical to voices in her other works, so that much of what she writes could be called the complainer with a thousand faces. Andrea Dworkin's *Mercy* represents a well-known form of feminist complaint and one that raises serious issues about extreme arguments and an author's relationship to audiences. When she died in 2005, some obituary writers muttered that she had set feminism back twenty years because women did not wish to be associated with her stances, but in addition to her extreme demand that women kill men are some more acceptable arguments as well. Roth, Dworkin, and Acker concern themselves with human inhumanity to humans as practiced along religious, gender, and class lines, all with dominance and subordination as contributing elements. Alice Walker and Frank Chin offer complaints shaped by race, gender, and ethnic identity. For contrast to these mostly self- and definitely human-centered complaints, we look at two authors who tackle human treatment of animals. Both William Kotzwinkle and Ruth L. Ozeki want us to change our behavior in this realm, but their techniques for making arguments and convincing the audience differ in important ways when it comes to persuading readers to continue reading.

Self-Centered Complaint: *Portnoy's Complaint,*
Don Quixote, Pussy, King of the Pirates

The very title of *Portnoy's Complaint* tells us what to expect in general tone. Through the narrative situation of Portnoy's talking to a psychoanalyst, Philip Roth is able to spin out a three hundred–page monologue on the damage done to Alex Portnoy by his manipulative Jewish mother.

> I would refuse to eat, and my mother would find herself unable to submit to such willfulness—and such idiocy. And unable to for my own good. She is only asking me to do something *for my own good*—and still I say *no?*
> Wouldn't she give me the food out of her own mouth, don't I know that by now?....
> I just don't want to eat, I answer.
> So my mother sits down in a chair beside me with a long bread knife in her hand. It is made of stainless steel, and has little sawlike teeth....
> Why a *knife,* why the threat of *murder,* why is such total and annihilating victory necessary—when only the day before she set down her iron on the ironing board and *applauded* as I stormed around the kitchen rehearsing my role as Christopher Columbus in the third-grade production of *Land Ho!*[8]

Portnoy's oedipal problems and his castrating Jewish mother are so famous as to need no further illustration. How does his complaint disturb us, though? Why do we keep reading? And what can it accomplish or persuade us to do?

In the division between self- and other-oriented complaints, this falls emphatically among those that focus on the narrative self and its problems. Insofar as those concern a man and his parents, we can be expected to do nothing except listen—as would a friend, relative, or psychoanalyst. If we can bring ourselves to listen as a friend or relative, our reward is knowing that we are trying to keep the social fabric from tearing, trying to reduce pressure on it through reducing the pressure on this individual. Insofar as the complaints concern tensions between Jew and gentile, we might find reason to alter our behavior if gentile, though presumably only if Portnoy manages to elicit sympathy, and his record on that is spotty; his complaints are not that attractive. They are upsetting to anyone with WASP notions of masculinity because this extended whine violates canons of manliness. Nor need one be WASP to feel the extremity of this self-exposure. Portnoy himself equates his complaint with lack of manhood, though he interprets that as a larger Jewish male problem. "Please, who crippled us like this? Who made us so morbid and hysterical and weak? . . . Bless me with manhood! Make me brave! Make me strong! Make me *whole!*" (40). He imagines himself and his "fellow wailers" wallowing across seas of guilt (in steerage), crying to one another "Poppa, how could you?" "Momma, why did you?" and "vying" among themselves as to "who had the most castrating mother, who the most benighted father" (132–33). He pictures men complaining to one another, their status determined not by bravery and power but by who has suffered the most—and he obviously feels that he will win, so he oddly recoups a bit of his hierarchical position by formulating unusual rules for masculine interaction. Unless his readers wish to enter this new contest, however, they will not respect him more for what he is doing. He is no David abasing himself before the Lord; David gained a certain dignity, if only from having a special relationship to God, but neither Dr. Spielvogel the analyst nor we as readers can ennoble Alex Portnoy.

Because of changes wrought in cultural consciousness, Portnoy is less funny than he once might have seemed in his treatment of women. Conceivably his half-hearted attempt to rape a Sabra in Israel was once amusing—and she certainly suffered no harm, being combat-trained (298). This increasing unattractiveness adds to the novel's repellent qualities, though, and makes us ask why we continue to read. Why should we follow this monstrous infant, whose parents still loom gigantic in his mind, and who is so narcissistically wrapped up in his own victimization that he adamantly refuses to admit that others can be victims too, especially gentiles? His most significant girlfriend comes from an impoverished Appalachian background. She can hardly read or write. She has made her way in the world through sex and good looks, but is getting too old for that to work much longer and wants to settle down. Portnoy rants: "It must be made absolutely clear, to you and me if not to her, that this hopelessly neurotic woman, this pathetic screwy hillbilly cunt, is hardly what could be called *my* victim. I simply will not bend to that *victim* shit!" (151). Yet she is a victim, even his victim, and much more victimized by society than he is with his education.

So what keeps us listening to this lament? What inducements does Roth offer? Readers who feel victimized by their pasts may relish finding a language in which to express their problems. When the book came out, the sex, the comedy, and even the misogyny had some attractions. If mental simulation of friend listening to friend operates here, as Feagin's theory of reading suggests, we vicariously feel that we are helping someone. Given Portnoy's unwillingness to take responsibility for any of his problems, we may just respond to him by testing our theory of mind, in Zunshine's terms. I would also suggest that we continue to listen—despite the ways we are made uncomfortable—because we derive a gratifying sense of superiority. Whether Jew or gentile, most listeners will feel that they have survived their parents in better shape than Alex has. Men and women are likely to look down on him for his positioning of himself as the loser. That boost to our sense of superiority is a little-discussed reward for reading some texts, and I think it functions in this case.

Roth appears to develop his literary complaint out of Jewish oral and scriptural tradition. While Kathy Acker is also Jewish by background, she seems to draw more on the European classical tradition for her complaint. Acker translates Catullus in *Don Quixote* and Propertius in her novel *Great Expectations*. Furthermore, her interest in mythologies suggests that she would have been familiar with Ovidian complaints. The complaint tradition offers her as a feminist many advantages. In *Abandoned Women and Poetic Tradition* Lawrence Lipking argues, for instance, that lamentations uttered by abandoned women threaten both Aristotelian definitions of literature and the status of the canon; Aristotle states (and Matthew Arnold and W. B. Yeats agree) that suffering unrelieved by action is not suitable for poetry, which Aristotle defines as action (3). Resolution is necessary in traditional literature, and such traditions being mostly male-generated, Acker happily breaks that rule. Her laments fail to produce coherent action and thereby destroy some of the male-dictated functions of poetry. Lipking, in discussing the ballad that Lady Gregory translates as "The Grief of a Girl's Heart," points out that "nothing in the world—not duty, not propriety, not God, and certainly not literature—ranks in importance with the grief of a girl's heart. Her love destroys all distinctions" (8). He claims that "the poetry of abandoned women is indeed so resistant to authority that it challenges the canon, so hardy and pandemic that it represents not merely one more poetic tradition but an insidious counter-tradition or alternative to traditional ways of thinking" (8). Acker certainly presents her case as if nothing mattered but the pain she feels. Duty, propriety, social tradition, order, and God do not begin to achieve parity.

In addition to this intense exaltation of personal woe, complaints can also be political. Scottish and Irish ballads and poems give us women who represent the land and who bewail the lost native or Stuart king.[9] *Les Lettres portugaises* equates the seduced nun with the territory being conquered by the expanding French Empire (Kerrigan 68), and Giuseppi Verdi's early operas contain laments for missing fathers and lovers that carry a political subtext about united Italy (Lipking 11). Indeed, Lipking argues that the antihegemonic properties of female-voiced laments make them a genuinely heroic alternative to the male pattern of heroism in their resistance and their refusal to be cowed by traditional social forces (67).

How does Acker manipulate this potential power of the female complaint? Whereas Andrea Dworkin, as we shall see, makes a simple, direct, anti-male argument, Acker offers no such clear enemy or goal. In *Don Quixote* she appropriates voices found in Cervantes, Lampedusa, de Sade, Charlotte Brontë, Frank Wedekind, George Bernard Shaw, Emily Brontë, Shakespeare, Dante, Andrey Biely, and other writers. Through them she crystallizes and focuses facets of the Kathy persona's thoughts as she undergoes an abortion. For a start, this separates Acker's persona from the seduced and abandoned women who must go through with unwanted pregnancies; she refuses to be bound to the natural course of events. At one level Acker's *Don Quixote* consists of the dreams and visions of a single night, but symbolically it represents the dreams and visions of a questing knight, or rather a female-male night-knight, searching for what she/he considers the ultimate goal: love. The persona's quest spreads over a whole life and recursively introduces the infantile relationships with her parents that make the absence of love so persistent and shattering.[10]

Complaint screams from the page: "It is the wound of lack of love. Since you can't see it, you say it isn't here. But I've been hurt in my feelings."[11] "I want love. The love I can only dream about or read in books" (18). "'I'm always miserable,' Don Quixote whined. 'It's the way I am'" (20). "*How can I stop loving you? I must stop loving you. You are my life. Please help me. I don't need help.* 'I won't go against the truth of my life which is my sexuality'" (33). "My family protests the way I am. The fact is that I *am* this way" (146). "There's no end to, because there's no escape from, my being-pain" (147). "Why am I lower than Jesus Christ? Why do I suffer more than anyone else suffers? Why is there human unhappiness?" (149). "I hurt because he doesn't exist" (155). "I hate myself. Do all other people hate themselves? Must every single person be apart from every other single person?" (156)

"Howl, human winds! Howl, all the atoms of this human skin. You do not love me!" (158). "This life which passes from desire to desire, desires which as I grow older I'm less able to satisfy, until I have grown to hate my very self? This life which becomes harder, then goes. I'm a mass of hunger lust loneliness unsure if I have value unsure of any meaning deeply bored helpless" (182). "Even freaks need homes, countries, language, communication" (202). Not all of these lines are uttered by the female Don Quixote persona, but as all the other speakers are basically emanations of her mind in various dreamlike sequences, they become one larger voice raised in such mostly self-centered lamentation. Listening to this as receptively as one can bears some resemblance to manning a suicide hotline.

Some of this complaint does arise from personal problems, and so we as readers cannot do much about them, though the speaker's projection of blame will make most readers feel that they too are being blamed, at least at times. The persona plays many versions of a primal rejection by parents in this novel, and other personae do the same in Acker's other novels. A mother is deserted by the speaker's genetic father when that mother is pregnant, and she is never able to forgive the child for ruining her life. Besides the absent father, there is a lustful stepfather who sometimes does and sometimes does not molest the speaker. One or the other of the parents commits suicide—which one varies from novel to novel. The parents talk about institutionalizing the Kathy persona, and she fears lobotomy. The absences, rejections, and refusals to love get replayed in her life as she throws herself at one lover after another who cannot reciprocate her passion on the same high, intense, consuming level. She turns lovers off with her extreme sexual and emotional neediness. We may be sorry that this has happened to a child, but at the same time, we may feel that worse is possible, and that the child at least was given an education and could have used it in conventional ways had she been willing to live within social constraints. This the Acker persona resolutely refuses to do. We may also be put off by the persona's ability to analyze her problems with great clarity while remaining unwilling to try to modify the self that so upsets her. The self seems sacred, never to be tampered with, even if it is highly impractical, causes much grief and unhappiness, and is recognized to be the result of shaping by others and hence not possessing any inborn authenticity.[12]

Acker also issues complaint on levels other than the personal. Those presumably have a larger claim upon us as readers, even though we may wonder whether the political discontents of her fiction are just transmutations of personal emotions. She herself admits that "on a political level, hatred is revolution. On a social level, it's chaos. On a personal level, self-destruction" (116). These other kinds of complaint concern men versus women, the hypocrisy of governments and other power structures, and the gap between the United States government's self-proclaimed excellences and the actualities. The persona goes off on political tirades that are larded with names: the Biafrans, Henry Kissinger, Eliot Richardson, Ambassador Ellsworth Bunker, and Lawrence Eagleburger (106). Richard Nixon gets a walk-on part spouting obscene denigrations of America, which he calls "a piece of diarrhea, no, of worm shit in the flux and flow of the music of the Third World. Rape America the Cunt! (I do. Yay.)" (108). The persona also demolishes the foundational myths of America: "These New Worlders had left England not because they had been forbidden there to worship as they wanted to but because there they and, more important, their neighbors weren't forced to live as rigidly in religious terms as they wanted" (117–18). In colonial Boston, Quakers were thrown into unheated jail cells during the New England winter and beaten twice a week, each whipping consisting of more strokes than the last (118). Little wonder to Don Quixote that a republic founded on such beginnings has become the hellhole she longs to obliterate.

When Acker moves into political complaint, then, the reasons for trying to remain open to her comments shift. Politically angry authors often serve the role Kurt Vonnegut claimed for them, namely, to be canaries in the coalmine. Their behavior warns humans that deadly coal gas is seeping into the air. My likening Acker to such a canary points to the possible outcome of her political rage: some kind of revolution or major social change. Acker's desire to raze the current civilization may seem extreme, but revolutions usually include some ideologues as extreme as she is, and when we get to other authors later in this chapter, we will see protests and warnings that may indeed bring about change, in which case the warning helps readers become prepared for such changes.

In addition to political walk-ons and demythologized history, Acker also uses pastiches from other authors to build her complaints. She is not assembling an anthology of similar complaints; rather, she grabs various literary characters and shows us that even if those characters did not think in her terms of their oppression, they were oppressed, and furthermore, that oppression of women by men is ubiquitous. The original Don Quixote, one of her appropriations, did his deeds for love, but he was mad without knowing it, whereas the Kathy persona "knows" her quest is insane. Wedekind's Lulu, merged with Shaw's Eliza Doolittle, exemplifies women being manipulated by men. Acker's version of Jane Eyre in the red room and in the charity school suffers from intolerant, bullying relatives and a rigid, unpleasant orphanage. De Sade helps her argue that most of us do not know our own bodies or minds, having been brainwashed by society into thinking and feeling only in certain ways. Since Acker alters and plays with her sources extensively, one cannot properly argue that these authors all support her grounds for complaint in their own centuries, but she uses them to extend the range of her complaint through time.

Pussy, King of the Pirates, a late Acker novel, carries out her complaint in both old ways and new.[13] She applies the names of Antonin Artaud and Gérard de Nerval to characters, drawing on their iconoclastic and tormented writings to locate her own in relation to literary models for desperate writing. Julia Kristeva's *Black Sun* expatiates upon Gérard de Nerval's castration anxieties, and Acker makes castration central to her Nerval's artistry. Her character Artaud describes Nerval: "*He hung himself from a woman's string in order to protest against political control. Suicide is only a protest against control....After he castrated himself, language came pouring out of him*" (21). This treatment of castration resonates with the lobotomy fears shared by several Acker personae. The persona is terrified of society cutting out part of her mind to make her more biddable and conforming.

Complaint also takes a new form in *Pussy,* namely, mythology. The cosmogonic myths work as complaint because they project a world hopelessly unpleasant from the first step. Incest generates the world. "A father's fucking his daughter. Night's fucking with morning. Night's black; morning, red" (68). The myth goes on, relating that the father once withdrew and ejaculated over nothingness, creating time. "Sperm is lying everywhere, in the world of time, on its ground. Lying in viscous pools. Since there's time now, the sun, the first being in the world, not yet quite being, cooks away all the sperm; black char and red earth are left" (68). Theogony follows as a boy, who disapproves of the incest, beheads the father; the boy, however, does not wish to multiply, though he is "continually screwing a girl who's as scummy as he is and looks like a rat.... The brat never comes in his girlfriend" (69), a girl who incidentally looks like the narrator, O. This relationship falls to pieces when the girl questions his love, and she cries, "What's the use of this sexual body which alienates what it desires? How can I bear to be conscious? Better not to be" (70–71), at which she burns herself up. The boy drapes himself in her remains, whirls until all the parts of her body spin off, until nothing is left but her cunt, which falls into a crevice and ends this world. The world then begins again with the boy, Orpheus-like, seeking her. A variant on this mythic story is told again in the book (97–101), with a continuation later (157–159). Gods have multiplied, and, "being gods, they were more hysterical, more fearful, more desperate, more emotional than humans" (157). To many readers that might seem a disparaging remark, but Acker exalts the hysterical over the rational and controlled elsewhere, so this is probably high praise.

Many of our world's cosmogonic myths involve incest or some other sexual irregularity or miracle, since they usually start with one god or a divine couple, and all creation emerges from those one or two bodies. Acker, though, personalizes this incest much more than usual. Few people remember that Zeus and Hera are brother and sister, for instance, and they are not described in the course of their marital coupling as siblings; the Greeks certainly made nothing of their kinship and did not value incest positively, as Oedipus's story makes plain.[14] For Acker, father, son, and daughter exist as categories in this beginning of the world, though no mention is made of mother or wife. Her function is elided, this being Acker's vengeance on an unloving mother who was a suicide. Someone not of the family, the rat-faced girl, remains unexplained, much like the giants in Genesis into whose lines Cain married, though on another level, she is the Acker persona and the gods are projections from her mind. The forces that cry forth at this world-birth are the incestuous drive of the father, a desire to kill him displaced from the daughter onto a son, and the desire to be loved that is unfulfilled for an alien outsider to this small family.

What, then, is Acker complaining about in these novels? What are we as readers supposed to do? In *Don Quixote,* numerous possibilities present themselves. Clearly poverty and lack of medical insurance constrain the life of Don Quixote, the Acker persona. One of her key distinctions is between tenants and landlords; landlords are owners and control wealth, and at some level she wants revolution against landlords and the economic structure of America and other first world powers. Acker embodies her attitude in a pirate's song: "There is no way we can defeat the landlords. But under their reins and their watchful eyes, 'I sail as the winds of lusts and emotions bare me. Everywhere and anywhere. I who will never own, whatever and whenever I want, I take'" (199)—a sentiment that says nothing about the fact that it is much easier to rob the poor than the wealthy. Generally, that pirate spokesperson struggles against pressures to conform to social norms, and this is where we hear the persona voice so loudly. It objects, for instance, to gender roles. In Don Quixote's dream, a voice identified as a dog speaks of Villebranche and De Franville, two ambiguous figures who change genders frequently and about whom others use both male and female pronouns (129–41). Indeed, Acker will take gender-bending to such lengths that in *Pussy,* Heathcliff is a woman, but she has a penis (108). In Acker's fiction, pressure to conform is equivalent to pressure by someone to control her. All of Acker's arguments seem to lead to the concept of control, and her personae and voices struggle against it. Opposed to any control is some kind of authentic, impulsive, emotional self, a self as little shaped by deadening social norms as possible, but one clearly formed and even deformed by its treatment in early life.[15]

No simple solution for control exists, whether for Acker or for other artists concerned with that problem. Control is also a key concept for Burroughs, Mailer, and Pynchon. Burroughs and Pynchon share with Acker a generally paranoid vision of politics.[16] When "They" control everything, making specific plans is difficult. Anarchy and wholesale destruction are the best tools but not easy to launch on a grand scale, and few readers would enter into such a plan. Local names for the controllers are legion—Nixon, landlords, the CIA, Americans, doctors—but how does one undo all hierarchy? Organization of large populations demands hierarchy, control, and coercion, as Burroughs laments in the introduction to *Cities of the Red Night:* "There is simply no room left for 'freedom from the tyranny of government' since city dwellers depend on it for food, power, water, transportation, protection, and welfare. Your right to live where you want, with companions of your choosing, under laws to which you agree, died in the eighteenth century," which Burroughs blames on "the overpopulation made possible by the Industrial Revolution."[17] He too sees pirates as an alternative, but the ideals of his pirate communes could not prevail against the population density of mushrooming cities, with their demand for food, water, and the constant availability of manufactured goods. Or, as Pynchon states in *Gravity's Rainbow,* "once the technical means of control have reached a certain size, a certain degree of *being connected* one to another, the chances for freedom are over for good."[18]

For all Acker's anguish over patterns of oppression, she presents few suggestions for changing them, other than letting our impulses rip and refusing to obey social rules, and of course if people followed that prescription, society would indeed change, though how chaos would be better is not clear. Revolution may be an ultimate goal, but she offers no blueprint. The point to her complaint seems more to complain, to release a growing, choking pressure within herself, and to sensitize us to the issues and to the world we live in and with which we collaborate. Lament might be another word; she sees no answers, and can only respond to the horrors she sees and feels with emotional protest.

Such protest does not meet with universal approval. Consider that offered by Robert Hughes in *Culture of Complaint: The Fraying of America:*

> In these and a dozen other ways we create an infantilized culture of complaint, in which Big Daddy is always to blame and the expansion of rights goes on without the other half of citizenship—attachment to duties and obligations. To be infantile is a regressive way to defy the stress of corporate culture: Don't tread on me, I'm vulnerable. The emphasis is on the subjective: how we feel about things, rather than what we think or can know.[19]

Even less sympathetically, he comments on the complaint element in performance art:

> In the performances of Karen Finley and Holly Hughes, you get the extreme of what can go wrong with art-as-politics—the belief that mere expressiveness is enough; that I become an artist by showing you my warm guts and defying you to reject them. You don't like my guts? You and Jesse Helms, fella.
>
> The claims of this stuff are infantile. I have demands, I have needs. Why have you not gratified them? ... I am a victim: how dare you impose your aesthetic standards on me? Don't you see that you have damaged me so badly that I need only display my wounds and call it art? (186–87)

Pretty clearly, Robert Hughes would not approve of Acker. Nor, for that matter, does he care for the more extreme writings of Dworkin, considering her work totally lacking in any qualities that would make it live as art beyond its own decade (109). He vividly articulates the objections that can be leveled at this kind of attack on the reader.

Of course the point of such complaints is to remind us that not everyone is lucky enough to avoid being victimized. Dworkin, Acker, and others work to prevent our cultivating ignorance of those who are thus damaged by culturally sanctioned powers. Given that Western society is based historically on male dominance and female subordination, and that complaint is one way for the subordinate to hold on to sanity, then we need to understand the functions of complaint. At the very least, Acker's use of complaint seems to ask us for understanding, and for the gesture of a friend or relative of listening patiently. While we might emerge from the experience feeling superior to the persona, the desired result is more that we feel harrowed, that we acknowledge our complicity with the system that is doing such damage. Ultimately, of course, we should do something to better the world, not just recognize complicity. While both Dworkin and Acker see revolution as desirable, neither is positioning herself rhetorically to make an effective pitch for that. If we are to improve society or even just protect our own interests, we will have to work out how to do that on our own.

Complaint about the Oppressor: *Mercy, The Color Purple, Donald Duk*

Whereas Acker's complaints, like Roth's, remain largely self-centered, Andrea Dworkin, Alice Walker, and Frank Chin offer examples of complaints that focus on a self that is less personal than representative of a much larger oppressed group. All of them bombard us with examples of the oppressors. Whereas we as readers may be unsure what response we are to offer to self-centered complaints, those concerning a group are easier to understand but all the harder to swallow if we do not wish to change our outlook and life.

Like Acker's complaints, Dworkin's *Mercy* also reflects European literary traditions. The obvious forebear is the Ovidian lament of the seduced and abandoned woman, though in Dworkin's narrative, the crime is rape and physical violence rather than honeyed seduction. The composite portrait that she assembles of men, however, also makes her book a modern mirror image of the medieval complaints against women. Hers is a complaint against men. John Peter discusses an exemplar of this tradition by Bernard of Cluny, a three thousand–line poem of recriminations, many of them against women, and reminds us that the tradition has classical roots in Juvenal's anti-female diatribes as well as Christian theological sources.[20] Chaucer describes a popular example of this literature in Jankyn's "Boke of Wikked Wyves," which the Wife of Bath's husband uses to needle her. In it, women do such things as murder their husbands. Like Dworkin, the medieval authors show no interest in presenting a balanced portrait or in admitting to exceptions. Total obloquy is the purpose of this form of complaint, whether misogynous or misandrous.

Where Dworkin differs from her forebears is in her particularizing and personalizing the accusations. Medieval complaints, especially when directed toward social groups, tend to be unparticularized and the speaker unidentified. The chapters in *Mercy* all concern a character named Andrea who makes much of her name because of its etymological relationship to manhood and courage. Parts of the novel may be autobiographical, and many people read it that way, but if all of it were autobiographical, then Andrea would stand convicted of invincible stupidity and inability to learn from experience because she puts herself at risk over and over. That may be the case. More plausible to me, though, is a reading that treats each chapter as a separate lyric outcry, each devoted to a different kind of rape, and to the different circumstances that can lead to rape and other forms of exploitation of women. The character Andrea speaks as if they all happened to her, because she is claiming an everywoman persona and because a first-person account is vivid. When she accuses a man of abusing the infant sucking reflex, he becomes more intensely shocking for being identified as her uncle. Whether Dworkin's relative actually behaved in this fashion is irrelevant given that no man should behave that way, but familial connection makes the threat greater, more intense, and more sickening.

For Dworkin, first-person writing makes us believe and respond more strongly because we feel we are hearing directly from a victim.[21] One inducement to read is the strength of her passionate tone. Reading this book gives one's emotions a thorough workout. She was always controversial, but even some male writers can pay tribute to her rhetoric if not necessarily to her argument. Madison Smartt Bell notes that "it's difficult to sustain a scream for over 300 pages, but Dworkin's narrator does quite a good job, using long tumbling run-on sentences to achieve a powerful effect." He likens her to Medea, and finishes, "Still, she is a brilliant and passionate theoretician, her anger is a polished and dangerous instrument, and even some of the people she's marked as enemies can hope she finds her way."[22]

She starts with a painfully effective account of being molested in a movie theater when she was ten years old; half the problem comes from trying to tell adults what happened and not having the vocabulary, and from their being too mealy-mouthed and ashamed to speak bluntly or clearly. "They ask if something went inside but when you ask inside where they look away and you are nearly ten but you are a fully desperate human being because you want to know inside where so you will know what happened."[23] She is furious and hurt when they decide that "nothing happened," because what happened was very scary and confusing (a strange man in the seat next to her in the theater, talking quietly—which means he was respectable and to be obeyed—but doing wrong things that cannot be described). He made her touch something strange and slimy, and felt her where no one had touched her before. The result is that she is banished to her room and not allowed out, punished because the only way she can break the tensions is to say "nothing happened" (9). And this is merely the first rape.

She describes many others, and for a while each is the first, which undercuts any claim that this narrative should be read autobiographically or as concerning a single person. She makes sense of this string of firsts by defining rape as "just some awful word. It's a way to say it was real bad; worse than anything" (46). Raped by teenaged boys, by the roommate of a sometime bed partner; sadistically abused in gynecological ways by jail doctors; raped by a Cretan lover with whom sex has been incandescently cleansing and beautiful before their different standards and assumptions ruin their relationship. Because she goes out alone at night and because she sleeps with whomever she wants, she is a whore by Cretan standards: "This means nothing to me. I've always lived on my own, in freedom, not bound by people's narrow minds or prejudices" (76–77). If she gives in to the local customs, then she is supporting them and helping in the suppression of women. If she violates them, however, then she gets the violent treatment meted out to whores.

Grounds for complaint continue to unroll before us. At times she is so poor that she must let herself be "raped" or not have any place to sleep. She fears walking the streets because of the young men playing basketball or the older men watching, to all of whom she is just gash. She complains, "If

I was famous and my name was published all over the world...it would still be cunt to every fucking asshole drunk on every street in the world" (224). She describes the experience of being bitten and cut on the genitals:

> I'm thinking that pain is a river going through me but there's no words and pain isn't a river, there's just one great scream past sound and my mind moves over, it moves out of my head, I feel it escape, it runs away, it says no, not this, no and it says you cannot but the man does and my mind just fucking falls out of my brains and I am past being anything God can help anyway and He's making the man stronger, He's making the man happy, the man likes this, he is liking this, and he is proud to be doing it so good. (132)

All forms of patriarchal power over women merge and flow together, so that God becomes a child abuser, and the original sin is not that of Adam and Eve but paternal abuse and incest. "God kept killing us [the chosen people], of course, to make us hard enough; genocide and slavery and rape were paternal kindnesses designed to build character" (274), as she says with heavy irony. Masada is his quintessential gesture toward his children, demanding that they kill themselves. She sees God as equivalent to the uncle who made infants suck his penis, an act she describes from the infant's point of view, giving voice for those who cannot.

She looks at excuses offered in court to keep men from suffering significant penalties for rape and concludes: "It is very important for women to kill men.... Amnesty International will not help us, the United Nations will not help us, the World Court will not help us.... They don't stop themselves, do they?" (331). Only the threat of killing will make men afraid to act on their impulses. She ends the book with a useful distinction: "The notion that *bad things happen* is both propagandistic and inadequate." Andrea offers the proposition that "*bad things are bad*" and must be treated as such in the courts and out of them (334).

In structuring her complaint, she works very much like Upton Sinclair in *The Jungle,* who frazzles our nerves both with the filth going into American-made sausage and with the inhumanity toward immigrant workers. Having worked on our sensibilities until we long for some kind of release, he then offers us socialism. We can sign up at his recruiting station and let our tightly wound feelings flow through that channel into action. Dworkin does the same here, trying to rouse us to such a pitch of horror, concern, and anger that we will accept her solution: murder those bastards who behave in the ways described. Join her revolution. Her *nom de guerre* is Andrea One, and she says many girls named courage are, like her, ready to kill.

Her problem is that this will not gain her many recruits. If your life as a woman has been torn to pieces by rape, putting yourself in jail for twenty years because you murdered the rapist or just some other man is unlikely to improve matters. She may indeed believe in her solution, but a secondary effect of her argument is to make audiences aware of the soft stance of the courts toward the male perpetrator, and to strengthen reader resistance to that leniency. She may fail in a revolution yet encourage a small step in reform. As rhetorician, she is too angry to compromise her stance and calculate how to gain the widest audience. In its present form, her argument does little to win any man to her cause, any more than Jankyn's "Boke of Wikked Wyves" won the Wife of Bath to her husband's way of thinking. Those women in Dworkin's readership who enjoy middle-class comforts and were raised to accept middle-class self-protecting behavioral patterns may feel that she indulges in risk-taking behavior, and may withdraw some sympathy, though her eloquence in expressing the feelings of victims has power even over the resisting reader. One innocent female student of mine felt that reading the book had permanently defiled her mind with the horrible forms of violence Andrea describes: that testifies to the force of the attack. As a professor now herself, however, that former student has taught the book, so something in it must have seemed worthwhile. Even if we resist Dworkin's solution, we are unlikely to forget her eloquence, and her heavy irony at the expense of the courts' lenience will leave us hypersensitive to such judicial rhetoric and (ideally) unwilling to accept it complacently. Dworkin also offers an important idea: she shows her middle-class readers that by avoiding danger and confrontation, they are colluding with the paternalistic system of values and are preventing any true equality or mutual respect from coming into being.

How might a man open himself to a novel like this, and why should he wish to? The same could be asked of Alice Walker's *The Color Purple.* Clearly the kind of man targeted as abusive is unlikely to open and change, but others not as heavily invested in dominance and misogyny might find some useful answers to the question "What does a woman *not* want?" as well as, perhaps, to the question of what she wants. Walker's novel came out early enough in the feminist movement for men to be surprised at her hostility and anger; in that sense the book offers a warning, and sensitizes willing readers to issues they may not have thought on seriously. Walker was indeed a canary in the coalmine when it came to warning that equality for black men was not enough, that male dominance over female was as bad in its way as white over black.

Walker starts her novel with a vicious situation: "He act like he can't stand me no more. Say I'm evil an always up to no good. He took my other little baby, a boy this time. But I don't think he kilt it. I think he sold it to a man an his wife over Monticello. I got breasts full of milk running down myself. He say Why don't you look decent? Put on something. But what I'm sposed to put on? I don't have nothing."[24] This man is her stepfather (whom she believes to be her father). He has raped her into bearing two children, and treats her thus. She gets similarly repulsive treatment from Mr.——, the man her father gives her to because he needs someone to tend all his children. While I do not mean to depreciate her suffering, much of this novel seems relatively quiet in tone compared to *Mercy,* more desperate than violent. That description would surprise early readers, given the wrath the book aroused in African American male writers such as Ishmael Reed.[25] Here we have a dynamic that is first female-male, but paralleled and echoed in other dichotomies: black-white, human-divine, and even just person-to-person. Throughout, those who are dominant struggle to impose their will and those who are subordinate resist that imposition. Most readers comment on the reiterated portrayals of men who violently abuse their women, but Walker does not offer a complaint as pure as Dworkin's in this regard. Not only does she present a couple of (admittedly brief) portraits of reasonable and supportive men, but also she undertakes at the end to transform Mr.——, one of the most fully articulated villains in the piece. If he can be rendered bearable, then the effect of this complaint is rather different from that of Dworkin, even if the main examples of evil are what we remember most.

What Walker sets up as the female answer to male dominance is, first, the achievement of self-supporting independence, and second, a philosophical attitude that lets one maintain personal serenity toward anyone of whatever gender who has dominated one's mind. As Celie says to herself of her long-absent female lover, Shug: "If she come, I be happy. If she don't, I be content. And then I figure this the lesson I was suppose to learn" (290).

Partly by force of circumstance, Celie lives largely outside the bounds of white society so has little to do directly and personally with white dominance, but her family suffers from race hatred, and she herself does suffer from her vision of God as an old white man. From various people in her life she learns to think of God as being in her, and of God as the creator of things to wonder at and admire—the color purple in a field, for instance (203), or sexual pleasures. The scenes of abuse by her stepfather and then her husband remain central to the book's impact, but the narrative does move out of the complaint mode toward the end, when Celie reaps the rewards of her stoicism. Possibly the complaint against black males remained so unacceptable to male writers because Celie's answer is not to find a *good* man but to find that she can do happily without a man at all, and even without a lover. She need depend on no one beyond a large circle of friends and relatives, and that attitude threatens all who wish some kind of dominance over her.

For contrast to Walker's gendered and racial plaint, let me briefly mention Frank Chin's ethnic complaint. In *Donald Duk,* he writes from the perspective of a twelve-year-old Chinese American boy cursed with that Disneyesque name. Throughout the weeks of the story, Donald struggles with his hatred of being Chinese and his hypersensitivity to racist slurs. Part of his problem is that he cannot make his world consistent; he would like to hate or despise his father, King Duk, for being Chinese and for being named King. His father, however, is a sympathetic and successful man who has reached accommodation with American values, and whose advice on how Donald should deal with gang boys in the streets proves very effective. Many an angry youngster wishes to hate his father and blame him for all that is wrong in the teenager's life, but Donald reluctantly admires his father, even though he resents his father's cultural comfort. Nothing seems right to this young man, which results in the novel's being a complaint.

One of Chin's grounds for objection is the way in which Western cultures consider the Asian man less than impressively male. Or as Donald puts it, Americans think that "Chinese are artsy, cutesy and chickendick."[26] No legends of Chinese heroes and warriors have breached the cultural barrier. Donald has trouble seeing his father, a chef, in a heroic light, and much the same goes for his other male relatives. Donald himself is not a brawler, and fears the gang boys, so is partly angry because he himself does not feel heroic. That the Disney duck runs around without pants and is clearly sexless adds to Donald's sense of emasculation. He learns about the contribution of Chinese men to building the railway, but sees that the Chinese got no recognition for their contribution; they were left out of the celebratory photographs and driven from their dwellings. What would be just a personal problem endemic to growing up becomes magnified because it is reinforced by such cultural prejudices. Chin's or Donald's solution, however, makes matters worse, both for Donald as character and for us as readers. Donald's string of complaints puts him in what Western culture sees as the feminine/subordinate position in relation to cultural power. He himself thus invites us to look down on him as less than heroically male. While this might seem an inevitable clash—if Donald does not complain, how will non-Chinese readers know what the problem is?—a few writers find a different solution. Gerald Vizenor, for instance, fiercely refuses all expression of "victimry" and causes any characters who indulge in it to come to a bad end. His favored approach involves bravery, imagination, and projection of a trickster ethos that refuses to be bound by rules. Through the complaint form, Donald creates and reinforces his own misery, while Chin, by presenting him through complaint, encourages the Western attitudes toward Chinese males that Chin so hates.

Chin's ending takes us out of complaint modality and into traditional novelistic territory: what Donald learns is low-key and common sense. Value your friends, and use holidays to cement your ties with others. Be generous. Do not hoard things. The complaint in this book is thus modified by a family- and society-oriented ending, but the tone throughout is irritating enough to make one consider putting the book down. One obvious reward for persisting is the insight into Chinatown life and Chinese American culture. Donald's age also makes us less bothered by the whine; he may be a male protagonist expressing distress, but that negativity is normal for his age. We remain uncomfortable with the drawn-out complaint in this book, however, because we are being asked to right the ethnic tensions but do not feel able to do anything effective, let alone wave a wand to produce an instant solution that would satisfy Donald.

Complaint is a frustrating genre because in its purest form, it does not offer a solution. Roth, Acker, and Dworkin embrace it in its angry purity, and readers must either start by being semi-convinced or must be willing to open themselves to an emotional storm for the experience of being all churned up. They must submit to the provocation. Possibly with a view to retaining readers, Walker and Chin modify the complaint form by offering resolutions at the end of their novels. Celie achieves philosophical balance, and Donald has been reminded that his family provides some support and understanding. The underlying inequities are not truly resolved, though, and we are implicitly told to do what we can to improve that social problem.

Complaint over the Plight of Others: *Doctor Rat, My Year of Meats*

We have seen how a self-centered and often female-voiced complaint, rooted in Jewish, Christian, and classical traditions, operates in contemporary fiction. We have fewer models for issuing complaints in the names of others. Jeremiah laments damage to Jerusalem, and he and other prophets castigate erring Israel. To worry about nonhuman feelings or even about mistreatment of natural resources, however, is a relatively modern development.

Speaking for animals demands different tactics. Who can speak for them, and how does one build any readerly sense of identification? William Kotzwinkle, in depicting an animal protagonist in *Doctor Rat,* claims license to speak for animals, but readers do not feel an automatic sense of oneness with such a speaker, particularly as he appears to be mad. We remain aware of the fantasy. Ruth Ozeki evidently recognized that sympathy would be a weak card to play. Her protagonist, Jane Takagi-Little, never tries to make sympathy for animals her chief line of argument and does not try to speak for animals. She works instead on readerly self-interest. She tries to make us understand what we will suffer if we continue to ingest the chemicals used on beef cattle.

In calling *Doctor Rat* a complaint, I am straining the term somewhat, because satire is the label that would come to most readers' minds. Complaint and satire are overlapping categories, and my purpose is not to divide such works into subgenres but to talk about novels that strike the reader as complaining about some wrong. *Doctor Rat* does complain vociferously, but does so mostly by means of heavy irony. Exactly where that irony originates is debatable. The character Doctor Rat may be producing it, or he may be truly mad, and the irony may be William Kotzwinkle's. The latter seems to me the better explanation. In that case, Kotzwinkle has a mad narrator glorying in the tortures that animals undergo in labs. Doctor Rat, the character, is not complaining in his own persona, but Kotzwinkle complains through his hyperbolic hymns to science and the professor. Though complaint and satire can be differentiated, the underlying subtext in this instance is basically the same: "How awful. How unfair and horrible. They do these terrible things to animals. If they don't stop behaving this way, the world will come to an end"—which in this book plays out in all non-human animals in the world dying. Also characteristic of complaint is the unrelenting pressure on the reader and the shrillness and extremity of the claims.

Doctor Rat is a pun; most of the experiments described are carried out by graduate students pursuing doctorates. Part of the target is the university system that spawns such experiments, as well as all the granting bodies that support it, the government above all. What is done to animals in this lab bears certain parallels to experiments carried out by the Third Reich on human subjects, so one of the first leitmotifs is Hitlerian. Rats' bodies are dissolved from their bones by a 5 percent formaline solution, which Doctor Rat terms the Final Solution. Rats cry out that they do not want to die as their spinal fluid is drained out ("The rat wants to die now, I assure you").[27] They are placed on ice in a thermos bottle to be cooled to 2 degrees below zero centigrade. Others are blind because one of the students is removing eggs from a female rat's body and grafting them onto male rat bodies, including onto the eyeballs. In Doctor Rat's version of "Three Blind Rats," *"We all run after the graduate life/And cut off your balls with a carving knife/Did you ever see such a grant in your life"* (6). Kittens are microwaved (48–49). One dog is made to inhale flames (27). Several others are made to run themselves to death in blazing-hot conditions that bring on sunstroke (24). Another is whacked on the leg with a rawhide mallet to induce shock: 573 blows so far, and at Columbia where this was first tried, it took 1,000 blows to achieve the goal (28). Another dog's leg is being crushed in a clamp (37). Doctor Rat gleefully claims that "it might also result in a better kind of plastic, or perhaps a new sort of aspirin. Housing projects will be more perfectly designed and detergents will improve. The applications are simply endless" (37). Dogs gassed in a glass chamber might produce "a better shoe polish for the army" (51).[28] No matter how pointless-seeming the experiment, we are told that it is necessary for national security.

Meanwhile, outside the lab, the animal kingdom is being stirred by strange psychic winds. Dogs flee from their owners and run wild in the forest, high on the scent of freedom. Pigs develop philosophical awareness as they are taken to slaughter, and hens talk with religious overtones of a paradisal new world they will find after their battery existence, but instead they get their throats cut. These psychic winds cause wild animals to congregate in huge masses and zoo animals to drop dead. This provokes a violent reaction from humans, who respond to the unusual by deciding to slaughter it. African dictatorships welcome the chance to try out new weapons on elephants and rhinos, while the animal food companies bid for the right to process the meat. The military-industrial complex swings into action, and when the dust settles, all or almost all the animals of the world are dead, man excepted.

Kotzwinkle can persuade us that the various preposterous-seeming experiments are real, in part because we are willing to believe that unpleasant and painful things are done, and we admit that as outsiders we might not see what knowledge such experiments could usefully provide. Grafting eggs to eyes could, after all, teach us something about rejection mechanisms and ultimately provide information useful in organ transplants. Kotzwinkle even supplies us with journal references, which make the experiments look real. Because the book came out more than thirty years ago, I had trouble finding proof in current databases. Even with help from a librarian, though, I could find no evidence that many of the journals he cites existed, and I found none of the articles I tried to check, so I postulate that at least some and probably all of the references are fake, a weakness in the construction of Kotzwinkle's argument. If the situation is as bad as he would have us believe, then offering documentation that stood scrutiny would help his cause. False pedantry is a common satiric technique, but that serves to satirize the pedantry. In this instance, the falseness undermines the horrors he is claiming to expose because they are evidently not as bad as he asserts.

The plangency of this complaint stays firmly fixed on humankind's cruelty toward animals. Some of this seems well argued, but some less so. Pigs are intelligent but are not likely to be capable of thinking, "Now that I have truly ascertained that I exist, am I to enjoy my new awareness?" (70). They are able to sense the dangers implicit in a slaughterhouse, as two British Tamworth pigs proved in 1998 when they dug under a fence and swam an icy river to escape from one. Hens seem even less capable of the visions given to them here, but the problems of battery containment—beaks burned off to prevent them pecking one another to death, the inability to hunt grubs and move about—seem likely to produce a wretched existence from the hen's perspective. Most animals will settle happily in relatively small quarters, provided that their food is well balanced and those quarters satisfy their need for territory. Even given that hens live in flocks, they need individual space as well as adequate group territory and exercise. Under conditions of crowding such as hens experience in battery boxes, most species exhibit destructive behavior and show signs of mental breakdown. Hence, I'm willing to accept his argument on that score. When he gets to dogs freaking out over freedom and finding that they do not need mankind, I become dubious. Most domesticated animals are not well suited to living wild. Long domestication literally changes their bodies, such that skulls become thinner, for instance. Dogs going feral in packs in cities can be a threat, but they are living off garbage and other human detritus, not running free in the woods and living off what they can kill. A few hunting breeds could doubtless revert to pack hunting, but the smaller breeds would not survive. Kotzwinkle romanticizes his animals in ways that are demonstrably fraudulent. A less strained argument would be more plausible and effective.

The same problems undercut Kotzwinkle's mass migration of the animals to meeting points. This movement does draw on some little-understood natural phenomena. We do not know why some members of the whale family will run aground as a group; that seems sometimes to happen naturally, though in recent years it has allegedly been caused by deployment of sonar in their region. Lemmings do not migrate with suicide as their object, but will, evidently, migrate when territory becomes too crowded, and have been known to go over cliffs into water and swim along in the direction chosen, and Kotzwinkle seems to be drawing on that migration myth. He credits animals with a collective consciousness that makes them join as one, their power growing as the minds of more of them come together. Alas, in hoping that man would join them and heal the rift, they were mistaken. Kotzwinkle ends on an emotional note: "I [Doctor Rat, a lone survivor] hear people talking on campus.... But no scurrying little feet in the grass. No softly sliding feline shadows. Not a single meow, not a chirp, not a solitary bark in the whole of creation. You can feel the emptiness out

there: the Final Solution gives you a sort of lonely feeling" (243–44). Again
the Hitlerian note, but does it work?

Kotzwinkle wrote in the complaint mode, and does produce some funny
or gripping or eerie passages. Overall, though, he seems to me to fall short
in his persuasions, and so serves as a warning of how this form of writing
can turn the reader against the arguer, however much readers may accept
the argument in general. The shrill tone of the accusations reflects hysterical thinking with no signs of willingness to discuss reasonably. He offers
no alternatives to laboratory testing, for instance. What does he think any
convinced reader should do? If we are to avoid contributing to the scenes
he presents, we would have to stop using modern medicine as well as turn
vegetarian. Few readers will feel that generous. He offers no inducements
but only moral and emotional righteousness, and those seldom crack the
shells we have built for ourselves. *Uncle Tom's Cabin* could move North-
erners to tears, but was rather less effective in the South, where personal
financial loss was a factor. At present, no bloc of states or countries has
forsaken laboratory use of animals and made it central enough to their
identity to wish to invade others and force them to comply. The large audience that could put his complaint into action seems lacking, though in
the years since the book came out, animal rights activists have grown very
considerably in power. In their attacks on labs, we may be seeing what
started as a fringe position when Kotzwinkle wrote turning into a more
recognized political stance, one that has affected legislation and that may,
in another thirty years, truly change the nature of laboratory experiments.
Time will tell.

For a rhetorically more effective argument we should turn to Ruth
Ozeki's *My Year of Meats*. This novel lies on the very borderline of complaint; only in patches does the "whine" present in others books discussed
show itself, though the pressure on readers is steady throughout. Perhaps
because she takes a more analytic than frantic tone, Ozeki avoids many
of the pitfalls of complaint as an attack on reader sensibilities. Readers
will feel assaulted by some of her grosser scenes of animal treatment and
slaughter, but we have been well prepared in advance. Furthermore, we
are less invited to decry the sufferings of the animals than we are to consider the damage to ourselves, a topic for which we might be expected to
have unlimited sympathy. Her protagonist, Jane Takagi-Little, notes that
"information about toxicity in food is widely available, but people don't

want to hear it."²⁹ She goes on: "I would like to think of my 'ignorance' less as a personal failing and more as a massive cultural trend.... Fed on a media diet of really bad news, we live in a perpetual state of repressed panic. We are paralyzed by bad knowledge, from which the only escape is playing dumb. Ignorance becomes empowering because it enables people to live. Stupidity becomes proactive, a political statement. Our collective norm" (334). This willed ignorance is what Ozeki must assault, and she does so with true wiliness, coming at us delicately from many directions until she can slap us with the consequences of the pattern we accept at present. The gist of her message remains that of complaint: people are doing horrible and stupid things, and something should be done to stop them. Moreover, she pushes us hard enough that we feel that she is complaining and we want to shut her up. Unlike the other authors in this chapter, though, she has budgeted for that response, and for some readers she may succeed in bypassing it.

Jane Takagi-Little is a documentary filmmaker, but she is a starving artist and can take on a job as "cultural pimp, selling off the vast illusion of America" (9) to Japan, because she is bilingual and bicultural. She is hired to do a series of programs on American housewives, each of whom will prepare a favorite meat recipe (preferably beef), the ultimate point being to sell American beef to the resistant Japanese market, although the ostensible focus is on the women as people, not on meat. The wholesomeness and friendliness of the housewives symbolically guarantee the wholesomeness of the meat. Jane is occasionally appalled by the gap between the ideals of the program and reality. One episode of *My American Wife!* nearly causes the couple being featured to divorce. Her program on a vegetarian lesbian couple upsets the sponsor, both for the lesbianism and for the lack of meat. Her boss objects to nonwhite housewives. Some programs, though, seem to work at a higher level than she could have imagined. The plight of a golden-haired child who revived from a coma to ask for her favorite lamb chops changes the entire town she lives in; its citizens decide to devote themselves to new ways of bringing such injured people back to life. Some programs affect people in unanticipated ways. Her Japanese crew teach a Louisiana Cajun cook how the despised kudzu vine can supply starch, salad, crispy batter for deep-frying, and a hangover remedy, and Jane later discovers that her being Asian American has made her a desirable role model for many of the ten Asian children adopted by one of her featured families.

Her first serious inklings that meat produced in America might not be good for us is when a Japanese director goes into anaphylactic shock from eating some fresh veal at a feedlot farm. The doctor comments that calves are kept "alive with these massive doses of drugs just long enough to kill them. What sent your director into shock was the residue of the antibiotics in the Sooner Schnitzel" (60). She gets another nudge when a poor family admits that they stopped eating chicken necks because the chemical residues made a baritone voice climb into soprano register and caused the man to sprout little breasts (117). Jane starts researching this and realizes a personal application. Diethylstilbestrol (DES), an estrogen used to castrate male chickens chemically, had been used on humans to help prevent miscarriages despite the fact that it caused sexual deformities in rats and cancer in female children affected in utero. Jane was one of those children whose mothers had used DES, and she attributes her inability to become pregnant to her DES-deformed uterus. With this personal curiosity to urge her on, she seeks out a beef feedlot where estrogens are still used for fattening the cattle.

Estrogens are not all she finds. Food additives include plastic, newspaper, cement dust, slaughterhouse wastes, and manure as well as the expensive formula food. She learns about the drugs and abortifacients used automatically on heifers coming to the lot. She sees that the man running the feedlot has himself been physically affected by the female hormones, as has his five-year-old half-sister, who has a mature body with full breasts and pubic hair, and who has started menstruating. Jane has been filming materials she knows cannot be used on *My American Wife!* When fired from that job, she edits the film on the dangers of estrogen-tainted meat and manages to bring national and then international attention to it.

Ozeki makes the unpleasant news—which still hits us amidships with a thud—more acceptable in a variety of ways. She leads up gradually to the full revelation. We are not surprised, just upset by details the knowledge of which we may have been able to suppress prior to reading the book. Most readers have not witnessed the slaughter process, nor seen an aborted calf corpse crawling with maggots, nor seen the unnatural, crowded, and filthy conditions of a feedlot and the unnatural and unsuitable food (including corn, which is not something cattle would eat in the wild) that make antibiotics necessary. Nor have we dealt with the economics of being a feedlot farmer, and the cold figures that mean making a very slim profit if you use estrogens and some of the other feed additives, or losing money if you do not. She does not simplify the storyline to good guys and bad guys. She makes her case, though, to our heads as well as our hearts and stomachs.[30]

Another tactic she uses is to interweave the investigative documentary work with a romance. Jane meets and enjoys in bed a saxophone player; she unexpectedly finds herself pregnant, despite having believed from long trying that this was impossible for her DES-damaged uterus. She loses the child, probably to natural causes, but aggravated by injury in the slaughterhouse. She learns more about her mother's inability to carry children to term that made her take DES, and that she, Jane, had been so big at birth that she tore her mother apart and made having further children impossible. Fertility, sterility, and the complexities of mother and daughter learning not to blame each other for the physical problems they have caused each other: these give us human faces for the problems caused, pains and consequences that we can assimilate on a personal level. Jane may marry and will consider adopting, but that is just a personal solution to the wider problem of what chemicals in meats may do in the long run to the populace that eats them.

Ozeki does not launch this as a crusade to cease eating meat as a moral decision. Indeed, one of the Japanese characters, an anorexic, abused wife, finds lamb chops the first meat she can tolerate without vomiting it back up, and she attributes her eventual pregnancy to her eating the Australian (and therefore less chemically treated) lamb. Jane admits that sometimes she longs for the taste and mouth feel of meat, and finds that nothing else will do. Ozeki avoids moral preachments. She keeps the argument practical and makes the primary victims human, not animal. She holds no brief for abusing the animals but clearly understands that she will lose the agreement of her audience if she bangs on that issue too persistently. Self-interest, she feels, will persuade more people than appeals to their sympathy, idealism, or generosity.

What does she expect us to do? What options are open? Ozeki depicts the lesbian couple's decision to convert to vegetarianism as not a matter of burning moral concern for animals but one of family-protective instincts, and then because further reading does make the women feel that eating meat is not morally the best decision one can make. She gives us enough information to know that cattle could be raised differently, could be grass-fed and not filled with hormones. She also points out, however, the vast damage done to the ecology of the West by overgrazing, and makes clear that even if we continued raising as many cattle as possible on grass, the numbers would drop and the price of meat would go up. If we protected the grassland as well by permitting fewer animals per acre, meat prices would soar. Raising meat for consumption is inherently inefficient; vast amounts of grass and grain are necessary, and the acreage could produce more vegetable protein. As beef is currently raised, "it ends up taking one gallon of gas to make one pound of grain-fed U.S. beef" (250), and "the average American family of four eats more than two hundred sixty pounds of meat in a year.... [That requires] two hundred sixty gallons of fuel, which accounts for two point five tons of carbon dioxide going into the atmosphere and adding to global warming" (250). The cattle themselves produce methane, another greenhouse gas. "But cheap meat is an inalienable right in the U.S.A., an integral component of the American dream" (126). Clearly the result of any reform will be very expensive red meat. The rich will be able to afford it if they so choose, but the poor will not.

For all Ozeki's carefully designed argumentation, the book does project the voice of complaint. The focal figure is herself DES-damaged and may still die young of cancer. She does not whine about this, but we remain aware of the damage that such hormones have done and can do, and her personal experience gives an edge to every mention of related subjects. Similarly in the complaint mode are the piled-up details of slaughter, of livers oozing hormones, the "viscous, thickened gruel of blood and offal" (280), the cattle still alive as they hang upside down. This hits us strongly and produces visceral revulsion. We follow Ozeki along her train of thought more easily than in any of the other books considered so far because we can enjoy our sympathy for the main character. Because the romance lacks depth, though, we might feel that it lessens the aesthetic level of this novel. The purity of the complaint is diluted. This book was very successful, however, and reached a wide audience; it was translated into ten languages and released in fourteen countries. Even if we resist the romance, we can admire Jane's thinking her way through the problems she faces in regard to meat. Enjoyment balances the assault on our sensibilities as readers; it mitigates the most off-putting effects, encourages us to listen, to ponder, to reconsider our own lives in light of the data. Because of the romance distraction and Ozeki's avoidance of thrusting her message down our throats, her argument may be able to reach a wider potential audience.

Why Listen to Complaints?

Plenty of people enjoy complaining, but few enjoy listening. A recent analysis of how to get tenure warns junior faculty not to fall into the habit of complaining, because that will make their colleagues dislike them. The medieval *planctus* may have had musical connotations, but those of "whine" are all negative. Authors who run the risk of alienating readers would seem, therefore, to be driven by powerful emotions they cannot (or choose not to) control, or they relish their own performance of indignation and enjoy the rhetoric of accusation, fulmination, lamentation, and awful warning. They enjoy being forceful and upsetting the reader. Fair enough. Playing melodramatic prosecutor to a full court can stroke one's ego, but how can one hope to win the case, except with those readers who start out already convinced? What are the techniques that let these writers persuade undecided readers?

For me, at least, the most effective is the reasoned argument, the careful building of a case. Ozeki does this, and it works to the degree that I would support legislation that banned many of the substances being used, and would put up with much more expensive meat. I can also enjoy those parts of Dworkin that work as an argument, even though I fight in my mind with her and totally refuse to accept her concluding call to murder men. I am held by the argument enough to listen and talk back, and appreciate the stimulus to thinking my way through the claims that she makes. I ponder the ideal world she thinks should exist, and how the realities of power make her dream of civilized equality seem unlikely. This idea-based approach obviously appeals to a phlegmatic personality who relies on logic; it will not go far with someone who prefers emotion and believes that feeling is more authentic (and therefore more valuable) than systematic organization of thought.

Emotional appeals are also possible, and present in all of these complaints. Dworkin, say, is probably persuasive for most readers when describing the child's experience in the dark theater; we may be more critical of the adult Andrea's behavior, but the child has done nothing to bring on what happens, and her anguish is searing. Even someone who will reject Dworkin's unswerving hostility to men and stop reading in disgust at some later point might read that far with some willingness to be persuaded. We may similarly feel some sympathy for the Acker persona's childhood problems, and for the pain of Alex Portnoy, especially early on, before Alex's outpouring has become so obviously a performance.

Another technique for persuading us that something is a threat consists of equating it with or linking it to an acknowledged problem. This tactic is the basis for scare journalism: some new illegal drug is always the "next crack cocaine." Kotzwinkle obviously tries to make us take him seriously by equating human treatment of lab animals with the Third Reich's treatment of Jews in medical experiments. While many Jews are understandably wary of any claim of equivalence to the Holocaust, they might feel the need to look hard at the evidence lest they find themselves cast in the role of Hitler, and gentiles who deplore the horrors of the Holocaust might be equivalently unwilling to find themselves taking a Hitlerian stance. If the author's evidence is strong enough, this tactic works; if we resist it, however, it not only fails but undercuts the whole argument as well.

We can be swept along by conventional entertainment woven into the unpleasantness that constitutes the assault. We find this in the humor of Roth, the romance of Ozeki, the family-and-holiday ending of Chin, the feel-good message of accomplishment and personal peace at the end of *The Color Purple*. Sometimes readers may be held by prurient or intimate materials; Acker, Roth, and Burroughs (another author who occasionally works the complaint mode) capture interest with those. The question is whether so much entertainment is added as to soften the attack to negligibility or whether the amount of entertainment is insufficient to balance the hostile material. One can also ask whether the entertainment lessens the aesthetic integrity of the work, and the answer would often be yes. Personally, I do not find Roth funny enough to balance some of the ugliness, particularly against women. A male reader might well feel differently, however, as might someone more attuned to Jewish humor and jokes, and the novel's original readers might have been pleasurably startled by intimate materials that now seem dated.

We can also derive pleasure from the vicarious breaking of rules. Acker vents her emotions, gives no thought to ordinary polite responses, and ignores social conventions. She invites us to throw back our heads and howl.

If doing these things (or even contemplating them) gives pleasure to readers who force their lives to fit the accepted social pattern, then some of those readers will gleefully respond to the possibility. We see a version of this vicarious rule-breaking when Roth invites men to experience the prolonged complaint; those who expend a lot of unconscious energy holding in their dissatisfactions and maintaining a stiff upper lip may secretly enjoy letting rip through mental simulation even though the spectacle renders them uncomfortable. Some gentiles who repress emotions may similarly enjoy the sensation of being aggressive with their feelings. Contrariwise, if readers do *not* get a thrill from overflowing their usual boundaries, they may derive a sense of superiority to the spectacle of those who do. That might not keep one reading, but it may provide a small bonus. One notes that much of the comedy in *Portnoy's Complaint* is based on that flash of feeling superior that is one of the four bases for laughter.[31]

And finally, of course, we may be kept reading to be sure we know what's in the argument for us. Ozeki, in particular, offers information that could have real-life consequences in our own lives. The hormones in cattle may contribute significantly to human cancers, not to mention hormone imbalances (with dire consequences). Possibly more alarming is the misuse of antibiotics on animals, which is rapidly removing them from our medical arsenal as bacteria become resistant. We have to consider how important cheap meat is to us compared to dying, young or old, of routine infections that only antibiotics at present can cure.

Deploying such techniques may keep one or more kinds of readers reading despite feeling that their values are being attacked. One cannot say that any one technique is better than another because it will be better for only some readers. I personally follow with the most attention and approval well-reasoned arguments like those of Ozeki, but for someone like Acker, that would presumably be the least effective technique. As she puts it in *Empire of the Senseless:* "Reason is always in the service of the political and economic masters. It is here that literature strikes, at this base, where the concepts and actings of order impose themselves. Literature is that which denounces and slashes apart the repressing machine."[32] While readers do presumably fall into the three categories of response—the already converted, the convertible, and the intransigently resistant—those who might be persuadable are far from uniform. Some will yield to one kind of assault but not to others.

The chief reason for wishing to respond is to become a more competent reader so one can garner the pleasures of appreciating a difficult novel. One can, of course, wish not to respond if one considers the argument evil or silly, so learning to expand one's sensitivities is always balanced by whatever moral limits one sets. The other factor that tends to dampen our reaction to complaint is our usual distinction between literature and life. We may agree that what is being done to cattle is bad, but our experience of it in Ozeki is vicarious, a print experience, whereas any changes we would have to make are in our lives and in the laws of our land. Assault tries to break down that distinction. It hopes to charge us with the energy that went into the novel so that we may carry that energy into life, but most such transfers get swamped by everyday problems. Harriet Beecher Stowe and Upton Sinclair managed to effect real-world changes, and this may be the goal of many writers of complaints, but at best they are likely to contribute subtly to a gradual change of political climate through influencing individual minds—a worthwhile process, but slow—and as the climate shifts, those very complaints become outmoded. One characteristic of aggressive fiction, indeed, is its relatively short shelf life, and the modern form of complaint shares that ephemerality. If gender relations or conditions for lab animals change even slightly, the plaint sounds too extreme to be taken seriously. Ozeki's criticisms are still timely, but should the laws shift just a bit in the direction she wants, her books on meat and agribusiness will seem outdated. Most authors hope their works will live for decades or longer; those who write complaints must take pride in how short a time their works seem relevant.

3

Conjugations of the Grotesque

In *The Place of Dead Roads,* William S. Burroughs describes the sex life of the lophiform angler fish: "During intercourse the male gets attached to the body of the female and is slowly absorbed until only the testicles remain protruding from the female body."[1] Simply as natural history, this is not grotesque, merely unusual and non-mammalian; I note with amusement that scientific descriptions of this intimacy refer to the male being parasitic on the female and physically incapable of surviving on his own, which puts a rather different spin on a relationship that horrified and fascinated Burroughs.[2] Only when we apply this relationship to our human selves does it create the *visceral shiver of uneasiness* that accompanies the grotesque. Consider Burroughs's fantasia on this idea: "A Lophy Woman slithers out [from an underground river], huge mouth gaping to show the incurving teeth fine as hairs. They eat into the victim's face to block his breathing as they feed in oxygen through their gills. So the lethal mating is consummated. She absorbs first his head and brain, keeping his body alive with her bloodstream" (273–74). By making her a lophy *woman,* by referring to her male as a victim and giving him a face and brain, by having her eat his face rather than having him attach to her body, and by using gendered pronouns, Burroughs humanizes this sexual consummation. He even invents a fine vagina dentata transposed upwards, modeled on a lamprey's mouth.

Sophisticated readers pride themselves on being unshockable, but the grotesque depends upon shock, upon visceral response that amounts to an internal shiver or sense of recoil. Critics such as Ewa Kuryluk consider the grotesque impossible in the present day because we no longer have a single dominant culture to react against, yet Istvan Csicsery-Ronay hails the grotesque as "the dominant sensibility of modernism—and of postmodernism."[3] If the grotesque cannot currently exist or is unable to disturb readers, then it cannot be offered as a transgressive technique or means of discomfiting readers. Obviously I think it does still exist, but some questions must be considered. How can it function if we have moved into a decentered world with no master narratives? Should not the fluidity of the new order lower our anxieties about the borders between human and nonhuman, the traditional ground from which the grotesque emerges? Or are some of us not as sophisticated as we would like to think? William S. Burroughs, Katherine Dunn, Chuck Palahniuk, Robert Coover, James Morrow, Donald Antrim, Gerald Vizenor, and Cormac McCarthy all produce grotesque fiction, but by what definitions and to what ends? If I am right that their fictions can trigger that visceral frisson of discomfort—a hallmark of the grotesque mode—then to understand this form of reader-unfriendly fiction, we need to understand the ways in which the grotesque can affect even the contemporary reader.

Defining the Grotesque

Definitions of the grotesque have proliferated in the wake of the very different studies of Wolfgang Kayser and Mikhail Bakhtin. A few definitions characterize the grotesque in absolute terms. Several of Kayser's formulations qualify: "the grotesque is the estranged world"; the grotesque is the manifestation of incomprehensible and impersonal forces; "the grotesque is a play with the absurd"; and the grotesque tries to "subdue the demonic aspects of the world."[4] Most, though, attempt to explain it in bipartite or tripartite metaphors. In the two-part versions, we have the forces for the normal or the ideal, and opposing them are the grotesque, archetypally a human body altered by the addition of animal features.

While many definitions set up a binary opposition, they actually function, or can be parsed, in three parts, consisting of the opposed extremes plus the middle space in which they confront each other or merge. This three-part scheme seems the most powerful of the conceptualizations, so I use it to analyze all the definitions.[5] In this way of conceptualizing the grotesque, we have two sets of values understood to oppose each other; in the space between grows a third possibility, the grotesque. It arises from tensions between the two value clusters. It may be a hybrid of the two; it may operate by reversing the poles; it may be neither-nor; it may represent a third option in its own right. Somehow, though, it emerges in the gap between the poles. In the tripartite system, the human and animal are the polar forces, while the grotesque is their merged form. Bakhtin's concept of the grotesque is often discussed as binary, the upper-body values (repressive, hierarchical society) and the lower-body values (the grotesque). The lower body and its functions, however, can operate discreetly in a decorous society. Only when they leave their toilets and privies, bedrooms, hospitals, and asylums and move out into shared public space do they become grotesque. The grotesque is the intrusion of the one into the other, or the invasion of that space between. I have looked at some eighteen discussions of the grotesque, many of which draw on one another and most of which describe their subject in multiple fashions. Meta-analysis permits me to extract some common assumptions and patterns. Then we can see how best to apply this definition to actual texts.

Treatments of the grotesque agree on one of the sets of values. Emphases differ, but this cluster includes *law, form, order, rationality, the classical body, the ideal, consciousness, meaning, state beliefs,* and *decorum.* These values may vary from being an ideal version of our world to a high-norm to a norm, or they may be repressively orderly and thus be satirically exaggerated and debunked. Usually these values are associated with masculinity and with the historical (as opposed to the mythological). The other set is more diversely conceived, yet shares some values if only because of opposition to the first set. Values claimed for this cluster include Georges Bataille's *informe* or the *formless* (though see Rosalind Krauss later in this chapter), *death, fragmentation, unity broken into multiplicity, chaos, the unorganizable, no-sense, the archaic, the mythological, Freud's unconscious, the marginal, the lower body,* and *the female body.* In two-way definitions, these themselves constitute the grotesque, but almost always they can do this only by intruding on the first cluster, by joining or merging with it to form a third entity. In the example with which this chapter began, Burroughs puts maleness and humanity in one set of values, femaleness and animality in the other. He links the female with oppressive order and control and the male with freedom. If they simply went their separate ways, these differences would not matter. They become grotesque only because they occur in a single species that must mate to perpetuate itself, and because that mating permanently conjoins the sexes in a physical configuration not suggestive of sexual pleasure.

Let me elaborate how some specific definitions generate the grotesque. The groups resist tidy divisions, but I clump some as being Bakhtinian, some as deriving from or parallel to the definitions of Geoffrey Galt Harpham, some that emphasize form, some that focus on human emotion, and then some that do not fit larger classes.

Bakhtinian approaches follow their originator in marshaling his lower-body, lower-class life-energies against upper-body and upper-class restraints. In noting this agon, Bakhtin created almost ex nihilo a strain in European literature that had not been seen as a tradition before he analyzed it. Both Sylvia Kelso and Margaret Miles draw heavily on this vision but give it a feminist inflection.[6] Kelso argues for tripartite structuring of the grotesque, and sees strong parallels between the grotesque and Homi Bhabha's colonized mimic in the middle space between colonizer and colonized. Miles traces ways that the female body is used throughout classical and medieval texts and Bakhtin's own work to degrade the male body and render it grotesque. She sees the exaggerated, mythically potent female body as the opposite pole to the masculine. Bakhtin's world is strongly binary, male and female, upper and lower.

Harpham's followers develop one or more of his thoughtful and flexibly varied definitions. Among those useful to me were his formulation of the grotesque as an excess of energy without containing form, the irruption of the unconscious into the conscious, the irruption of the archaic or mythological into the historical, and the distortion of an ideal type, all of which can be laid out in the three-way structure. Istvan Csicsery-Ronay took Harpham as a starting point and looked at science fiction, with superb results.

He says the grotesque is "life set free of law" (82), and science-fiction grotesquerie concerns the "uncontainable metamorphic energies of the world"
(79). Both statements establish the usual opposition of containing structure
and formless energy, but the science-fiction version of the formless existed
long before humans imposed taxonomies. The grotesque arises in the specifically metamorphic, or form-changing, activities that can be recognized
as a threat only by the humans who rely on scientific taxonomy; in other
words, the formless alters humanity's forms or intrudes upon the system.
Csicsery-Ronay also places the grotesque in the gap between the two poles
that generate most science fiction: cosmos (the world as apprehended by
the scientific method) and chaos.

Wilson Yates takes up two other definitions of the grotesque mentioned
by Harpham: distortion of an ideal type, and an inward possibility that
becomes a universal possibility. Thus we might pit the law-and-order side
against chaos, and the savage human behavior that resulted from the disappearance of all law might be grotesque and upsetting to the degree that
it could represent a universal possibility; we shall see this pattern when I
discuss grotesque worlds. Yates also develops the idea that grotesquerie
can emerge from the mythic intruding on the historical.

In addition to definitions deriving from Bakhtin and Harpham, we
find that some critics stress the *concept of form,* either in the abstract or as
the shape of a creature that qualifies for their definition. Mark Dorrian
cites Rosalind Krauss as claiming that Bataille's *informe* reduces meaning
"not by contradiction—which would be dialectical—but by putrefaction."[7]
This sets form against death as the poles, with the putrefaction of form
as the grotesque middle term. Putrefaction of a dead body may be natural, but it does cause revulsion because it degrades the norm and disorders
the ordered. Because dead bodies exemplify a grotesque merging of something lifelike with non-life, we find uneasy laughter attached to morgues,
graveyards, and gallows, and some cultures add zombies as another grotesquerie based on death. Dorrian defines a masculine theory of monstrosity as rebellion against the father, and a feminine theory (exemplified in
Frankenstein) as the father's desire to replicate his resemblance without
female contribution. Monsters generally embody the grotesque, and in
those definitions, the opposed values are those of father and son, or man
and woman. The grotesque—or monstrous event, creature, or behavior—
emerges from their clash. Another critic who emphasizes physical form is

Bernard McElroy, with his strong though not exclusive focus on human-nonhuman mixtures, which he agrees with Harpham in tracing back as far as Neolithic cave paintings.[8]

Three theorists seem to me to locate grotesquerie in *human emotions* rather than in bodily form or clashing clusters of abstract values. John Ruskin stresses the combination of intellectual play and terror, Philip Thomson the similar combination of horror and laughter.[9] Leonard Cassuto sees the grotesque arising from two contradictory human impulses: one degrades certain people into things, the other exercises a hardwired anthropomorphizing impulse to treat as human anything remotely human.[10] His examples of racial grotesque show the racist ideology undermined again and again by anthropomorphizing vocabulary, thus producing an unstable, disturbing, and disturbed image.

Oddly enough, the first major theorist of the grotesque in the twentieth century, Wolfgang Kayser, is both everywhere and nowhere in current thought. He leads my *ungroupable* theorists. His definitions do not fit the three-part organization without considerable tweaking and extrapolation, but insofar as he also talks about the fusion of incompatible forms, he overlaps others. One thing that differentiates him is that his vision relies less on humor than any of the others'. For him and for Wilson Yates at times, the purely horrifying can be grotesque, exemplified in Goya's *Saturn* (Yates) or Kayser's demonic. Such demonic visions produce the frisson of revulsion, and any laugh is the involuntary response to something bad, not to humor as such. These definitions that shade into pure atrocity will matter when we look at Cormac McCarthy's *Blood Meridian*. Also useful, though not easily groupable, is John R. Clark's study of grotesque satire.[11] His most useful contribution is a list of standard topoi, and among those, cannibals and Armageddon occur in some of the texts I discuss.

These, then, are major recent ways of conceptualizing the grotesque, and they can mostly be discussed as the product of clashing values.[12] Clashing cultural values, however, do not complete my definition. The grotesque has emotional dimensions, and those need to be understood in terms of both audience response and authorial intention. Although reader response is more central to the definition, let me deal briefly with authorial intention. Basically, something will seem grotesque if the author supplies social standards that register the offense within the story and shows characters who call our attention to the phenomenon. Without such pointing, we will rely on our own standards, and according to those, something might or might not seem grotesque. We can, though, be persuaded of a grotesquerie if the writing is powerful enough. The classical story of Leda and the Swan means nothing emotionally to most readers today, but Yeats managed to reimbue it with some of its original power to upset when he imagined it truly as a rape, starting with a sudden blow and going on to "terrified vague fingers" trying to push away the powerful feathered assailant. He does not descend to gross physical detail of a bird's copulatory organ and how it might join with human; such detail would have supplied humor as well as queasiness. Even without a full grotesque treatment, however, rape by an animal can produce the shiver of revulsion that typifies the grotesque.

Why an author should wish to make readers uncomfortable with grotesquerie can be answered in many ways. Some writers live in a world that seems grotesque to them, so they represent that world, and they may enjoy pushing their nightmares on what they perceive to be smug, satisfied, and blind middle-class readers. The class element of this attitude saturates Dunn's *Geek Love*. Writers may enjoy the feeling of forcing a reader to respond strongly; Coover is avowedly one of these. They may wish, as Morrow does, to make some ideological or moral point and use the grotesque to pierce reader defenses and shake the reader up.

In addition to authorial intention, reader response must be considered in any definition of the grotesque, and it is here that attack on the reader's mind and emotions becomes evident. Theorists who have stressed the reader's investment (Thomson, McElroy) insist on an ambivalent response: horror *and* laughter, terror *and* play, rejection *and* a certain sadistic glee, repulsion *and* identification. That grotesque material should produce such a response is itself an attack, for these reactions contradict each other and cannot be held comfortably at the same time. Most people's sense of decorum forbids laughter at something horrible, so laughing in those circumstances renders us uneasy. The more we are repelled by what we are forced to contemplate, the more uncomfortable we find our impulse to laugh or even to enjoy the forbidden. In this regard, most of us seem to identify consciously with the decorous set of values unless they are presented as extremely oppressive. A reader harboring revolutionary sentiments might identify with the second, chaotic set of values and welcome the horrible if it meant destroying some aspect of the decorous world, and such a reader might not find the phenomenon grotesque, or might do so only if ambivalence remained about some other aspect of the clashing values.

When one's own values are upset, one perceives the process as an attack. Csicsery-Ronay offers the multiplication of subatomic particles as something perceived by early-twentieth-century scientists as grotesque (79–80); the particles did not fit the paradigms, and seemed a horrible excess, a violation of perfect form and simple equations. They certainly made classical physicists feel attacked; their entire mental world was disintegrating and betraying them. Now that the particles are better understood, and simpler basic units to build from have been identified, those many particles have become part of law and form and have gained a new beauty in their own patterns. Or take a traditional example of the grotesque: a human body that seriously departs from norms, whether through a stutter in the genetic code or because the body has been maimed. Why should the mere sight of such a body make us uncomfortable? Rationally, we know that it does not threaten us, yet many people are likely to feel repelled as well as curious. Such an unusual body is not contagious, yet the nonrational response is fear of becoming "like that." Emotionally, we dread a kind of infection or contagion, the spread of deformity, and authors can play upon this primitive fear.

For the grotesque to work in literature, the reader must assent to the author's formulation, must feel the clash of values and sense the attack. A reader can resist, or the attack can go wide. Scholars in disability studies have resisted Dunn's *Geek Love* as unsympathetic to the unusually abled. If the reader simply fails to understand an assault, then puzzlement will result, as can happen with Coover's *The Adventures of Lucky Pierre*. If the reader is not moved by the values espoused, then indifference will produce neither horror nor humor. Readers may also actively resist an argument that something is grotesque: people of our era reading nineteenth-century scientific pontifications on race or gender will probably refuse assent. That women leech intellectual strength from men through sexual intercourse or that some African tribe represents either lack of evolution or devolution from the Anglo-Saxon male norm would mostly meet with derision. If the nineteenth-century author is making the argument with sarcastic confidence, presenting the women or tribespeople as grotesque, we can refuse to laugh salaciously (and may find the mental gyrations of the arguer a form of unintentional grotesque). We must assent or be overwhelmed for grotesquerie to operate, so that audience compliance is an important part of the definition.

I proffer the following elements of a definition:

- Two clusters of values set in opposition to each other (one concerning law and form, the other concerning something perceived as chaotic by the orderly side, though the author may treat it as life-giving or positive).
- A third space somehow enterable by both, in which the values transform each other, their interaction or merging causing the reader discomfort.
- Reader compliance, signaled by a mixture of laughter and repulsion, the latter producing an ephemeral physical frisson of unease the first time one is exposed to the material.
- Authorial intentions to create the grotesque. Except when we reject the values and decide that an author's own mental gyrations are unintentionally grotesque, we can assume authorial intention to upset the reader and provoke at least some recoil.

To test this definition, we will have to see if the two value clusters do indeed manifest themselves in the literature. Do the same tensions that work at the theoretical level govern the actions within a story? Can looking for such forces within the story affect our reading of it or help us choose among interpretations?

In what follows, I look at the grotesque from three perspectives. One focuses on the *bodily grotesque* and considers how and why these alterations of the human body can still work in the contemporary world. The second perspective projects values into *grotesque worlds;* this approach uses the body but pushes us to consider disturbances in society. The third acknowledges that the grotesque is not immutable and can be *transformed,* even nullified. Since some theorists see our responses to phenomena such as deformed faces or hybrid bodies as instinctive or hardwired, the strategies used to disable that reaction will help us understand better the mechanisms that make the grotesque work.

Bodily Grotesque: *Geek Love, Invisible Monsters, The Adventures of Lucky Pierre*

Bodily grotesque is the oldest and most deeply rooted form. If Harpham and McElroy and their scientific sources interpret the "Sorcerer" in the Trois Frères cave correctly, we have human and animal merging fifteen thousand years ago to represent an eerie figure of spiritual and magical power. Even modern viewers can feel the combination to be uncanny, and disability studies exists as a field because too few people control their aversion to distorted human forms. Classical myth has its satyrs, centaurs, and other mixed forms, whether part human or, like the chimera, entirely animalesque. While we have domesticated and Disneyfied those images to the point where they have mostly lost affective power, a statue or story can recapture it. The statue of Pan and Daphnis in the National Archeological Museum of Naples pits the physical shyness and modesty of the human boy against the goatish lust of the god, and viewers derive an unwelcome sense of Pan's power as something ancient, nonhuman, and ugly. Dante's Satan is the more disturbing for having three faces on his head, and the Green Man for having vines growing out of his mouth. Gulliver's Lilliputians and Brobdingnagians achieve their effects through size distortions in relation to normal bodies. How many otherwise realistic fictions use minute manipulations of the body to tap into our primitive response to physical difference? Different-colored eyes symbolize mixed blood and ensure lack of acceptance, for instance, in Leslie Marmon Silko's *Ceremony*. The texts to be discussed all use bodily distortion, physical or symbolic.

Bodily grotesque takes at least three forms. Katherine Dunn's *Geek Love* concerns people who are physical prodigies whom the public pays to see. Chuck Palahniuk's *Invisible Monsters* exposes us to voluntary surgical re-formations of the body. Coover's *Adventures of Lucky Pierre* shows us a symbolic equivalent to the classical Greek satyr play in which satyrs flaunt their erect phalluses on stage. All of the novels use topoi that turn up in definitions of the grotesque, and even while introducing modern values that challenge traditional responses, they illustrate the mechanisms that encourage us to see the material as grotesque.

Geek Love might be called classical grotesque in that it focuses on performers with physical deformities in a traveling carnival, the freaks who constitute the freak show.[13] This novel attracted instant attention, and has generated several different interpretations. Most critics agree that Dunn forces us to see that her freaks are full-fledged humans, with their sibling rivalries, obsessions, loves, ambitions, and feelings. In addition, critics have variously argued that Dunn is attacking evangelical fundamentalist Christianity, American individualism, patriarchy, capitalism, and the values of 1980s America. We are also told that Dunn's freaks have learned the hard way a lesson that most of us need to learn: to love and accept ourselves and not project our problems onto others.[14] Can looking at the structure of the grotesque here help us make choices among these possibilities?

The orderly values are easy to spot: ordinary society, the "norms," small-town American people and their values. These people are portrayed not in idealized terms but rather as ignorant and narrow. They live in one place and hold conventional notions of the human form. What does this cluster of values press against to produce the grotesque? The elastic, free, wandering life of the carnival. That life is nomadic; it mixes creative thinking with chicanery; it collects strange individuals, many of whom have made themselves unpopular in normal society. This opposition appealed to Dickens, too; in *Hard Times* he confronts the number-and-fact-crunching industrial and bourgeois society with a circus, and like Dickens, Dunn shows loving family life among her carnie folk. If this opposition of norm and carnival is the plot's primary dynamic, then we should look here for our principal interpretation; other oppositions such as patriarchy and feminism are secondary.

Why, though, should forcing norms and the carnival into close proximity create the grotesque? In this instance, primarily for monetary reasons. The show was edging toward bankruptcy until Al Binewski got his idea for breeding his own freaks. His monsters, like Frankenstein's, represent his determination to create an image without letting nature and his wife do their part unaided. We are encouraged to feel the grotesquerie of his enterprise by the contrast between Al's genuinely loving behavior as a father and his tender collaboration with his wife to administer poisons, radioactive substances, and known teratogens to their embryonic children. Their results include Arty, a boy with flippers for legs and arms; conjoined twins; an albino hunchbacked dwarf; several abnormals who did not live but are preserved in formaldehyde as carnival displays; and an apparent "norm" who proves to be telekinetic. Dunn does not obviously encourage us to join the gawping public in reveling in the children's freakishness (and the man who tries to shoot them is not presented in a way that would gain him much sympathy), but more subtly she encourages the voyeur in us by feeding us intimate details that titillate voyeuristic curiosity. The marks want to know about freaks and sex; Dunn tells us.

What does Dunn gain from thrusting her grotesque upon us? The relish with which she piles up bizarre details suggests that she enjoys making the reader squirm in primitive discomfort at deformity. How often can an author achieve a visceral effect? Get through reader defenses? One of her targets is the middle class per se, and bodily grotesque lets her challenge the morality of the compulsively orderly world that prefers to exile these and other aberrations to peripheral lives in carnivals and jails or homelessness on the streets. Or as Arty puts it: "You know what they do with people like me? Brick walls, six-bed wards, two diapers a day and a visit from a mothball Santa at Christmas."[15]

In addition to being a mode of art, the grotesque is also an authorial sensibility, and Dunn enjoys being able to push the buttons of the reading classes. Culturally, if not always individually, middle-class readers are conditioned to accept certain limits on the nature of the human, and to be rendered uncomfortable by violation of those boundaries. Whether we stare or avoid staring because we believe it impolite, we are not indifferent or unaware. If Dunn were primarily concerned with making us more humanely disposed to those with visible deformities, her unpleasant portraits would not be the most effective means. Arty's cynical instructions to a man who lost his legs may be practical but is distinctly unattractive: "You ought to tan your thighs and walk on them. Wear silver sequin pads and dance on a lit stage where they can see you. All those soft girlies come knocking on your door borrowing sugar in the dead of night and sliming for you" (170). He gloats at how much power such stumps can exert. Those Binewski children with visibly non-normal bodies are not very lovable, yet lovability, presumably, is what some disability studies specialists would prefer. Making a case for the deformed seems not to be Dunn's purpose. If her primary target is a form of Christianity or the Me Generation of the 1980s, she fails to make them prominent enough, and fifty years from now they may not register for readers. What will remain is the story of physical abnormalities that were deliberately created, their genesis rendered more affecting by the conceptual clash between family love and poison. Readers will probably accept Arty's claim that freaks use themselves to gain power over "norms," and insofar as readers respond at all to reading about the physical deformities of the freaks, they can attest to that power.

If we consider various definitions of the grotesque, we find many that seem to operate in this novel. Bakhtin's grotesque body is present, and insofar as his ultimate grotesque is the pregnant hag,[16] we have Olympia, the hunchbacked albino dwarf incestuously pregnant by telekinesis, giving birth to a girl child with a tail. *One Hundred Years of Solitude* also brings its closed world to an end with the birth of a child with a tail, a traditional grotesquerie that merges human with animal. Mark Dorrian's masculine concept of monstrosity—son rebelling against father—is played out in Arty's destruction of his father, even as Dorrian's feminine concept is embodied in Al's method of creating artificial children of his own devising, rather than letting his and his wife's traits mingle naturally. We find plenty that is horrible in Arty's followers amputating their limbs to resemble him, the grotesquerie made more revolting as we learn about the problems of disposing of the surgical detritus. We find similar gruesomeness in Miss Lick's defacement of women, who agree to her surgeries for money. Like Arty, she gains followers who will share her peculiarities, in her case sexlessness and achievement in a man's world. Like Arty and Al, she creates offspring without the natural contribution of a partner. McElroy expects the grotesque to exhibit a touch of magic, which may appear in primitive or childish modes of thought, and we have that in Chick's telekinetic abilities. We also get an irruption of the mythological in the apocalyptic end of the carnival, as Chick's powers overwhelm him, and most of the family and followers go up in flames. Arty boils to death in his tank. All of these add to our sense of the grotesque, even though we are constantly reminded of the humanity of those with unusual bodies.

What happens if readers do not assent? Disability studies encourages such a response; David Mitchell sees the book as exploiting the disabled and rejects it for the unflattering portrayals, for the artistic use of the disabled to symbolize problems with society.[17] Someone heavily invested in normal births, such as an obstetrician or a pregnant woman, might also reject it and be unable to respond to the gusty humor. If one assents to the uncomfortable mixture, however, one feels the power of grotesquerie in *Geek Love*. And if one grants the grotesquerie to be the generating structure of the novel, then this relegates to secondary importance such elements as the satire on evangelical Christianity argued by Michael Hardin, or at least suggests that it be read within the dynamic of the grotesque: the patterns of evangelical fundamentalism disrupted by the intrusion of new myth (Arty as savior) producing grotesque amputees who pattern themselves on their leader.

Chuck Palahniuk offers us a different form of physical grotesquerie. Dunn's freaks are grotesques in a classic sense; freak shows paraded just this kind of prodigy. Arty's cult, however, with its surgical amputations, carries his abnormalities into the normal world and makes his particular characteristics contagious.[18] We see both such contagiousness and voluntary surgical alterations explored in Palahniuk's *Invisible Monsters*. The title signals Palahniuk's awareness of the uncomfortable side of his material. Three of his four main characters are men at various stages of turning into women or being feminized; the fourth is a woman who has shot off the lower part of her face and jaw to escape being glamorous. If these are the grotesques, what forces within this novel clash to produce them? On the one side is the heteronorm, the classical male body: one of the men comes from a wealthy Texas background, one comes from small-town America, and one was a body-building cop who was considered good-looking. All therefore are symbolically well ensconced in cultural circumstances associated with order and form and normality of a patriarchal sort. The other side might be women, but women can be contained within the patriarchal system of order if they are submissive and obedient. I would say instead that it is femaleness mythologized, femaleness with a capital F. Femaleness in this sense is contagious; it can infect and contaminate maleness. Shane McFarland is cast out of the parental home because a sore throat proved to be caused by the gonorrhea bacterium, and he has thus taken what is seen as the receptive/female role to some other man. His masculinity is contaminated by his female receptivity, the infection being proof.

One reason we see femaleness as transferable is the analysis of what Brandy Alexander (Shane in training for sex-change surgery) has to learn in order to seem female. She learns how to raise her voice and how to alter speech patterns. Men stress the adjective ("so *attractive*") but women say "*so* attractive."[19] His sister, Shannon, experiences femaleness as a series of poses, the sort called for by a fashion photographer:

> Him yelling, Give me lust, baby.
> Flash.
> Give me malice.
> Flash.
> Give me detached existentialist ennui.
> Flash. (13)

Having been a fashion model, Shannon handles all scenes by imagining the photographer giving her such instructions for projecting her female beauty in different emotional situations, all of which illustrate Palahniuk's emphasis on this fragmentation of her beauty (101, 109, 111, 112, 150, 152, 158, 173, 176, 181). Beauty "is power the same way money is power the same way a gun is power" (16): female beauty thus fits one definition of the grotesque of multiplicity within unity.[20] Like the atom, femaleness is found to explode into a multitude of separate particles, and each of those can stick to male bodies, thus spreading femaleness.

Femaleness is also chemical; both Brandy Alexander and Shannon feed Manus Kelley female hormones without his knowing it. He becomes fat, develops breasts, and cries easily. Because this is being done out of vengeance for his two-timing and his having abused Shane as a minor, femaleness is thus a punishment. Shane also looks at it for himself as the ultimate self-mutilation of one who has no great desire to be a woman (258); the final genital surgery will force him to change his unsatisfactory life—and, incidentally, it will transform him into what his parents feared most, an unmanly man who acts as a woman would to other men. Evie (formerly Evan) evidently made the surgical transition early and completely, thanks to wealthy parents, but they see her as a problem that now needs to be contained: "We've gone along with her little obsessions, but enough's enough, so now we're gonna marry her off to some jackass.... The biggest wedding in the world is worth the cost if we can shove Evie off onto some poor man" (267–68). If she can be recouped into southern womanhood of the sort of background she comes from, she should be more manageable, more submissive.

The strangest revulsion at femaleness is that of Shannon McFarland, the model, who shoots off half her face, explaining that

> you look at burn victims and think how much time they save not looking in mirrors to check their skin for sun damage.
> I wanted the everyday reassurance of being mutilated. The way a crippled deformed birth-defected disfigured girl can drive her car with the windows open and not care how the wind makes her hair look, that's the kind of freedom I was after. (286)

She could have let herself get fat, but apparently that was not permanent enough, so she severs herself from any conventional female life irreversibly. By doing such damage to herself as ideal body, she puts herself well along the continuum of form putrefying into death. And although she talks breezily at one time of becoming a great doctor or artist now that she is freed from distractions, we see no signs whatever of the hard-minded determination that such a course demands. The predilection for drugs she shares with her sibling, Brandy Alexander, suggests that she may just pursue distractions of a different sort. Basically, Palahniuk treats essential femaleness as horrifying enough that Shannon maims herself to escape. By doing this, she also imitates Shane's initial rebellion of letting a can of hairspray explode in his face, and she punishes her own femaleness, carrying out her parents' unconscious wishes, given their marked preference for their son.

Palahniuk does not treat sex-change operations for those who want them as monstrous, but he cannot avoid his material's becoming grotesque, given the mixed, vengeful, self-damaging motives of his various characters and the humor with which their goings-on are chronicled. Nor does he keep mythic femaleness from taking on an amusing but malign power of contagion. Csicsery-Ronay points out that science-fictional grotesque reduces form to "goo" (88), and as we watch Manus's body (note "man" in his name) softening and bloating, we feel that process of deliquescence starting.

Identifying the opposing value as femaleness does not exclude chaos in the cluster of values that oppose order and form. Shannon says that she shot off her face "to be saved by chaos. To see if I could cope, I wanted to force myself to grow again" (286). Perfect body against chaos produces the monster that she becomes, identified as such by small children who see her in the supermarket (55). The plasticity imposed on male form, a term many times invoked with reference to plastic surgeons, is one step toward goo, chaos under another name.

Shannon likens herself to a deadly virus (121), and the end of the book certainly leaves us wondering what will emerge from the chaos that these four characters have created. Shannon seems to think that all will be well, that she is acting from love and making possible the new life that Shane desired. She leaves him her identity and her career as a model. And yet...She makes us acutely aware of his big hands throughout the text; even her own are a size too large for hand-modeling jobs; his will probably disqualify him from any modeling, and that goes for feet, too. We are told how beautiful he now looks after his various adjustive surgeries, yet as a teen he deliberately damaged his face with the hairspray explosion, and surgery rarely removes all traces of such a disaster. Shane has admitted that undergoing the final genital surgery would be the greatest mistake he could make; Shannon seems to be trying to ensure that he takes that step. She wants to force him to burn his bridges as totally as she has destroyed hers. Is that love? Would Shane become a successful model and enjoy it because for him that would be a hard-won achievement as it was not for her? Or is she still a deadly virus, destroying lives all around her? She is the one genetic female of the four, and it would seem that her gender is indeed metaphorically equivalent to plague. Femaleness is contagious and destructive.

A different form of bodily grotesque presents itself in Robert Coover's novel *The Adventures of Lucky Pierre: Directors' Cut*. This version does not derive from poisoning embryos or self-mutilation. Coover's main character is not physically deformed. While his penis is always erect and ready to perform, it is not out of proportion to his body the way those of ithyphallic satyrs were in Greek drama. What makes Lucky Pierre (LP) grotesque is more behavioral than physical; this character is really just an appendage to his penis. The events might be said to represent a penis-eye view of the world: if it's female, try to fuck it. His life as a porn star is one grapple after another.

If a Bakhtinian male life force is one set of values, the other appears to be our normal business world, coupled with its ability to turn sex into a commodity. This novel makes much of business clothes, office routines, schedules, film shoots, ads, traffic, theories of art, and civic functions featuring the mayor. Where Coover gets some disquieting effects is from his treatment of this world. The infectious quality of LP's sexual activity has permeated our everyday world and transformed it. All film is pornography. All ads are pornographic, and they feature four-letter words and full nudity or copulation. Pornography is Cinecity's main product, and everyone including the female mayor is flashily, publicly active sexually. Practically all conversation concerns fucking or filming it. While many Americans believe themselves to have jettisoned old taboos on sexual matters, those strictures remain in attenuated form. One may be able to stroll naked down a town street during a heat wave in Denmark, but not in the United States. In some kinds of films, genitals may be visible, but not in most, and in many Western nations, performing sex in public is a crime.

Like Pietro Aretino, who thought that if men were honest about it, they would flaunt an erect cock as a talisman on a necklace or pinned to their cap, Coover turns the ruling notions of the public and the private inside out.[21] The grotesquerie of Pierre's always bared cock is thus echoed at the social level, with disturbing results.

Consider this early scene. LP strides along a city sidewalk on an icy winter morning, expensively dressed in a stylish business suit, but "poking forth from his thick herringbone wraps like a testy one-eyed malcontent—his penis, ramrod stiff in the morning wind, glistening with ice crystals, livid at the tip, batting aggressively against the sullen crowds."[22] He accidentally prods an old woman from behind with his cock as she stands at the curb; she falls into the rushing traffic and is flattened to a pulp in the slush (5). This gruesome accident means nothing to the onlookers. She has simply become something that the street cleaners should clean up; evidently someone that old is outside the sexual realm and so meaningless.

If LP's activities exert force on society, society exerts its force on LP through his career. As a porn star, LP deals with nine muses, who are also his cinematographers. He made early pornographic films with all of them as his sexual partners, and is now being filmed by them in turn, sometimes redoing the originals, sometimes setting up different kinds of cinematic adventures. He is helpless as they move him around or discard him at will to create their art. When they are done with him for the moment, he usually finds himself out in the snow and cold again, until he drops into another adventure that proves later to be a scenario one of them has set up. LP loves all of these muses in different ways, and collaborates gladly most of the time, but his life is marked by a frantic inability to keep up, an inability to understand what is happening or to live up to their demands. He suffers all kinds of damage, physical and psychological, in this sexual rat race; what might sound like a male fantasy idyll is more a nightmare. Toward the end, the muses are filming what they sinisterly refer to as his last fuck. Although these muse-cinematographers cause pain and confusion, they are not the monsters one would find in the fiction of Burroughs. Neither Coover nor LP seems hostile to them. Coover is, among other things, a film expert. The muses' manipulations of LP are lovingly and lavishly described in a manner suitable to art, and Coover does not seem to be challenging the desirability or importance of art.

Coover's grotesquerie, here enlarging the role of the penis to the point where it subsumes all other human activities into its routines, is a comic rendering of the human that makes us aware of what we repress. He also shows all forms of art concerned with this same sexuality. Readers will respond very differently to this vision. Some women will resist this completely male-centered vision of life, but it is, as I suggested, a penis-eye view; another writer would have to produce a female equivalent, as, indeed, Eve Ensler did in *The Vagina Monologues.* Those who refuse assent on feminist grounds will miss the humor, and consequently the grotesquerie, because it will simply become the unacceptable.

The task that Coover sets himself in all his fiction is to break bonds, deny generic expectations, and fracture patterns.[23] In *The Adventures of Lucky Pierre,* he overthrows sexual repression and forces us into awareness of the limits on our actions that we have absorbed. He values rebelliousness over passive acceptance, and has expressed his preference for communication that breaks through the reader's defenses in terms that make that authorial intrusion a kind of rape, at least of the ear.[24] Breaking the social bonds governing sexual expression naturally produces grotesque situations as forces held separate by those bonds now rush together.

Freaks, sex-changers, and ithyphallic porn stars: these all represent versions of bodily grotesque of a more or less traditional sort and can generate conflicting responses. Contemporary unshockability does not protect against an author determined to get past most of our defenses. Despite our supposed lack of master narratives, we have not freed ourselves from some of the most basic such systems of meaning—human and animal, man and woman—and these can still be manipulated in ways that cause momentary uneasiness. Writers can still use the human body to upset reader sensibilities, to break into our comfort zone and leave us disturbed.

Grotesque Worlds: *Towing Jehovah, Elect Mr. Robinson for a Better World, Bearheart: The Heirship Chronicles, Blood Meridian*

We have seen how manipulations of the body can be used to make us uneasy. When authors want to highlight social issues, they create grotesque worlds. Wolfgang Kayser indeed makes the grotesque world central to the very nature of the grotesque. McElroy elaborates on Kayser, arguing that "the grotesque transforms the world from what we 'know' it to be to what we fear it might be."[25] The texts grouped under bodily grotesque and grotesque worlds do not divide cleanly. *The Adventures of Lucky Pierre* could easily have been discussed in the second, given its overt sexualization of our business-oriented capitalist world, and *Towing Jehovah* focuses spectacularly on a body yet uses it to make us consider a grotesque world. My reason for dividing them as I have is to emphasize the different nature of what is rendered grotesque. Geoffrey Galt Harpham and Wilson Yates recognize a kind of grotesque that shudders at something dreadful being presented as a universal possibility, and that seems to me what gives the ultimate frisson to grotesque-world books: a concern with deformed worlds that might be our future. *Towing Jehovah, Elect Mr. Robinson for a Better World,* and *Bearheart* all concern near-future worlds; *Blood Meridian* concerns a past world, yet barbarous behaviors could easily recrudesce in a post-catastrophe future, as happens in a later McCarthy novel, *The Road.* These novels establish their value systems in terms of religious, social, and historical order rather than physical form. The body remains an important tool for upsetting the reader, but the aim of the attack is social, not just physical.

We find numerous definitions of the grotesque at work in James Morrow's *Towing Jehovah*.[26] The values related to order cluster about the Judeo-Christian God, who is ideal, a representative of perfect order (if you consider male, patriarchal order perfect). He happens to have died, however, and his corpse is two miles long. With death and chaos as the focus for the opposing values, we have the obvious grotesquerie of form putrefying, fragmentation of a former whole, intrusion of the mythic in the historical world, and a terrifying glimpse of behaviors that result when the inhibiting influence of God, sin, hell, obligation, and conscience disappears; these behaviors might readily become universal possibilities. We also deal with a traditional topos, cannibalism, the terrible disintegrative death of the Archangel Michael (358–60), and even gruesome jokes, such as Captain Anthony Van Horne's reference to his hated father's frozen corpse as a "pop-sicle" (347).

Reading *Towing Jehovah* for the first time is a strange experience. I am an atheist raised in the Protestant tradition, and would have thought myself immune to any discomforts roused by God's having died and having a body that can decay, but as I read, I definitely felt an acute sensation of uneasiness, deriving in part from the exaggeration of human form to monstrous size. The second reading was much jollier, my attention drawn to Morrow's skill at working out the implications of his grand fantasy. I admire the discomfort that Morrow manages to produce simply by imagining a body two miles long and identifying it as belonging to God, thus reifying the oft-repeated statement about deity being deceased in the modern world. The effect would not have been nearly as strong had this merely been the corpse of an unexplained or extraterrestrial giant. Neither Donald Barthelme in *The Dead Father* nor J. G. Ballard in "The Drowned Giant" gets a response as remotely intense with their giants of lesser significance.[27] Morrow's plot concerns attempts to manage the mountainous corpse, contain it, and prevent dissolution of an *indecorous* sort, since its being God makes decorum feel necessary.

The extreme corporeality of this God is one of the fascinations of the book. Divers go into God's ear (noting his Darwin's tubercle, with its implications for evolution), and see "stalactites of calcified wax" in the ear canal, along with the sea fauna that have welcomed this cave (89). One can drive a jeep up to the "great glassy lake" of the eye (117). People note "how each predator had staked out its own culinary territory. From on high came the Cameroon vultures, swooping down like degenerate angels as they laid claim to the corneas and tear ducts. From below came the Liberian sea snakes, ruthlessly devouring the succulent meat of the buttocks" (107). Sharks eating at bearded cheeks and "tender webbing between the fingers" (107) had "wrought such terrible destruction, stripping off the foreskin like a gang of sadistic *mohels*" (115). God mysteriously has a navel (115), and Father Thomas stops briefly to observe "the great veiny cylinder floating between the legs (a truly unnerving sight, the scrotal sac undulating like the gasbag of some unimaginable blimp)" (115). Father Thomas and Sister Miriam stare up God's nose: "Marshes of mucus, boulders of dried snot, nose hairs the size of obelisks: this was not the Lord God of Hosts they'd grown up with" (119). This corporeality excites and disgusts us.

A strange, Atlantis-like island rises from the sea and temporarily strands the oil tanker that had been towing the corpse. The crew members mutiny. If no God exists, they reason, they are free and can do anything they like. The island contains the remains of a pagan civilization: statues celebrating drink, drugs, sex, food appear. This Atlantean Pompeii has what Father Thomas terms a museum of unnatural history (190)—all sexual perversions illustrated in mosaics. The mutineers establish gladiatorial combat in an arena and kill off those they like least, though they willingly cheer an intended victim who manages to kill the armed man with a forklift rather than a trident. One day finds them indulging in "binge, bacchanal, orgy, brawl, and disco tourney" as well as eating and smoking marijuana, while eight men, "each plugged into another," form a "carousel of sodomy" (190). So totally lacking in reason are they that they wantonly destroy their limited supply of food, heating the cheese wheels to tar, fighting with the fresh eggs, and popping off tops and showering one another with the soups and desserts (192).

This chaotic destruction of food necessitates eating the slowly decaying *corpus dei*. The captain and his loyal followers carve portions out of the breast and eat it, gilding their theophagy with full Latin Eucharistic liturgy adapted to this situation (226). They ponder the meaning here of "Lord, I am not worthy" and worry about whether eating the body is a sin (for those who still believe in that concept). Moreover, the human shape of the body makes this meal a species of cannibalism. They wonder why it should taste so like a Big Mac rather than something more refined. Their cook shows his genius. "The body itself supplies other essentials: wart fragments for mushrooms, mole scrapings for garlic cloves, tear duct chunks for onions. Most astonishing of all, by combining a fresh-water condenser and a microwave oven into a contraption that causes rapid fermentation, our chef can now distill His blood into something that tastes exactly like first-class burgundy" (240).

While this might look like an attack on religion, and on Catholicism in particular, the tone throughout is remarkably respectful and reasonable, and not the obviously skewed reasonableness of the speaker in Swift's "Modest Proposal." If you accept the first monstrous premise of God's gigantic corpse, the reactions and turns of plot that follow are fairly plausible. Liberals, a feminist, a Jesuit, a member of the Vatican, a nun, a Jew, and a born-again Christian might well respond as these people do, at least until the historical reenactment buffs get hired to bomb the corpse, at which point we veer into frantic farce.

If this is not a satiric assault on religion, then what kind of aim does the author seem to have had, aside from undoubted cleverness and originality?

The violence, brutality, and irrationality of the mutineers suggest a concern with what holds society together. Captain Van Horne at one point finds statues of gods and friezes that indicate how human sacrifices are to be carried out at the altar. "Thus far on the voyage he'd failed to work up much affection for their cargo, that sour old smiler, that grinning judge, but Judeo-Christian monotheism suddenly seemed to him a major step forward" (167).

The leaders decide by a narrow vote to keep the body hidden, once they realize that entombing God in arctic ice was a scheme of the archangels, not God's express wish. Father Thomas thinks that if the body is displayed, humanity will exhibit "denial, terror, grief, everything we observed on the *Val* when we told the sailors the score," but will ultimately enter euphoria, celebrating their freedom and adulthood, once the eternal father has removed himself from their lives (364). Others, however, fear "something far sadder and bloodier" than the euphoria Father Thomas first imagined (368), and that fear keeps them from revealing the truth to the world. In other words, the wantonly destructive chaos resulting from the withdrawal of all moral sanction might become the universal norm, might destroy all order except those local orders established by strength and greed. Humanity might take centuries, even millennia, to crawl out of that to something more civilized, repeating all the same mistakes that had marred its social evolution the first time. Purely scientific and social sanctions seem inadequate to prevent human savagery from wiping away the world we know. Human society governed by its religions is undoubtedly flawed, and of course religion can have a malign as well as a beneficent influence. Without such a belief system, however, humans might quickly make life nasty, brutish, and short.

The body grotesque here serves a larger function of making us think about a world without sanctions. I prefer rational to supernatural decisions, but Morrow's material forces me to admit the historical inadequacy of reason to make large-scale action civilized. Although his argument worked for me, I can imagine audiences that would resist. A Christian unwilling to see serious issues fictionalized might simply recoil and reject this as blasphemy. If one can permit oneself to smile as well as recoil, though, one sees the grotesque at work, serving to open our eyes to the larger implications of a grotesque world.

One can ignore religion yet still worry about the forces that make society cohere. Another grotesque world that looks in secular terms at the nature of civilization is that of Donald Antrim in *Elect Mr. Robinson for a Better World.*[28] His first set of values are those of American towns and suburbs; this suburban town is unnamed, but it resembles what one would find in Florida, ecologically and socially. This is order and the norm. The opposing values combine formlessness and nature freed from man's constraining engineering, both implicit in the chief manifestations for this side, water and the ocean. When these sets of values clash, a grotesque community emerges.

Our first contact with the grotesque lies in what we are not told. We realize that something is wrong. The community seems to have no contact with a larger world. Utilities have failed, and the machinery they use to make keepsakes from black coral is powered by generators. We see no tourists who might buy such mementos. Schools have closed. Library books are thrown into no-man's-land to detonate land mines. Despite what appears to be a complete breakdown in economic order, we do not learn where food comes from, other than the sea, or where the people get fuel for their cars. Despite their isolation, they manage a semblance of their old lives, including meetings of the Rotary Club at the Holiday Inn and playing tennis. What happened that wiped out the rest of the world or cut off contact? We never find out, and nobody refers to anything that might explain the change. The banalities of small-town life become grotesque because this huge question remains unanswered. As Csicsery-Ronay notes, narrative grotesque derives from "incongruity between manner and matter," a tale "told in a tone at odds with its subject matter, as in Gogol's 'The Nose'" ("On the Grotesque" 84).

Other strange developments add to our uneasiness. The Rotary Club sponsors a workshop on theriomorphic trances—trances in which one becomes an animal (the merger of human and animal being a traditional grotesque trope). The narrator's wife, Meredith, is gifted at making the shift, and becomes a coelacanth, a living-fossil fish known from only a few specimens caught by chance. While this New Age practice clearly imitates some shamanistic spirituality, the author invites our skepticism. Meredith's complacence may make us suspicious, and so does the humor with which she is presented; her husband, Pete, the narrator, achieves the transformation once—as a bison—but he joins her in her water world and so nearly drowns (96). She takes their totemic differences to indicate fundamental incompatibilities that may be surfacing in their marriage.

Another grotesquerie involves excessive violence. Neighbors quarrel and sow the middle ground with land mines. A former mayor, having launched a Stinger missile that killed several people, is punished by being attached to four cars that pull him to pieces, thus imitating the practice of drawing and quartering of the Middle Ages (12–13).[29] Although we see no violence expended against individual homes, the homeowners have developed an urgent desire for fortification, and most have dug moats that they fill with sharpened bamboo stakes or poisonous snakes. Thus do the tidy suburban bungalows sprout indecorous accretions.

In this vaguely apocalyptic landscape, the schools have been closed, and Pete wishes to open one in his house. On the first day, however, his pupils punish one of their number by pulling her to pieces on Pete's model torture rack. We may know that kids are capable of committing such atrocities— William Golding's *Lord of the Flies* and Marianne Wiggins's *John Dollar* leave us with no illusions on that score. What renders the scene grotesque, however, is Pete's benign and unmoved supervision of this action. We do not know how to reconcile his apparent desire to be part of the structure of order as teacher and mayoral candidate with his detached engagement in this monstrous event—and, of course, with his having such a working model in his house. He refers to this event as an "unfortunate incident" (185) and "awful things" (2) when speaking from his padlocked attic. Has he been imprisoned, or has he withdrawn from awkward social intercourse? Is the padlock inside or out? We do not know for sure.

The broken body of the child, the theriomorphed body of woman into fish, the cut-up, frozen body of the man drawn and quartered: bodies and their limits are Antrim's key tools. He also employs the animalistic with a touch of magic (at the bison's near-drowning, for instance). The alterations in bodies here do not put pressure on the difference between normal and abnormal body; they target the normal in society. Whereas *Towing Jehovah* questioned society in its religious mode, this novel challenges America's social mode and its mythic ideal, the small town.

On first reading this book, one uneasily seeks the logic for the society being presented. That uneasiness, that distrust, is part of the tactic for discomfiting the reader. This novel has a postapocalyptic air, but no apocalypse is mentioned or deducible. We want to know; we feel threatened by society crumbling for no visible cause. We are also unclear whether the narrator is simply insane or whether he represents a new norm in society and is therefore a threat. Pete wants to be mayor, and we assume that he has no chance, but a previous mayor was the man who loosed the Stinger missile for no justifiable purpose and killed fellow citizens. Pete is in disrepute at the end, but as the houses begin to rot, the drains back up and start filling basements with water and filth, and the land becomes waterlogged, his sins may come to seem minor. He seems very self-centered and unable to recognize feelings in others, especially children, and in that sense appears psychopathic. The public execution, however, suggests that other men of the town are similarly unable to imagine the experience of another person, even a fellow Rotarian, when they draw and quarter him. That fellow Rotarian, incidentally, insisted at a Rotary Club meeting, "We're all murderers here," as his contribution to an argument on human nature (57). We are being shown that civilization is a very thin veneer indeed, and what lies underneath is horrible—as Morrow also notes. Morrow ultimately attributes such little progress as we have made to the concept of a God and hell or heaven, but Antrim gives us no equivalent. When his social world crumbles, nothing will hold it together, and the disintegration and devolution point to a grotesque "universal possibility."

Another postapocalyptic world, one that is truly disturbing, unstable, and bizarre, appears in Gerald Vizenor's *Bearheart: The Heirship Chronicles*. Though few readers would deny the novel's thoroughgoing grotesquerie, the opposed forces do not emerge immediately in the usual form of order versus chaos. In an attempt to see what the dynamic is, we can turn to an episode featuring a traditionally grotesque topos, sexual intercourse between human and animal. While Lilith Mae's relationship with her two boxer dogs produces uneasiness for me, many of Vizenor's values on first appearance seem to argue for a different interpretation, and cultural differences might also demand our rethinking that repulsion.

All of Vizenor's fictional worlds are fundamentally grotesque. His trickster focal figures blast through largely unattractive worlds, upsetting law and order, indulging themselves, wantoning in the fullness of their overflowing spirits. Much (but not all) that makes his worlds grotesque is that they represent for him white cultural values, themselves repulsive and astounding from a Native American standpoint. Insofar as he shows Indian life on the reservation, however, much is strange and wacky about that too, and not all that is bizarre can be ascribed to white oppressions. Besides, Vizenor has declared war on whining about white oppression, on self-pity, on victimry. He also categorically refuses to define either Native American or specifically Anishinaabe values. To do so would be to make them into terminal creeds, something that causes one to conform to an external force rather than develop one's own life force and imagination.

Rather than see the opposition as being Native American versus Euro-American, we should look to the underlying values that Vizenor associates loosely and undogmatically with each. The values he upholds include life, change, flexibility, imagination, adaptability, hybridity, pleasure, and zest. As Vizenor conceives these values, they are completely indifferent to American laws, and almost as indifferent to the values of many contemporary Indian organizations as well. The opposing value cluster consists of death, rigidity, thoughtless adherence to laws, and what he sees as the life-denying assumptions of Western civilization. The trigger that sets his grotesque world in motion is the sudden disappearance of all the fuel that makes modern civilization possible. While this catastrophe might seem somehow to push the second set of values even further toward death rather than toward the middle ground where the grotesque takes shape, the disappearance of fuel breaks down so many social patterns that in fact new possibilities for life do irrupt into the rigid and rule-bound civilization. In this middle ground of shift and change and violence, a band of mostly mixed-blood characters make their way from the headwaters of the Mississippi to Pueblo Bonito, one of the earliest large Indian civilizations in the country. This journey the novel celebrates is a pilgrimage, a dance of death, and a quest, as well as being apocalyptic road fiction.

Lilith Mae is one of the pilgrims, and she has not had an easy life, sexually speaking. She was abused by her stepfather and gang-raped by members of the school board attached to the reservation where she was teaching, yet was driven from the reservation by the women for having had sex with their husbands. Her means of escape from men has been her boxer dogs:

> Her buttocks were elevated and glowing in the copper aura. The first boxer mounted her with his leather padded paws about her waist and began his sexual motions near her glowing cheeks until his penis bloomed like a stiff flower and slipped between her wet and waiting vaginal lips.... The first boxer ejaculated in powerful bursts and shuddered against her buttocks. The band of muscles on the head of his penis bulged and throbbed between her contracting vaginal muscles.[30]

Since the boxers have been licking her vulva and nosing her nipples, they have evidently learned what pleases her, and they seem to enjoy the activity.

Most readers will not blame the dogs, since they are only doing what their mistress has evidently taught them to do. Our views of Lilith Mae's stance are likely to be more ambivalent. A few extreme feminists might say that she had found a way around the evils of intercourse with men— and all Lilith Mae's experience with human males has evidently been very bad. Most readers will be bothered, though, that she insists that she hates the dogs because they remind her of her stepfather. While she also says she loves them, the relationship is not one of easy affection. We are unlikely to believe that in this instance, love justifies all. Furthermore, they remain genuine dogs; she cannot communicate with them in any way beyond the normal. Were this a man having intercourse with a dog or sheep, we might well wonder how much it hurt the animal, and would doubt any claims of reciprocity, but at least the boxers pursue the transaction enthusiastically.

We might just be shocked and resist this as bizarre and repulsive, but Vizenor twice tells a Plains Indian legend about a woman who had a dog for a lover (61–64, 93–94), and in context this is not repellent. In an interview with A. Robert Lee, Vizenor insists with what he calls "totemic irony" that Native Americans consider all species equal and tell stories of such interspecies intercourse, and so (by implication) no obloquy adheres to Lilith Mae's unconventional arrangement.[31] Given his joyous insistence that humans would be better if they masturbated with animals,[32] totemic irony would seem to affirm a position as well as undercut it. In the context supplied by *Bearheart,* however, the hostile women of the reservation do not use the epithet "dog-lover" affectionately. The nickname, they say, meant that the woman cared for the dogs, but it was also a standard insult, meaning half-dog, with the implication that she had sex with the animals.[33] I point out that in both of Vizenor's versions of the legend, the woman dreams a lover, and the dog turns into a human in the dreams and makes love with her in human form. This changes the valence; if she beds the human form, that action is clearly different from taking the four-legged dog as lover. The mythological versions are variants on the incubus legend; supernatural lovers take many guises. Her children come forth as puppies, but again in one of the two versions, the children learn how to be human and are, therefore, were-dogs, a form of magic recognized in many cultural traditions. In that version the woman even destroys their dog skins so they must stay human, which would seem to put some extra value on the human form, despite Vizenor's all-species-are-equal claim.

Divine figures in myths do copulate outside their own species, and divinity doubtless reduces resistance we might otherwise feel about Leda and the Swan, or Europa and the Bull. Vizenor's dogs are not gods in disguise, however, and he supplies a lot more gross physical detail than the poets of Greek and Roman myth. He pushes the grotesque at us. The only way in which he could be said not to stress the prurient side is that he expends about the same amount of gross physical detail on human-human couplings and does not make them more attractive. As for where in the middle ground between value clusters all this falls, I would say rather close to the negative values. Lilith Mae is no Bakhtinian roisterer through life and sex. Nothing in her actions makes them life-affirming. She is inclined to whine and feel sorry for herself, always a danger signal in Vizenor. Hers is not an act redolent of life, flexibility, change, zest; rather, it comes across as a dispirited, self-centered pleasuring that is as much hated as wanted.

This is only one of many grotesque episodes; others involve cannibalism, witches, passionate love for a bronze statue, bizarre murders, and all forms of shattered social order. We need to ask, however, how Lilith Mae's behavior fits in with other activities in the tension between Vizenor's forces of life and those of death and dead cultural values. The few positive characters grow spiritually as they pass through the tribulations of this trip. They cultivate detachment and good humor, no matter what catastrophe strikes. Those characters make it to the final transfiguration, whereas most of the rest die along the way, as does Lilith Mae. In the grotesque world that Vizenor creates, they do not have enough life force to survive and thrive. This world, like those envisioned by Morrow and Antrim, is one where greed and power quickly consolidate to offer the only order that can be found in the chaos. The life is horrible, and most people will end up dead because they lack the flexibility and imagination to escape traps. For these reasons, I think that we are free to take the sexual scenes as deliberately grotesque, and see them as an indicator of Lilith Mae's inadequacies, though Vizenor would doubtless say that they also serve as a statement on species equality and even a feminist solution to the evil of men. Overall, though, in a grotesque world that has become "universal possibility," her behavior exemplifies the forces of rigidity and death rather than resisting them.

The grotesque as "universal possibility" is a dark vision, and one that can push the boundaries of the mode. Cormac McCarthy's *Blood Meridian, or The Evening Redness in the West* stands on a border between the grotesque and pure atrocity.[34] Nonetheless, that border rests on reader assumptions and responses. We produce involuntary laughter when witnessing disasters that befall others. Some readers might experience that kind of recoil while reading of the horrors here. We may also feel something faintly comic in the author's zestful heaping up of his atrocities. The very density of horrible matter can rob it of some of its impact and may make one blasé: "Ah, here comes another horror scene; ho-hum, anything new? Men hung upside down over fires until their brains boil and steam comes out their nostrils? Well, yes, we haven't seen that before." Bodies pile up, sometimes in battle but mostly from the slaughter of unarmed people, complete with scalping, and sometimes with extended torture. People are shot for no reason if one of the desperados happens to come into a bar. Indians get it badly, but dish it out, too, with a fine lack of racial discrimination, torturing members of other tribes as well as whites. The landscape itself is merciless, and we see the bones of animals, humans, and their wagons thick upon the ground.

If this is to be considered grotesque, and it would be by Kayser and Yates, I would locate one value cluster as the heroic myths that prettied up the winning of the West: brave explorers, mountain men, courageous pioneers and their wagon trains, cowboys, order, the spread of law, the schoolmarm and her mission of civilization. The opposing cluster consists of the powers of death, brutality, greed, and chaos. While the heroic version has been discredited for its omissions, elisions, and selfish lies, it remains part of the national imaginary through films and TV. The complaints of legislators about a Smithsonian show that demystified that myth attest to its still sacred status.[35] The violence in the novel is driven by greed, and it parodies the heroic stories. The result is appalling and arguably grotesque. As a "universal possibility," this portrait of behavior can produce shivers of uneasiness, particularly because everything is related in flat, affectless prose that mitigates nothing. McCarthy gives us an elaborated depiction of the life Morrow described as life without God, the life Antrim imagines when connection to an outside world is gone, and the life Vizenor proffers if fuel were to disappear and government structures break down. All such guarantors of law are totally absent in McCarthy's Southwest. Readers grant voyeuristic assent to the extent that they keep reading. As we absorb abominable details, we may even find ourselves wanting to know more, curious as to whether it could really have been as bad as this. Form putrefying into death also seems a good descriptor for McCarthy's material. Nearly all the actions are indecorous, and seem more so by contrast to the Judge's occasional sartorial splendor. The quasi-mythic elements are compatible with grotesquerie. So is the archaic sense of life: anyone experiencing the events described would have to assume that life was mostly painful and unpleasant, and that moments of pleasure and happiness were transitory and far apart. Much in this novel, therefore, fits definitions of the grotesque.

McCarthy does not use deformed bodies; rather the mentality that could act this way seems grotesque. In the context of Morrow, Antrim, and Vizenor, however, what stands out is that McCarthy simply gives us more of the social chaos that makes up grotesque worlds. They give us vignettes of natural man; McCarthy produces the epic, all the more engrossing for his historicality. The Glanton gang really did scalp peaceful villagers to get the bounty offered for Apache kills. In the absence of any explicit ludic element, one could argue that this narrative is not really grotesque; rather, it embodies the ironic in demonic form, and given Northrop Frye's mapping of such mythic forms on a circle, we are not surprised to find twisted, ironized mythic elements in McCarthy's story.[36] His Judge is frequently called satanic, for instance. I am more inclined to read the Judge as an unsympathetic embodiment of Western civilization. His education, his scientific interest in nature, his ruthlessness, his cold-bloodedness and indifference to others as people, his ability to appear the well-dressed gentleman: these are all accusations leveled at Euro-American expansionist society at its higher levels. Nothing implies that McCarthy enjoys the descriptions of murder that he bestows so lavishly, but we have to wonder whether the violence is a predictable result of human nature when no sanctions can be brought to bear upon it, and if so, how we should respond to this portrayal, aside from our internal shudders.

Grotesque worlds alter our relationship with Bakhtin's lower-body functions, or they oppress us with violence, brutality, and threat. Some dystopian and many apocalyptic fictions would qualify as grotesque worlds, the feared becoming universal. Many such plots are plots of idea, not of character or action. The point is to make us think, make us worry that such a fate might overtake our own world, and challenge us to rethink the actions we unthinkingly take. Grotesque bodies are good at stirring up emotions; grotesque worlds use our emotions to waken political or philosophical or ethical thought.

Normalizing the Grotesque: Octavia Butler, Elizabeth Moon, Vonda McIntyre, Anne McCaffrey and Mercedes Lackey, Ted Mooney, Rachel Ingalls, Marge Piercy

If McElroy is right that the grotesque arouses very primitive responses to physical difference, one would expect considerable conditioning to be necessary to remove our visceral responses. How, then, do various writers of speculative fiction manage this trick? What are the elements they can alter to make situations like those I have described seem unexceptionable? Among the grotesqueries discussed, several are quite common in this kind of genre fiction: humans altered by surgery or genetic tampering; humans dealing with sentient species equal to humans; hybridization of humans with other species or with machines and electronics; and sex with nonhumans. We have seen how these operate when intended to disturb us; what can modify the disturbing element and disarm these traditional threats to our sense of order?

Many science-fiction novels figure sentient aliens equivalent to humans in intelligence, language capabilities, and cultural advancement. An author wishing to retain our resistance need only make the aliens more powerful than the humans and also give them qualities that remind us of snakes or spiders or other creatures that many humans find distressing. In *Dawn*, Octavia Butler covers her Oankalis' heads with tentacles instead of the features we are used to. Readers find this futuristic echo of Medusa made more repellent by the protagonist's revulsion, since we tend to resonate to the emotions of an attractive focal character.[37] Lilith learns to control her response, and I have discovered that students mostly join Lilith in getting over their reaction, though a few remain human-chauvinist to the end.

Elizabeth Moon uses occasional modified humans in her Vatta's War series, and such "humods" ought to repel us as grotesques but do not. One with an extra forearm plus a tentacle turns up as a customs official. The protagonist "managed not to blink in surprise; that was a humod form she hadn't seen before."[38] When someone comes to assess the value of a diamond to pay docking fees, we see another humod. "When he opened his mouth to speak, his tongue was dark and heavily furred" (94). This modification proves, however, to be economically and professionally useful. He puts the diamond in his mouth and can then announce that it is carbon and the impurities are too minor to affect value (95). His apparently modified eyes also let him comment on the cut, crystalline structure, and flaws, and he renders a precise figure for its value. This might be *rule one* for modifications: if they are obviously useful, even valuable, then such modifications are much easier to accept than alterations in human form that seem valueless. We can see the point to doing chemical assays by tongue; we are less convinced of the value of shooting off one's face because one is tired of being a model. We might initially cringe at a furry tongue (or one that turned into a centipede, as Sartre imagines in *Nausea*),[39] but if we find such a change economically worthwhile, we repress our revulsion fairly quickly and easily. If the modification were extremely valuable, we might even be brought to wish we had it ourselves.

The *second rule* for reducing response to grotesquerie is to impose the modifications on more than one person. For anyone who likes dolphins and is interested in the possibility of communicating with them, the physical modifications in Vonda N. McIntyre's *Superluminal* seem well worth undergoing; a human can put metabolism into overdrive to survive cold water, and change breathing so as to follow delphinic patterns of swimming.[40] Depending on the degree of modification, such a human swimmer will still look mostly human, but having the company of others who undergo the transformation as well as the company of the dolphins makes one part of an elite, dedicated group. Numbers supply companionship, understanding, and acceptance. That makes deviation easier on the variant, and being part of a recognized group that uses the modification improves public reception.

How we respond to hybridization of humans will depend very much on how the characters in the book respond. The *third rule* for lessening repulsion is to show characters responding cheerfully and calmly to the grotesquerie. Something that feels normal to them will rouse little resistance from us. If they resist, as Lilith does for much of *Dawn,* then we will too. Lilith passionately regrets losing pure humanity, but humans nearly destroyed life on their planet, so her being alive at all is courtesy of the aliens. The return for humans from cross-breeding is offspring with improved mental abilities, the capacity to understand complex chemistry and genetics through tasting, and freedom from cancer and many other diseases. The more practically we look at those gains, the more readily we may be willing to adapt our reactions to facial tentacles. Like Lilith, we might dislike being seen as a valued pet rather than an equal, but the Oankali are so far superior to humans in technology that this may be inevitable, and no such disadvantage accrues to hybrid offspring. Accepting a disadvantage for oneself might be equivalent to realizing that emigrating to another country will leave the immigrant generation feeling alien, but may gain advantages for subsequent generations. In other words, the characters and readers can negotiate differences if positive value attaches to them in the long run.

Androids present some challenging forms of human modification, joining as they do humans with non-living mechanism. Anne McCaffrey and Mercedes Lackey collaborate to invent a human-machine hybrid in which the brains of damaged babies and children are given bio-electronic connections. All sensory and intellectual engagement with life is carried out through an electronic interface, and such shell-people become the core of spaceships or systems for governing planets. Known as "brains," they have "brawn" partners to handle matters that take a body. McCaffrey and Lackey deal briskly with any initial resistance readers may have, since shell-people would have had limited and impoverished lives without the transformation, and the authors then cheerfully explore the complexities that could result, such as a brawn falling in love with the personality of the shell-person but being unable to satisfy the physical side of such passion.[41] Each book covers a different problem and kind of relationship to normal humans. Occasional characters do find shell-people a repulsive concept; pure-human cultists and Practical Darwinians think the original defective infant should have been allowed to die. The Practical Darwinian, however, is quickly discredited by his cowardly actions, and this does much to condition reader response.

One form of grotesquerie involves humans having sex with something nonhuman. Edward Albee shocked audiences with his protagonist who falls in love with a she-goat in his play *Who Is Sylvia?* No one in this man's life is able to accept this passion. Since speculative fiction sometimes makes cross-species sexual relationships acceptable, what are the variables that permit that switch? The *fourth rule* for transmuting the grotesque into something acceptable is to make these sexual partners as equivalent to humans as possible. Albee's goat is just a goat, and so the situation remains grotesque. Ted Mooney's *Easy Travel to Other Planets* starts with a woman having sex with a dolphin, one that she has been trying to communicate with in experimental circumstances.[42] Most readers realize that dolphins are extremely intelligent. Mooney amplifies our sense of delphinic intelligence by speculating on the ways that they gather data through their skin, and he tells us snippets of delphinic "sagas" about culture heroes and their early contact with humans. In other words, his animals approximately equal humans in intelligence if not in material culture. Each step toward humanity reduces our objection to the sexual contact.

Rachel Ingalls in *Mrs. Caliban* describes the love affair between an oppressed housewife and a humanoid with froggish or aquatic features.[43] He can speak and talk to her, but he is some other kind of natural life form, not an adapted human. His ability to communicate is limited by imperfect grasp of the language, but in that regard, he is little different from an immigrant. We are encouraged to sympathize with him over his being mistreated in a lab. Such factors quickly lessen reader resistance to this crossing of species lines.

We get much closer to perfect equivalence to humanity with Marge Piercy's *He, She and It,* in which an android is so good that all kinds of issues suddenly become pressing.[44] Should he be paid for his services? He was designed as a defensive weapon, but can he be sent to his sure destruction if he has developed enough humanity to fall in love and understand what he would be losing by losing his life? Since he comes into existence in a Jewish kibbutz, can he make up a minyan? And should he be a sexual partner? The woman who sleeps with him finds him an ideal partner; he uses his tongue well and has no hang-ups about penis size and no need to show off as a sexual athlete or to dominate her. But should she be satisfied with a programmed lover rather than a man?

When analyzing how the effect of grotesquerie can be negated, one might invoke the Turing test for computer sentience: if you cannot tell the computer's responses (on-screen) from a human's responses to your questions, then the computer deserves recognition as a sentient entity and should be entitled to legal protections. Likewise, if the android seems in all ways human, why should one worry about its originating in a laboratory rather than a womb, as long as having offspring is not at issue? In Philip K.

Dick's *Do Androids Dream of Electric Sheep?* and the related film, *Blade Runner,* our sympathies are with the androids who are being assassinated simply because they can pass as people, not for any wrongdoing on their part. Only if the androids desire to eliminate humanity do we need to fear them. Their likeness to humanity can, over time, nullify our resistance to recognizing an equal.

The normalization of the grotesque in speculative fiction represents one way of generating new material for plots. Take an experience that cannot be readily assimilated in real life or more realistic fiction, and make it acceptable. What leaps out as key is that modifications, if they are professionally or economically useful, would quickly lose their power to upset us. Indeed, they might become desirable. If the issue is sex with a nonhuman, our resistance diminishes to the degree that the alien can be considered equivalent to humans in intellectual and cultural terms, and to the degree that it seems beautiful, or at least not ugly. If a modification of humans is apparently unthreatening, and if many people share it, then they are likely to be acceptable to the majority. Therefore, when authors wish to upset readers, they must avoid these mitigating factors. We can see why certain of the grotesqueries described earlier remain grotesque—for instance, a woman having sex with her boxers, or Arty the flipper boy's followers voluntarily amputating their extremities until they become limbless, helpless torsos. Uselessness in this case outweighs whatever acceptability might have been gained through their numbers. The floating corpse of God by definition lacks a peer group, and is not exactly an economic or professional boon to anyone. Palahniuk's gender-benders are less shocking than the freaks of *Geek Love,* precisely because they seek the modification, and they are not unique; indeed two of them met at a sex-change support group for others seeking the same goals.

The degree to which we feel assaulted will intensify if the grotesque object is unusual or unique. We will find it revolting the more the change seems useless or actively harmful. When we think of the grotesque in terms of joining the decorous with the unexpected and gross, the latter has this element of excess, of being useless and destructive. The palliative effect of economic benefit suggests a reason why the grotesque can be used to demystify society and its values; our society judges things in terms of economic benefit, efficiency, cold cash. The grotesque is, by its nature, hostile to that mode of judgment because it embodies excess; hence the grotesque is capable of disrupting society, to our disquietude.

In the previous chapter we saw that complaints might irritate readers into putting the book down, and that readers wishing to overcome purely personal reactions of that sort could try at least two tactics: one can recognize that some complaints can be taken as warnings from canaries in coalmines, so one should listen out of self-interest; alternatively, one can practice one's social skills by serving as listening ear to someone needing a tolerant friend. Neither of these tactics would help a resistant reader open up to the grotesque fiction in this chapter. Admittedly, since most of these books produce relatively mild discomfort, the struggle to read on is not severe. Perhaps the hardest to continue reading is *Blood Meridian* because of its violence. What helped me plow on was a desire to know what had been hidden from me. This, after all, was not the American history taught in high school. Being given so radically different an account satisfied an itch I did not know I had until faced with this chance to recover the historically repressed. Alternatively, my politics were such that I was willing to read a demystification of white frontier behavior, a motive that obviously would not work for chauvinistic western congressmen who would consider McCarthy's version unpatriotic. I suspect that to be an unpersuadable audience for this book.

Politics guides objections to several of the other grotesque novels too. An inflexible feminist would probably find *Lucky Pierre* too irritating to read; one less doctrinaire might be able to give the novel a chance by focusing on the feminist cinematographers and their manipulations of Pierre. While some figures in disability studies disapprove of *Geek Love,* others might find it possible to admire the extraordinarily complete lack of shame and self-loathing enjoyed by the unusual Binewski children, and use that as something to hold on to while reading. Their comfort with themselves is stronger than that enjoyed by most non-disabled readers, so this attraction might help many readers. With these novels, finding something to approve of or identify with can lower resistance.

Possibly the most general tactic for engaging with grotesque fiction that repels one is simply to ask oneself how one would behave if thrust into the world of the novel. Being in Antrim's world, or Morrow's, or Vizenor's becomes a challenge to one's sense of survival. If one opens oneself in that fashion, one is basically following Feagin's theory of practicing social interactions.

Ewa Kuryluk thinks the grotesque is no longer possible because our postmodern existence has lost master narratives, presumably the systems of order and ideal that constitute one of the opposing forces. With body grotesque, however, we still make distinctions between man and woman or human and nonhuman. We may be less rigid in our distinctions than previous generations might have been about male and female roles and about same-sex couples, but we can still be made uneasy when those polar values are merged or forced into contact. The very fact that we have lost many master narratives—patriotic zeal, belief in the government, a shared moral code—does not make most people comfortable with fluidity. Our anxieties may even be stronger precisely because we lack unthinking belief in certain values. Without agreed-upon rules, we must keep judging situations and trying to decide what values to apply. This is wearing, and having to keep making decisions leaves most of us careworn. Hence, postmodern decentering does not seem to have made the grotesque impossible. If anything, it feeds the anxieties, even as grotesque worlds make us worried about the future of our own world.

Why assault us with the grotesque? Insofar as members of society in good standing tend to associate themselves with orderliness, radical writers may wish to rattle their assurance and make them look at the underside of law-abiding society. More radical readers may enjoy seeing the chaos enveloping social order. The writers in this chapter all side to a greater or lesser degree with the anti-orderly values, which significantly differentiate contemporary grotesque from that of the medieval or Renaissance periods. Then, the animal additions to humans did not free the humans but rather made them figures for sin and probable damnation. Contemporary grotesque tends to see damnation as inhering to the side of law and order.

4

VIOLENCE

In the context of fiction that repels readers, a chapter titled "Violence" might concern horror fiction. Genre horror in fiction and film does indeed exploit physical and sexual violence, and some readers or viewers are horrified and even terrified. Overall, though, genre horror is extremely popular: in four years, the first five films of the *Saw* franchise grossed over $668 million, though they cost only $36 million to produce.[1] Audience responses to violent acts in the films include cheers as well as fainting. The *Saw* and *Hostel* franchises permit people to watch acts roughly comparable to those in *American Psycho*, but they do not arouse national furor and viciously hostile reviews in the intellectual media, or calls for their originators to be killed. Nor have these films and others of the sort called "torture porn" had to linger years in storage before being shown, whereas Samuel R. Delany's *Hogg* waited twenty-six years to find a publisher. When serious artists take up violence or outré sex, they tend to produce something different from the genre norm, and their works are likely to provoke audience resistance and critical recrimination. Robert Mapplethorpe's photographic artistry both transcended and intensified the pornographic elements of his pictures. Pier Paolo Pasolini's *Salò* is still banned in several countries. Danish art-film director Lars von Trier's *Antichrist,* with its scenes of blood ejaculating from a genital injury and of a woman cutting off her own clitoris with scissors, has gotten very mixed reviews in both Europe and the United states but has been taken seriously because von Trier contextualizes these visuals as art and psychological exploration rather than peddling them as gore- or torture-porn. A genre-fiction-transcending element is central to the literature discussed in this chapter.

Genre horror mostly upholds the status quo, the norm, and the law. Stephen King describes the horror tale as showing "the outbreak of some Dionysian madness in an Apollonian existence, and that the horror will continue until the Dionysian forces have been repelled and the Apollonian norm restored."[2] Richard Slotkin's monumental three-volume study details the American literary pattern of indulging in redemptive violence, violence that justifies itself because it saves the community and returns life to orderliness and safety.[3] Martin Rubin says that our film violence mostly supports the status quo, with the result that America is a land with a Latin American level of violence but a Scandinavian level of stability.[4] Granted, not all genre horror ends with the positive characters emerging into sunlight. Also true, aficionados delight in having their adrenaline aroused as well as enjoying the relief when the dread ends. At least initially, however, reviewers did not get this kind of thrill from *American Psycho* or *Hogg.*[5] In the kind of brutal and unpleasant material to be discussed in this chapter, we do not emerge from the nightmare to find norms reestablished. Violent fantasies are part of most people's unconscious, repressed by the laws and rules of our culture.[6] Why should we read fiction that touches on these hidden horrors? And if we must, why not settle for genre horror?

A book like *Hogg* takes us outside the law and maroons us there. This produces a way of repelling readers that differs from speeding too fast in the narrative, complaining, or rendering readers uneasy with grotesque alterations in human form. When critics and theorists contextualize violent and horrific material, they tend to link it to alienation from our machinic world,[7] to late capitalism and consumerism,[8] or to uneasiness over gender-role changes.[9] I want to propose an alternative perspective. The way these texts manipulate our relationship to the law obliges us to think about the nature of law and about which laws seem justified. Another way of putting the issue is that these texts question the relationship between individual freedom and community well-being. These texts also invite us to ponder what makes us human and humane.

Most horror theorists agree that genre horror intends one of three possible effects on the audience: *terror*, *horror*, and *revulsion*.[10] Terror is the rarest and (according to Stephen King) the hardest to achieve. It consists of fear of what is about to happen and involves atmosphere, looming catastrophe, and nameless dread as much as any actual acts. Horror, more common, is our response to the ghastly sight of some brutality already perpetrated; horror involves a lot of fear, since we know that whatever happened to the tortured body could happen to ourselves. Revulsion is our disgust at what we see, in extreme examples an impulse to vomit rather than to scream, but it may represent nothing more than resistance to excreta or disgust at bad behavior. These responses need not be separate or pure. Terror and horror can mingle, as can horror and revulsion, and revulsion covers responses that range widely in their strength. All three can produce a desire to put the book down or stop reading it altogether. In this chapter I discuss examples of fiction that elicit the three responses, then look at the larger issue of how we are pushed beyond the law by this fiction and what that does for us as readers.

Terror: *Dark Property, The Road*

Brian Evenson's *Dark Property* evoked terror so well that I found one of the opening sequences all but unreadable. We are in a desert landscape, and we quickly surmise that some catastrophe has changed the world, since we see three men openly kill a boy with a bayonet and a woman gather stones to defend herself. Life is primitive and technology largely gone if a bayonet and stones are the best available weapons. The men are clad in hats, trousers, and boots. The people have clothes left from earlier times, or their society is advanced enough to support weaving, since they do not dress in animal skins. The men prepare to eat the boy, however, so cannibalism is part of their life.

The narrative links us to a woman on the road who is carrying a dead or dying baby in her rucksack. She observes the boy's murder, but she is too far away from the violence for us to see details or feel horror. Instead, we worry more about the threat those three men pose to passersby. The road the woman follows will take her close to the group as they dismember the boy's corpse. Probably in a landscape as hostile to survival as this one, the woman would be unwise to leave the road, but she may be killed if she comes any closer to the three murderers. She follows the road, and is accosted. The initial queries are not overtly threatening. She is offered a meal, asked her name, asked if she wishes to join them. Her silences or monosyllabic answers offer no encouragement, and she threatens to throw a stone whenever the lead man tries to approach her. "If you throw that stone, you force a reckoning," he warns her, and then he casually cracks the spine of the dead victim.[11] The two younger men do not engage in the charade of politeness played by their leader. As far as they are concerned, the woman would be useful as food, nothing more. She escapes only because she can throw her stones powerfully and accurately, and does them enough damage that they let her escape.

The three men seem to belong to a religious sect, which makes them even more macabre.[12] They all have "dark closed collars," "dark ministerial shirts," black trousers, and dark boots (8). The leader wears a hat. His name, Honeybone, probably combines the smarmy, specious politeness of his honeyed words with the death and rape threats implicit in "bone," used as a skeletal unit and as slang for penis. If they can catch her, the woman stands no chance. She survives this encounter, but I could not read more than a page at a time because of anticipating what *could* happen if she were to make any mistake. The atmosphere and the nature of the dialogue make clear that this is the way life is now led, and no help can be expected. The woman cannot hope for cars coming along the road; she cannot phone the police. Cars, phones, and the police no longer exist. This appears to be an impoverished, post-catastrophe world, in which the ruthless and greedy have the best chance of surviving. Even the fact that she is a woman capable of childbearing gives her no protection; two of the men clearly think she should be raped and eaten, not kept to produce the next generation (12).

Most of the other episodes in this strange book rely more on horror or revulsion. The woman meets Kline, a man who carries a large sack that he kicks to stop its contents wriggling. The woman with the baby escapes from his rape and attempt to asphyxiate her only when a nude woman wriggles free from the sack and tries to run. Kline recaptures his burden, ties her foot up next to her buttock, knifes her in various places, and then slices off her big toe (37). He makes her walk on the bleeding foot until she is exhausted, knocks her unconscious, and stuffs her back in the sack. We see Kline and the bagged woman actually talking, and see evidence of his suffering venereal disease ("His return revealed the member to her vision, its flectubile scaled and red, the cracked bullet weeping a spunk-less pus" [44]). He proceeds to slice off more of his captive's toes (45) and then stuffs her back in the sack. He tries to turn her in at a depot where captured women can be exchanged for bounty, but the man behind the counter will not accept such badly damaged goods and persuades Kline to kill her, which Kline does by having her buried alive. The boys who dig the grave put up token resistance, more to extract extra pay than because they object to the deed itself (60–61).

What are we to make of this sadistic sequence? Characters express no feelings, so we get no sense of motivation. If anything, the people seem deadened by the nature of their experience. Saul Bellow refers to life in the archaic mode as living always threatened by hunger, thirst, injury, disease, violence, and death. Affliction is "accepted as the ground of existence, its real basis."[13] Someone in that state wastes no time wondering if he or she can find more happiness; knowing where the next meal is coming from or shelter from the next rain is enough to make a day seem good. In Evenson's created world, surviving is not attractive enough to motivate the characters. They endure rather than think, and seemingly do not project their thoughts beyond the present moment. If we read scholarly or journalistic accounts of genocidal violence or tribal headhunting, their context gives us some sense of why the people involved behave brutally: they have community identities of nation, religion, or tribe that "justify" such enmity and behavior. Here, though, we see too little interaction to figure out what community may still exist to give meaning to acts. All we can deduce is that money is paid for runaway women who are recaptured. The fortress/town has inhabitants, though when one of them is stabbed with a knife, this act has no effect (119), so we do not know whether they are ghosts or unexplained beings in a horror fantasy. They do not bear the marks of the resurrected corpses we see later, but readers are given no explanations for the nature of their reality or of the town's organization.

With no comprehensible community, what men seem to have is freedom to act in any manner. Not surprisingly, those who are strong think nothing of damaging and killing others. Those strong people, however, do none of the organizing that would protect them against loss of strength as they age or are injured. They do not even follow the Darwinian imperative to pass on their own genes, let alone think more abstractly about continuing the species. The stronger men actually gain remarkably little from their perfect freedom. If Kline is at all typical, such a life is disease-ridden, damaged by injury, pointless, strenuous, and often boring.

Whether arousing terror or horror, Evenson writes with so unengaged a tone that we have no way of guessing his view or aim. We can only brood and draw our own conclusions as to what we may think about such an existence, and what it suggests to us about the functions of community with regard to the individual. In this respect, his extremes raise different issues from those in horror films, where physical reaction is more prominent than sociopolitical rumination.[14] In such films, we identify with characters who are trying to escape, trying to stay alive. Evenson's mysteriously neutral emotional tone ultimately puts the audience in a different relationship to the ugly deeds from the relationship in horror and splatter films. We are trying to figure out what the situation is; we want to make sense of what we are reading. Also in keeping with a more intellectual engagement is Evenson's relish for strange, arcane, and invented words: *spartle, stammel, fremented, sprenting, flench, slecked, woozed, scrudded, flittern, stoured, flizzed, burze,* and *corneous* all appear within the first twenty-two pages. Aesthetically he satisfies us, but philosophically he gives us no answers.[15] If we wish to go beyond the plot and escape in a fashion other than just closing the book and trying to forget, then we can rethink our way through the social contract and decide what freedoms are worth sacrificing in return for what protections.

Putting us beyond all law might seem necessitated by a postcultural setting, but lawlessness is not endemic to all denuded and impoverished apocalyptic landscapes. Cormac McCarthy's novel *The Road* (2007) features a similar landscape. The towns are mostly deserted, and only a few people live in the ruins. All commerce and communication have disappeared, and those still alive scavenge for what they can find. The lowering threat of disasters that never quite happen stirs terror throughout.

What makes McCarthy's postcultural setting entirely different from Evenson's is the focus on two people together, father and son. By themselves, they constitute a community, one in which they care for each other, worry about each other, try to help each other, reassure each other. Furthermore, they seek a larger community and wish to join it, so they are always planning with that future in mind. They talk; they express emotions, hopes, and fears. Their desire to find a group keeps them from random or selfish killing. While the threatening figures who try to steal their food or eat a baby act with as little compunction as those in *Dark Property,* the man and boy desire no such liberty from restraint. Within *The Road,* community is upheld as both necessary and desirable and manifested in their actions, so we never find ourselves outside any law despite being in a world without enforceable restraints. Thus, violent disaster scenarios need not push us into the world beyond our sense of community, and need not produce any uneasiness of that sort, though uneasiness, of course, depends on the reader. A friend of mine found *The Road* almost unreadable, but to me it seemed standard catastrophe fare because that terror was redeemed or softened by the community of two. McCarthy's father and son stay well within the law and do nothing that forces rethinking the rights or obligations of the individual. Evenson chose to explore those freedoms that McCarthy's characters do not want, and he forces us to examine such lawlessness without giving us any guidance on how to feel or judge. The implications of freedom are forced upon us.

Horror: *American Psycho*

Horror is relatively common compared to terror. We have seen one form of it in *Blood Meridian;* that book's lack of overt humor puts it right on the borderline of the grotesque and violent horror. We find ample opportunity to feel horror in Bret Easton Ellis's *American Psycho.* Like McCarthy and Evenson, Ellis uses a detached voice to describe horrifying events. The author's views are not explicit. This puts all obligation for interpretation on the reader. Nor does Ellis wind up the action with a release of tension. Patrick Bateman still roams New York, and women, gays, minorities, and white male financiers just like Patrick are all potential targets.

One of the lesser controversies surrounding this book is the level of "reality" at which the violence takes place. Does Patrick Bateman kill all those people, or are we simply inside his mind while he fantasizes the violence? The two best responses I have seen to this question deny that we can properly treat Bateman as a "person" whose actions are "real" within the story. Elizabeth Young points to many oddities: the psychological implausibility of one man's being a sexual murderer who will kill anyone, man or woman, rather than obsessing over a single type of victim; his being both a spree and a serial murderer; and his present-tense accounts of his deeds. That last pushes him perilously close to Shamela's first-person-singular present-tense epistolary account of attempted rape, and this voice best makes sense as a satiric technique.[16] The other is a comparative essay on Dennis Cooper and Ellis by Mark Storey. Storey argues that the principal characters of *American Psycho* and *Frisk* are not fictional people but embodiments of ideas. Postmodernism has broken down the values that supported traditional masculinity:

> In its most explicit form, Bateman's fear of his own subjugation expresses itself through the violence he enacts on "others"; this loaded term is important here, as what Bateman sees as "other" is linked to the position of normative masculinity in the postmodern era. Women in particular, but also homosexuals, blacks, and other ethnic minorities, all suffer his wrath at some point; we have already established the unreality of these murders, so we can presume that Bateman singles these people out in his mind for a reason. From a quick glance at the list, it is obvious why: These are the groups who, in a postmodern society, find their place in the margins being brought into the center. To Bateman, the rise of the marginalized threatens his central position as hegemonic male; to protect that position, he lashes out, attempting to eliminate the threat.[17]

Storey notes that the traditional male fears the postmodern breakdown of hegemony caused by women entering the male sphere of action, and comments on how, even while resisting women, Bateman is coming to resemble them in his morning beauty routines. When characters embody an ideology or set of ideas, we are reading the kind of intellectual satire that Northrop Frye called "anatomy," a disquietingly accurate term when applied to this book.

Storey also explodes the supposed realism of the descriptions:

> The state of Bateman's apartment on the morning after a particularly horrific night (290–91) is typical: The smell emanating from the mangled corpses (he opens Venetian blinds covered with the fat of electrocuted breasts), would

be hard to cover up. As he seems never to do any cleaning, we can only presume that his maid, whom he mentions more than once, does it for him. Would she stay silent about finding a decapitated head wearing sunglasses on the kitchen work surface? Or were there no remains to find because the murders never took place? Or perhaps there is no maid? (60–61)

Does Bateman kill or merely imagine these murders as his personality disintegrates? This question teases readers, but the more closely we examine the details, the less the plot seems to represent action on the plane of fictive reality.[18]

Another issue that dissolves under scrutiny is the "responsibility" that Ellis must bear for launching such horrifying detail on the world, telling the deranged how to carry out loathsome acts. Violent films often get bad press (though may become quite popular), but horror films usually do not draw the same obloquy, partly because we know that their grisly tortures of humans are the products of special effects and computerized creation, and partly because they often end with the reassertion of order.[19] What happens on a page is just ink on paper, yet in the case of *American Psycho,* those words were held culpable by early commentators. Julian Murphet quotes Ellis to the effect that his details on murder all came from real cases: "I didn't really want to write them, but I knew they had to be there. So I read a lot of books about serial killers and picked up details from that and then I had a friend who introduced me to someone who could get me criminology textbooks from the FBI.... That's why I did the research, because I couldn't really have made this up."[20] These murders have already taken place in the real world, and he has assembled them for his aesthetic and fictional purposes. Before rushing to judgment, we should try to see what those purposes might have been.

The pileup of nastiness will horrify most readers the first time they expose themselves to Bateman's descriptions, and part of the gut revulsion comes from the way we see this through Bateman's eyes. Bateman kills an old college lover by nailing her fingers to boards with a nail gun in a kind of crucifixion, biting the other fingers off, stabbing her torso and slicing off parts of her breast, using Mace on her at intervals, and cutting out her tongue with scissors.[21] Jumper cables, a car battery, and matches bring another woman to her death; in the morning "her mouth is lipless and black and there's also a black pit where her vagina should be (though

I don't remember doing anything to it) and her lungs are visible beneath the charred ribs" (290–91). He uses a Bic lighter on another woman's eyes until the eyeballs burst. He cuts the flesh off around her mouth and uses a power drill to widen the hole so he can force his hand and arm down her throat and pull out the contents of neck and upper chest (305). For another, he stuffs cheese up her vagina and shoves a rat inside through a pet store animal tunnel. Then he saws off her lower half with a chainsaw, and she remains alive long enough to see him pull the lower half away (328–29). Toward the end (344), he gets into cannibalism, not just the incidental gnawing off of digits and biting off of nipples, but eating intestines. Portions of some corpses end up being baked, probably for consumption.

Can one argue for a positive value to reading this novel? One can read purely out of curiosity to see how much mere words can upset one. The more revulsion and discomfort they cause, the more praise the author deserves perhaps? Fredric Jameson condemns postmodern writing for its loss of affect, and Ellis is indeed deliberately affectless in his descriptions, but emotion has not disappeared when we take reader response into account. Ellis provokes something stronger than mere "decorative exhilaration."[22] One could read to see how the author aroused so much response. These would be aesthetic appreciations of effective writing without regard to whether the effect is pleasant or not.[23] One might enjoy being upset because of the sense of relief afterwards; in *Brave New World,* people take violent passion surrogate treatments periodically to awaken and then purge adrenaline-fueled emotions, and this novel or numerous horror and slasher films may operate in that fashion. *American Psycho* can also be read for its satiric elements. The attack on yuppie life might be said to make the nastiness acceptable as exaggerated symbolic criticism of capitalism and consumerism. Bateman famously says he is in "murders and executions" instead of "mergers and acquisitions." One can read out of wide-eyed innocence as to there being such people, though very few, if any, serial murderers are attractive and wealthy in the style of Patrick Bateman. Nor do they resemble the mesmeric Hannibal Lecter as played by Anthony Hopkins. The profiles of those known and captured are considerably less appealing. Some readers may read *American Psycho* with a degree of positive feeling; someone whose fantasy world is violent, as is the imagination of Cooper's two characters named Dennis, might find this a stirring source for new fantasies. One cannot even count on horror being a universal response.

I have argued that the books analyzed in this chapter push us as readers to consider our relationship to the law and to community. Evenson make us long for order and wonder which rules would help most, particularly since Kline's freedom from such restraints offers so little pleasure or reward. We may be moved to think about exactly what protection we might wish to build into a law code if starting from scratch again, as would be necessary after Evenson's postcultural world. Readers face more options concerning order and society with *American Psycho*. Some are devastated that Bateman is not captured at the end; they are rooting for the police and forces of the law and feel betrayed by the law's ineffectiveness. They may suffer from realizing that laws, no matter how draconian, could not protect victims from a killer like Bateman. Readers, however, who feel unswerving hostility toward the police functions of our country could wish for his escape on those grounds, and others who share Bateman's values with regard to the homeless or gays or women may enjoy entering a fictive world in which such prejudices are being acted upon. Because the narrative is given through Bateman's perspective, antisocial views are more readily allowed than in a detective story where we side with the detective. Instead of giving us the comfort of aligning with law enforcement, Ellis not only puts us nominally outside the law because of our narrative point of view but gives us a different sort of tingle as well. We put ourselves outside the "laws of decency" by continuing to read, by letting those agonizing images enter and dwell in our imaginations. That, of course, assumes that the law governs what goes on in our heads, and the degree of discomfort we feel reading tells us just how much we have internalized such laws. Reading this book with any appreciation at all is a form of breaking rules, as is reading and enjoying various extreme forms of pornography. Reconsidering how much we wish our thoughts to be bound by cultural rules is another version of reconsidering the laws and their limits. This seems to me a positive value to be gained from reading this novel.

Revulsion: *Hogg, Frisk, Try, Blood and Guts in High School*

The third kind of response evoked by horror literature is revulsion. While this may include an element of fear, as it does when we look at some terrible dismemberment, fear is not essential. Samuel R. Delany's *Hogg* and

Dennis Cooper's *Frisk* and *Try* all give us a world that mostly repels us rather than scaring us out of our skins. Again, though, we read without an obvious reward for doing so. Why should we?

Hogg portrays a man who lives in his truck, always pisses in his pants, and picks up an eleven-year-old boy to serve as his sexual convenience. Most of the laws we question when reading *Dark Property* or *American Psycho* involve protection of property or life. Those in *Hogg* are the rules of toilet training and the taboos on incest and sexual use of children, although we also see plenty of murder and violence as well. *Hogg* features thirty-one deaths—one murder carried out by Hogg, the rest by one of his sidekicks. The spree murders mostly take place offstage, and the media commentators induce more revulsion than the mostly invisible corpses of unknowns. The violated laws that matter are those relating to excretion, to assault, and to outré (and illegal) sexual pleasures.

For someone from a middle-class background, the impact of flouting those laws is considerable. Rob Stephenson's introduction to *Hogg* states that "Maurice Girodias of Olympia Press, famous for first publishing Nabokov's *Lolita* and the novels of Sade, told Delany it was the only novel he 'ever rejected solely because of its sexual content.'"[24] The body count was not a problem, and I suspect that even the commissioned assaults and rapes were not the issue; though brutal and unsavory in every way, they do little permanent damage—no broken eardrums or destroyed eyes, amputated limbs, or rape carried out with a knife blade. They exhibit none of the artistic pleasure in gruesome mutilations found in *American Psycho*. I would argue that the spectrum of physical violence mostly just defines the hellish world in which the characters operate. The excretory and sexual materials are what push us beyond some limit of tolerance and comfort. They include, as I have mentioned, using children sexually, incest, and the thoroughgoing exploitation of all bodily secretions.

Michael Hemmingson presents Hogg as follows:

> The narrator first encounters Hogg raping and beating a woman in an alley; next, he couples with Hogg through fellatio and sodomy. Hogg, we learn, is a thug, a "rape artist" and terrorizer for hire, with inclinations more homosexual than heterosexual. Hogg may very well be the most vile, disgusting personality to emerge from contemporary American fiction: he never bathes or changes clothes, urinates and defecates in his pants, eats his own various

bodily excreta, drinks a lot of beer and eats plenty of pizza to "maintain" his large gut—he has worms and likes it—and enjoys bringing suffering to others, male or female, mostly for pay but sometimes for his own delectation. Yet he is also fascinating: the embodiment of what our society can turn people into, the decaying condition of the human soul.[25]

I doubt that society is entirely to blame for Hogg's attitudes and actions. What makes him so startlingly original is his success in freeing himself from all laws but the laws of physics. In this regard he is an intriguing creation. The degree to which one enjoys entering that state of freedom explains some of the book's attraction.

The unnamed eleven-year-old boy who serves as focal figure is simply called a cocksucker. He consumes the sweat, semen, saliva, phlegm, tears, urine, shit, blood, foreskin cheese, snot, belly-button fluff, and toe jam of Hogg and his rapist friends. Those adults interact with one another sexually, and they collaborate in the rape-assaults, but the boy is the sexual nexus of the group and focus of the narrative. The tastes and smells and textures in the mouth plus pleasure in doing what other members of society cannot contemplate are what seem to matter most to these men:

> "Shit stinks. But it don't taste like anything.
> That nigger shit a horse turd too!
> I bit. It mashed out against the corner of my mouth. I chewed. It was like sour starch paste. And grainy....I spit out about half of what I still had in my mouth into my hand. I looked at it a few seconds. Then, kneeling back on the floor, I put it inside my open fly and rubbed it around on my cock and nuts. It felt good; but it only got me half hard. (176)

Many readers will be too repelled to wonder whether fresh shit—the most generally tabooed substance—would feel good if massaged into one's sexual skin.

Sucking cocks is the least unusual of the activities shown. The boy's companions live a life in which they piss on one another or one pisses into another's mouth; Hogg always pisses in his pants; he also shits into them and shakes his trouser leg to dislodge the turd, and does not change the pants until they fall from his body. Members of a motorcycle club get new members drunk, piss on their clothes, and insist that the new members wear those clothes and not shower. The boy drinks the piss spurting from a man who has been shot in the head, and this is considered a rare treat. In one another these characters recognize a brotherhood of body and clothing filth. These tastes not only revolt middle-class sensibilities but also break down any traces of the hegemonic values the men may have preserved from their upbringing or schooling, thus freeing them from those inner constraints. Given their exclusion from the middle class by tastes, income, training, skills, and now by stench, they glory in freeing themselves from its values.

Aside from murder, the challenges to the law in this book consist of consuming bodily fluids, injuring women, and familial incest. Enjoyment of bodily products is an infantile joy, characteristic of the period before a child is conditioned to reject them. Feces have not yet been termed "yucky" and met with a wrinkled nose and expression of disgust at smell. Infants do not yet know how to control urine, or that it should be loosed only in sanctioned locations; they only know that being relieved of the pressure feels good. Regulating bodily functions constitutes one of the earliest forms of law that infants learn to obey, their first training in purity and dirt (as Mary Douglas calls it), the system of taboos that defines an infant as part of a particular cultural and biological group versus the rejected Other, be that animal or other cultural groups with different patterns.[26] Deriving adult sexual satisfaction from excretory functions can be called a positive perversion, but for readers the shock value seems to be in undoing some of our earliest social conditioning, however vicariously or speculatively.

By repealing these laws of toilet training, Delany radically rewrites the world as we understand it, and shows us just how arbitrary our supposedly natural world is. If we take his word for it, enjoyment of excretions can bring delight, sexual excitement, and extremely varied kinds of sexual contact. Were he hymning a mechanical sex toy (which does not violate such taboos), plenty of readers would be interested in buying it, given the pleasures he promises. He gives us no adverse evidence concerning these ingestive practices—problems of infection or buildup of toxins, problems that *Gravity's Rainbow* illustrates by killing off the coprophagous Brigadier Pudding with *E. coli*. To the degree that we are willing to let our conditioned barriers down, we can experience vicariously the sense of freedom that discarding that training might produce. While the life Hogg and his henchmen lead does not appeal to me, I do respond with curiosity to the fact that they depend on no one; they can act on impulse; they look up to no one; and they must obey no one. Their source of money—the contracts taken out on women—provides them with the pleasure of violence, so they can truly be said to enjoy their work. They are free in strange ways that few people achieve. Given the emphasis on freedom in the American imagination, this offers us the opportunity to reconsider how we rate that value and what we mean by it.

For a certain kind of male reader, the violence against women can be seen in the same light. William S. Burroughs saw women as a virus that infected men and limited their lives with prissy rules and enslaving regulations designed to ensure female safety and social predictability. *One Flew Over the Cuckoo's Nest* gives us a famous heterosexual version of the resentment toward women and their social control (exemplified in Nurse Ratched). Those men who feel constrained by what they see as female laws might enjoy the fictive freedom to strike back. Many men hate the social demands for politeness, nonviolence, neatness, cleanness, sexual restraint, heterosexuality, and self-control: these behavioral patterns marked a "gentleman" in the nineteenth century but are also the patterns that made Huck Finn and other American men light out for the territories. For men who resent these demands, then, women are an obvious target, and Hogg makes what money he needs by assaulting and raping women. He has no qualms about these acts and will beat up a girl in a wheelchair as readily as any other woman. The women's usual alleged transgression is infidelity or getting tired of the man who has purchased this punishment. Such belief in sexual ownership is common enough that fiction exploring the freedom to act upon it presumably offers a pornographic pleasure for someone who represses such attitudes in his attempt to seem civilized.

Paternal incest appears three times in *Hogg*. Some authors favor it as the primal experience behind the violent phenomena they present, but Delany's presentation is not easy to pigeonhole. In *Hogg,* incest occurs in the introductory basement scene when a brother is selling his sister and the cocksucker to bikers and drifters for twenty-five cents a go. The siblings' father appears, drunk and indignant, and eventually has sex with his daughter while the bikers look on, taken aback, amused, and even a bit admiring at this violation of taboo. The act is not offered as the cause of the children's precocity. It merely sets the tone for the cocksucker's world, and puts readers on notice that rules will be broken, with no moral outrage expressed and no particular sympathy shown for the child thus victimized.

Victimhood is not Delany's point, and that lack of indignation leaves all response and evaluation to the reader, a tactic that in itself creates uneasiness, since we are used to being guided by implicit or explicit standards. Judgment does seem suspended within the book.

Two more instances of incest provide children's first sexual experience in *Hogg*. Hogg's was with his sister, but all his family members seem to have had sex with one another, parents with children and children with children, his father with children of both sexes. His mother had at least one child by one of her own sons. We do not see any repugnance on the children's part; this is simply how life as they know it is lived, and they all participate, sucking one another off, learning to eat and drink secretions, giving pleasure and getting it from these activities. Honey-Pie is the other child whose sexual experience began with incest. She is used by her father, Big Sambo. Honey-Pie never says anything, no matter what is done to her, and as literary voyeurs, most readers probably feel horrified at what she undergoes. Our boy narrator is unclear how comfortable she is with these activities but notes without comment her lack of response to Big Sambo's statements:

> "He cute," Big Sambo repeated. "Ain't he, sweetheart?" He glanced at Honey-Pie.
> She just blinked. (169)

> "I run her momma out of here about eight or nine years back when I couldn't put up with the old lady's complainin' at me all the time about me wantin' to fool around with the little girl here." Big Sambo grinned. "Been pretty happy since then, ain't we, baby? Prettiest little pussy you ever seen, huh?" His knuckles kept working.
> Honey-Pie blinked, scratched her ear. (170)

Since she is about twelve years old, Big Sambo has evidently been using her since she was three or four.

When an outsider asks whether anything is wrong, she only says, "Nothin"—her one utterance in the book. When the nameless cocksucker is secretly thinking of leaving Hogg, Hogg queries his abstraction and is similarly told, "Nothin" (268), the boy's only spoken word. The similarities found in Hogg's childhood sexual experience, Honey-Pie's abuse and silent behavior, and the silent behavior of the boy suggest that the boy probably experienced incest or very early sex with someone who had parent-like authority. The import of that "Nothin" for both of them is ambiguous. They may be afraid to answer truthfully. They may find impossible the act of trying to describe their state, especially to outsiders. Possibly they feel that nothing is wrong, that this is just how life is, even how life should be. Outsiders find that difficult to comprehend, but they have not been conditioned by such experience.

Delany does not moralize, and that lack is something that tells us we are beyond the law. He invites no shock, but neither does he laud the incest or child abuse and present it in an attractive light, as is seen (about adult incest) in Theodore Sturgeon's daring "If All Men Were Brothers, Would You Let One Marry Your Sister?"[27] If anything, Delany seems to portray a life that is so weak in any sense of community that all relationships are ad hoc and ungoverned by larger community rules, such as those on incest. This life has no refinement and few actual pleasures, but it does offer freedom and sensual gratifications. Delany strips away much of what we consider civilization as inessential.

We may declare that Hogg has been victimized by his parents and in turn victimizes the boy, but is "victimize" an accurate term in either case? When we see them, neither Hogg nor the boy expects or seems to want anything else, at least until the boy thinks about leaving Hogg at the end. Presumably the boy felt victimized the first time he was sodomized, but he has gone past that either into sporadic enjoyment or into a quasi-mute survival mode, simply living for the moment.[28] Possibly the boy's silence reflects his having been reduced to Saul Bellow's "archaic standard" of life. If so, most readers would consider moral indignation the appropriate response. Alternatively, one can accept that many people in the world suffer that kind of life and ask instead whether or not the boy can move on without penalty. Hogg did, after all, kill someone who tried to leave his band. Does the boy enjoy the liberty to do as he pleases, or is he enslaved to Hogg until he proves strong enough to break free? Emotional mutism and slavery or the liberty to please himself: which defines the nature of the boy's life?

My relatively unengaged response to much of *Hogg* is probably not a typical reaction. It would have been different had I not, a year before reading *Hogg,* read Delany's novel *The Mad Man,* where the sexualized ingestion of all bodily fluids is similarly enjoyed. This diminished the shock value of some parts of *Hogg,* though not the impact of the child abuse. Here is a more typical reaction:

> Delany is one of my favorite writers, and yet it took me weeks to read *Hogg.* I read quickly; the problem was, I found it too upsetting to continue reading for more than a half-hour at a time, or to return to the book until the effect of the last reading had dissipated. The strength of the book's emotional, physical, and psychological impact is due, to a large extent, to the quality of its writing. It evokes, in the reader, an extraordinary range of emotional and physical responses: from sexual arousal, to laughter, to nausea; from empathy, to sorrow, to fear. *Hogg* is a story about sadomasochistic (s-m) and submissive-dominant (s-d) sex, sexual exploitation, racial fantasies, assault, rape, and serial murder. It is also a strongly erotic pornographic novel.[29]

This reader obviously reads with her moral senses alert, ready to apply them to action. Delany himself calls his book pornography, but also admits that it probably does not prove sexually stimulating for most heterosexual women, heterosexual men, homosexual men, or homosexual women. All he can say is, "It is the most rigorous and honest fictional exploration I can render of what crawls and wriggles and grubs among the roots of my own scorpion garden," while insisting that "it is *only* a novel."[30] Delany interestingly links *Hogg* to de Sade's *Juliette* in his essay "The Scorpion Garden." He describes *Juliette* as a pornographic novel in which a woman becomes aware of the hypocritical pressures placed on women by men so as to rule them, and proceeds to break every rule and law she can in order to get whatever she wants. Only thus, and doing great damage to others, can she win her own freedom. While Delany agrees with the marquis on the situation of women, he focuses instead on a man who similarly wins freedom from the rules that society would impose on him. Insofar as we follow Hogg imaginatively, we too experience a reflected version of such freedom.

Hogg is unusual for taking us beyond much more elementary taboos than the laws that protect property and personal safety. For readers marginalized by their sexual or predatory interests, the books may just represent a pleasing relief from oppressive rules not consented to, a cheering violation of regulations. For the norm-accepting reader, the result is likely to be deep discomfort and possibly a disinclination to continue reading, or

a teasingly perverse pleasure from indulging in the forbidden. What readers gain is exposure to an outlook not often represented in books. One sees
in *Hogg* a set of people whose lives are governed by sensation, by physical
feeling more than by intellect, ambition, community spirit, or planning,
but they have to live inside a civilization with very different values. Clearly
they reject the repressions analyzed by Freud that are the price we pay for
civilization, since they do not care if civilization crumbles away. Even if
one's taste does not go in the direction pursued by Delany's characters, the
freedom to act on such drives may provoke thought about what exercising
such freedom might mean.

Clearly such freedom can mean abusing the weak. Are we to claim that
freedom as an individual's right? Hogg obviously does, though we have no
evidence for Delany's views here. Given the eleven-year-old-boy's deadpan
exposition, we are pushed to produce our own answers. Most readers are
unlikely to identify with the spree murderer Denny, one of Hogg's cro-
nies, a slightly older version of the narrator. While many readers will reject Hogg's violence toward women, what he and his sidekicks do among
themselves sexually seems mutually accepted and so of no concern. What
they do with children, however, upsets many readers. A boy is raped in
one of their raids; Honey-Pie and the narrator are the other sub-teens who
presumably had no choice when they were originally forced into sexual
activities. Insofar as the narrator ever expresses a personal sentiment, he
seems willing: "He liked the way he was getting it. I liked the way he was
giving it" (58). Delany offers us several options. First, we can draw on our
internalized social rules and feel horrified at child abuse, treat it as open
and shut, and pass judgment. Second, we can recognize that some children
are on their own, and some belong to adults who think children owe a
return for care and support: they pay their way by means of sexual service,
and, like the child Ludwig in Pynchon's *Gravity's Rainbow,* they find that
the fate worse than death is negotiable.[31] This puts it crudely, but unless
you can guarantee all children a loving upbringing with adequate material
wealth, then alternative power dynamics will inevitably exist. That leads
to other choices: Change the world so that no child is ever dependent on a
sexual predator, which would mean income leveling and extreme state sur-
veillance. Queasily shrug and note that the children shown are managing
somehow, and the very position of the boy as narrative voice might mean
that he has survived and even matured into a writer. Or recognize that

some children survive this treatment, however damaged by the experience, but others will not.

Then again, we can remind ourselves that these actions and characters are just words on paper, in which case these responses are beside the point. They also don't help orient us in regard to the book. None of the answers that assume relevance to the experience of real children is attractive or desirable, so where does that leave us with our moralistic bluster? Indignant but ineffective, in all likelihood. Delany thus takes us not only beyond the law but also beyond the world of morally satisfying solutions.

The strength of our revulsion or discomfort is probably less strong, though no less pervasive, when we read Dennis Cooper's *Frisk* (1991) and *Try* (1994). Unlike his novel *Guide* (1997), in which the violence does happen in the fictive world, *Frisk* presents the violence as sexual fantasies, though, as in *American Psycho,* we are not sure for some time what level of reality to assign to the ugly deeds. The main character is called Dennis, and his erotic fantasies are extremely violent. He wants to kill partners; he imagines, for instance, forcing one hand down a lover's throat and the other up the anus and shaking hands with himself somewhere in the middle.[32] Apparently Dennis cannot repress his fantasies or change their nature, and he implies their origin in snuff porn photos he saw at an impressionable age. He obsesses over a particular physical type of man, one like the subject in the snuff porn. In *Guide,* several people do die, but in *Frisk,* the murders remain in Dennis's mind. He even writes a narrative describing killing several rootless young men as if he had really done so, and sends this account to an acquaintance, inviting him to visit and take part in such murders. The acquaintance and his young brother do visit, despite some qualms as to whether their host is indeed a murderer who might murder them, but they disprove the narrative from internal evidence and, if anything, find the account and its ideas rather cool.[33]

The violence seems here to emerge mostly from consensual, casual sexual encounters with same-sex strangers. Sadism looking for an outlet and masochism looking for pain and submission are common. While for some readers this material might provoke repulsion, I find that largely muted by the degree to which ordinary cities exist within the novels. The actors in Cooper's worlds may feel no attachment to family, church, or workplace because they have chosen to follow sensual rather than professional drives, but complex social structures do exist all around them. They can telephone the police, as one cannot in Evenson's novel. They have choices.

Cooper poses an interesting problem with broad applicability. What if someone is driven by erotic fantasies, the nature of which he cannot control? Dennis finds his life dominated by this seductive inner violence. Because sexual response would be heightened by committing physical violence, the temptation to act is constant. All of his routine encounters operate on two levels, one a fairly ordinary physical one of easy exchange of sexual pleasure. The other is a violent mental world, where an act that might in other circumstances express love or cheerful lust and desire for release is instead a thin front for actions that would usually be ascribed to hatred or to berserk fury or malignant aggression and pathological self-centeredness.

Both *Frisk* and *Guide* make us see that plain vanilla heterosex is a social construction, something fostered for the sake of community stability and comfort but inadequate and irrelevant to many members of society. Porn is the most available way of satisfying forbidden desires, but viewing it may have consequences. In *Frisk*, we see how a sequence of snuff porn pictures ensorcels young Dennis's imagination. In later life he meets the model who posed for the pictures and realizes that he was not really killed; later still, at the end of the book, Dennis and friends can reconstruct the pictures and dwell on the artifice: "The 'wound' is actually a glop of paint, ink, makeup, tape, cotton, tissue, and papier-mâché sculpted to suggest the inside of a human body. It sits on the ass, crushed and deflated" (128). Dennis acknowledges that his life has been totally shaped by something whose artifice was as shoddy as that of their reconstruction. Even his fascination with insides and guts apparently stems from this pornographic picture seen at an impressionable age. He shows no particular regret, no hostility toward pornography. Porn is simply omnipresent in these characters' world.

Because we have seen paternal incest in *Hogg*, we should note that Cooper also explores this theme in *Try*. Ziggy is the adopted teenaged son of a gay couple who subsequently split up, and both his fathers have used him sexually. Although Ziggy has had some kind of therapy, he is still in the custody of one father and visits with the other, so the law has not taken steps to protect him from such abuse. He is far from being a happy boy, but he has little sense that life could be otherwise, and Cooper walks a fine line between inviting outrage on his behalf and treating this simply as a case of how life is for some people. Unlike Hogg, Ziggy is not trying to free himself from ordinary rules of behavior. Rather, like most teens, he wants to belong and yearns for love. The opposite of the wordless boy in *Hogg,* Ziggy both talks and writes compulsively. His battered perkiness keeps him going, keeps him hoping, talking, and trying to connect rather than just enduring. In Cooper's world, paternal incest is not the source of all ills, though it does seem slightly more frowned upon than it is in Hogg's world. When Ziggy quotes the school therapist on how he uses people because he's afraid he can never get anyone to love him, his father Roger answers, "You're a disaster....It enriches your beauty so much."[34] Even with a father like that, Ziggy manages to be caring, though he is certainly emotionally needy.

I mention paternal incest because several writers see it as the "original sin" of their disturbing worlds. In *The Alphabet Man,* Richard Grossman's multiple murderer spends his boyhood involved in his parents' sadomasochistic routines.[35] Kathy Acker also offers a paternal incest sequence. Unlike Delany or Cooper, she does not use affectless description or invite us to make up our own minds. Rather, she screams at us, demanding sympathy and encouraging revulsion at such paternal misdeeds. *Blood and Guts in High School* starts with the incestuous relationship between Janey (who claims to be ten years old) and her father, Johnny.[36] The realism of the scene quickly disintegrates, however, when Janey talks like someone in her twenties or older. She analyzes the ups and downs of their relationship in a mature way. She considers Johnny naïve for believing Sally to be "a minister's daughter from Vermont" when Janey knows *"that Sally's a rich young bitch who'll fuck anyone until a more famous one comes along as young WASP bitches do"* (18). Moreover, the drawing that Janey does of her own genitals shows them to be anatomically adult, supplied with pubic hair and with more visible labia minora than a young girl would have.

Shocking though the situation seems at the outset, Janey is no Honey-Pie; Honey-Pie's father is horribly real-seeming, whereas Janey's quickly comes to seem just symbolic of patriarchy and the way it abuses girls, destroying their confidence and abilities. Acker does blame patriarchal incest in various guises for her female characters' problems, but in this instance the incest appears to be metaphoric and is used for shock value. I started rethinking my initial sympathy the moment I ceased to believe Janey to be ten years old. Her emotional neediness, like Ziggy's, is obviously a product of psychological problems with her upbringing, and is not something you would wish on anybody of any age. Janey is old enough, however, that we might expect her to have gained more control over her behavior—if, that is, we consider getting along within society a practical and useful approach to life. Acker clearly does not; she prefers as author to scream rather than compromise and fit in.

How does this incest operate in conjunction with the motif of taking readers beyond the law? In this sequence, Janey seems unworried by the incest itself; rather, she does not want the relationship to end and feels devastated when her father finds another partner. Later, though, Janey deliberately tries to get beyond the patterns and rules of ordinary life. She tears around with a teen gang doing outlawed things. She scribbles baby-talk obscenities on a wall, evidently regressing to an infantile state. She fantasizes scurrilously and scabrously about President Carter's anus, genitals, and sexual proclivities. The paternal incest represents not just fathers but society as patriarchy; hence Janey's need to break all rules and laws. Unless like de Sade's Juliette she succeeds, she can never win free of oppression. As she despairingly puts it, "The only thing I want is freedom. Let me tell you: I don't have any idea what that means" (112).

Cooper certainly takes us outside norms and laws, and raises questions about the rights of the individual as opposed to the community. Cooper's incest does not seem as metaphoric as Acker's, and we wonder what protections the community should offer. The violent fantasies underlying the sexual acts also take us outside cultural assumptions about sex. Our social conditioning tries to control such acts by associating them with love and partnership. We have culturally chosen to stress those positive elements, and have built them in as restraints, but we need only think of medieval attitudes toward lust and sin to know that our culturally favored version is not universal. In *Guide,* characters struggle with a very immediate manifestation of the individual-versus-community clash of values: AIDS. We see some characters who resist limiting their sexual activities, even though they know that such activities may cause them to contract the disease or to pass the disease on to others. Again, we are challenged to consider what individual freedoms should be sacrificed for a greater good. Cooper offers no answers, but we are put in a position of having to think about our own stand on such issues.

Eat or Be Eaten and the Nature of the Law

Before trying to decide what we can gain from reading horrifying fiction, we need to recognize something troubling. Fiction meant to shock rarely retains its full effect on second reading. Even as *Hogg* was leached of half its impact on me by my having read *The Mad Man,* so the effect of reading *American Psycho* the second or third time around is very different from first exposure. What can we make of this loss of impact? In theory, one characteristic that makes works of art classics is their ability to reward multiple rereadings and re-viewings. I might reread *Hogg* for its eleven-year-old demotic voice, but not for other content the second time around. I might read new works by Dennis Cooper, but would probably not turn again to those already read. Insofar as we internalize these books on first reading, we gain the maximum release from our inwardly assimilated laws and are unable to gain further freedoms the second time we read through. Aesthetic pleasures may remain, but far less relief from the pressures of the law.

In addition to their putting us outside the law, I note something else common to most of these novels: consuming (in various senses) and being consumed. While consumption to most critics automatically signals a critique of capitalism, capitalism seems more relevant to *American Psycho* than to the other books.[37] Were the works discussed supporting the status quo, as do popular-culture horror films involving zombies or malevolent aliens, then capitalism might be subtextually relevant. It would be presenting itself as the desirable, safe world; early horror films are now interpreted as reflecting cold war fears, wherein the aliens represent communism. For these repellent fictions, however, extreme forms of consumption and even cannibalism might also be interpreted as relating to our gut sense of what it means to be without law. Cannibalism literalizes "eat or be eaten." Those who achieve comfort in their outlaw status do the eating. The boy in *Hogg* survives because of his willingness to consume bodily substances. The scariest portion of *Dark Property* concerns the cannibalism, carried out on the slaughtered boy and as a threat to the woman. Some of Cooper's more violent fantasies involve consuming "blood, piss, vomit" in the course of killing someone (*Frisk* 38). Patrick Bateman literalizes his embodiment of the ultimate consumer by eating parts of his victims. The most impressive form of consumption in any of these books is the teenage Dennis's viewing a porn sequence and having it take up residence in his mind, changing everything. That consumption goes both ways. He consumes the pictures and they consume him, his life, and his imagination. No mind-eating alien could have bonded more intimately with him. Most horror texts try to consume and possess us, and our awareness of their power reminds us that we might well not survive outside the laws.

"Eat or be eaten" is what we would expect to find in a life without law. Laws are what make community possible, but their demands on and damage to individuals are great—unacceptably so for those who do not match the norm. Unlike most creators of genre horror, these authors all seem to consider that cost too high. They deny us the relief that comes with reinstating the status quo. Instead, they push us to reevaluate the laws or cultural patterns, asking that we question which laws may be necessary for what benefit, and that we consider ditching some in the name of individual liberties. Only Acker does little with outré images of eating. I think perhaps that her mind does not reduce life at its most basic to "eat or be eaten" because for many women, the third possibility is be fucked and buy your way with sex, or be victimized through sex rather than by being eaten. The eating imagery seems more a male than a female image for life.

All law presupposes violence. One cannot uphold a rule without being prepared to use force against those who disagree, yet what many laws try to restrict is violence. Violence is everywhere, in the laws as well as outside them. What do we gain by reading ourselves outside the laws? Why should we persist in reading a book or watching a film if we find the material repellent?

One thing we gain is a new perspective on the individual's relationship to community and its laws. We are forced to consider whether certain of these laws are justified or desirable. If so, which ones? Very few readers are likely to want the total breakdown of all social order that would make power the only motive or justification for any action. Evenson's vision of such a world does not offer joy to anyone. Perfect freedom leads to a far from perfect life by most standards. How much, though, do we give up to make ourselves conform and belong? Is the resulting society worth the cost? What is individual difference worth? After all, as Burroughs made clear in *Cities of the Red Night,* the world population is far too large to permit the kind of communes or small anarchist enclaves that would give the inhabitants genuine liberty. How, then, can we adapt what we have?

Cooper too longs for anarchism: "All structures created to impose order of any kind are inherently corrupt and ... the quest for personal power within the context of America's notion of democracy is at the root of every extant problem here." His advice: "As soon as you get power, disperse it."[38] Anarchism may be an ideal, but what is real and practical?

Mind-cleansing can be another result of reading such material. Popular culture and political ideology have long upheld the sacred and community-protecting qualities of violence. Richard Slotkin's extensive research shows just how embedded that myth is in the American psyche. By refusing us a return to normality rendered attractive by contrast to the horrors, these books challenge the desirability of the status quo. Instead of hiding from the implications of violence, we have to face them.

The fact that most of these texts refuse to guide us can encourage us to consider our own answers to the problems they pose. Their emotionless descriptions and affectless narrators leave us no choice but to think if we are to derive any sense of meaning from the texts. We cannot win the sense of achievement that comes from a satisfying interpretation or even just appreciation unless we make our own choices and assessments. The longer we hold back that judgment, the richer the array of possible answers we may come upon. Delaying judgment and distinguishing between fictive and real-world violence seem to be the important issues in current discussions of violence.[39] Condemning too quickly is just a version of imposing a law by force, and that is what we are being challenged to avoid doing. This delay, though, does not guarantee us satisfactory answers. As we saw in the possible lessons one could derive from *Hogg*, people will get hurt no matter what you decide to do to prevent a child from being sexually abused. The quick critical judgment against Patrick Bateman's deeds caused numerous critics to overlook Ellis's political argument, and also caused them to overlook the tyrannical power that social values have within the confines of our own imaginations, forbidding us to look at the obscene. Indeed, the violence of critical responses should remind us that we may be posthuman according to some theorists, but many people's responses to fictional violence are strong enough that they do not treat even cardboard characters as mere constructs. Many readers, including, in the case of Ellis, sophisticated critics, insist on a human-centered, humanist reading, if only because they can imagine the violence happening to themselves.

5

ATTACKING THE READER'S ONTOLOGICAL ASSUMPTIONS

Having seen in the last three chapters tactics designed to arouse unpleasant emotions, we turn now to attacks aimed at our intellect, our sense of what is real. To function efficiently, we rely on a set of beliefs about the nature of reality. These ontological assumptions provide stability as we deal with day-to-day living. They govern our responses to sights, sounds, and events; they keep us from expending all of our energy on permanent fight-or-flight readiness. Authors who challenge our ontological assumptions with the aim of destroying our faith in them are trying to undermine the foundations of daily comfort and confidence. Many aims may produce this impulse, from political wakeup call to contempt for readers' naïveté to sheer mischief or playfulness. The more a book succeeds in provoking discomfort, the more it qualifies as a kind of attack on the reader. Identifying ontological destabilization as aggression, however, raises practical problems. In *Postmodernist Fiction* (1987), Brian McHale proposed such ontological destabilization as the goal and defining feature of postmodernism, so by that definition, all postmodern novels qualify as aggressive.

McHale made us aware of the extent to which contemporary fiction constructed worlds and used them to undermine or contradict consensus reality. He articulates the methods of creating a zone of conflict between what we consider our world and another: *juxtaposition, interpolation, superimposition,* and *misattribution.*[1] His example of *juxtaposition* is Guy Davenport's "Haile Selassie Funeral Train," which train passes stations in Europe, Asia, and America. This postmodern way of destabilizing ontology puts the two worlds on the same plane and treats them as unbrokenly contiguous; a train can go from Russia to the United States. *Interpolation,* McHale's second technique, gives us Mark Z. Danielewski's *House of Leaves.* An alien world opens up within a bounded space, a house, making Danielewski's tour de force (in part) a variant on the haunted house topos. In *The Universal Baseball Association,* Robert Coover's living baseball world emerges (to the reader's surprise) from within the paper world of the baseball game being played by an unemployed accountant.

Superimposition, McHale's third technique, works geographically. Juan Goytisolo's *Landscapes after the Battle* superimposes Alexandria upon Paris, and their landmarks intermingle. In the film *Donnie Darko,* the two alternative versions of the universe intersect and come together at key points. In Coover's *Public Burning,* the prison yard at Sing Sing is superimposed upon Times Square; Nixon has a private interview in the prison and backs out of the room, only to find himself on the scaffold in Times Square. *Misattribution,* the fourth technique, builds strange worlds by going against stereotypes and attributing, say, tropical jungle or Venetian canals to Boston rather than showing us the terrible traffic or the John Hancock building. Among the authors McHale mentions for this technique are Donald Barthelme, Walter Abish, and Ronald Sukenick.

Granting that ontological instability has been the cultural dominant for some time, what do authors get out of disturbing readers in this fashion, and why should readers put up with this treatment? In order to answer these questions, I shall leave the question of how destabilization is executed literarily to McHale and look instead at the various ways destabilization can be used to render readers uneasy. The places from which the assaults are launched seem to me threefold.

The mind of a character offers one method for undermining reader comfort. We assume that a character's mind works the way our own does if the character is even remotely person-like, so if that character's relationship to reality proves false, then possibly our perceptions may be flawed too. We know that our ability to perceive depends on our brain and senses, but what if they are not reliable? Authors who pose this problem in very different ways include Mark Salzman, Chuck Palahniuk, and Philip K. Dick.

The second textual location for damaging reader confidence lies in the text as something traditionally meant to represent reality. Postmodernist texts mostly invoke reality only to deny that they imitate it at all. "Ceci n'est pas une pipe," as René Magritte wrote along the bottom of his painting of a pipe. Whether literature, painting, or film, such postmodern texts emphasize their constructed, arbitrary, and conventional nature. In a sense, they scold and hector us for willingly suspending our self-consciousness, if not actual disbelief, for pretending that a story (a bunch of words on a page) can have any relation or application to our lives. Danielewski's *House of Leaves* will serve as my example here. Its challenging textual and typographic games made it a cult classic almost immediately, and how Danielewski gained this popularity is of some interest as we try to understand why such literary provocation can be pleasurable as well as distressing, or at least frustrating.

The third basis for upsetting the reader lies within the storyline; a novel may appear to represent the world, but then it departs from consensus reality with additions that are impossible by ordinary logic. Thomas Pynchon's *Against the Day* portrays much that is technically possible (if improbable), but throughout, Pynchon hammers on the existence of another reality or multiple set of realities, and calls in question our culture's materialist minimalism. Some of his alternative visions of reality are fugitive, more or less forgotten quickly, but at times he departs entirely from reality as we know it, as when the airship travels through the hollow earth. Given the bulk and complexity of both *House of Leaves* and *Against the Day,* the books put extraordinary pressures on readers. The authors must have great confidence in their writing or feel great urgency in what they wish to achieve that they should risk turning readers off with such demands for time, attention, memory, and thought. My overall questions in this chapter are simple. How do ontologically aggressive books challenge readers? What do the authors gain from that sustained assault? What do the readers gain that keeps them reading?

Reality Lives and Dies in the Mind: *Lying Awake,*
Fight Club, Ubik

Ontology destabilized through a character can be our old friend the unreliable narrator. That destabilization can, however, encompass many kinds of experience, and these need not strike the reader as overtly hostile. The damage to reader comfort may just take effect if we accept that the story can apply to our own lives, an assumption that is not encouraged by the postmodern ideology that ignores any such connection to "real" life. Usually when the attack takes place through a character, we expend a certain amount of pleasurable thought trying to figure out what explains the lack of connection between the focal character and reality. In Lisa Zunshine's terms, we keep trying to apply our theory of mind to the character. We can enjoy being detectives, and can also enjoy the problem of a strange reality because it afflicts someone else. When the problem proves insoluble and reality cannot be pinned down, though, we have to wonder about wider applications to us in our own world.

My inclusion of Mark Salzman's *Lying Awake* (2000) may seem inappropriate, because aggressiveness is not what strikes the reader. Indeed, I would call its atmosphere benign and sensitive, and we are invited to sympathize with the protagonist. Far from being repulsed by what it offered, I was intrigued and happily entertained. The novel does, though, raise a terrifically large question, and it undermines the assumptions of many religious readers with upsetting force, despite the gentle presentation. Salzman respectfully portrays a nun who discovers that her vivid mystic experiences and her overwhelming sense of God's love are the by-products of a minor brain tumor. She reluctantly consents to have the tumor removed, and with it goes the ecstasy of God's precious presence. She copes through faith and community as best she can, and in that sense, the book has a happy ending. Her response and that of her fellow nuns is sensible; if she has written so lyrically about experiencing God's love, now she may do yet more for souls by showing them how to live when that assurance is taken from them.

Part of the attraction of this novel is the meaningfulness of everything in Sister John's life before the operation. When she hears biblical phrases during the service or edifying texts read aloud during meals, she sees how they apply to her life and to God's love. They vibrate with meaning.

Almost everything in her day is luminously intense. Sister John's actions make even the nonreligious reader sense what strong faith and a seriously contemplative life might be like at their best. When she reviews her day, she asks: "Have I acted and spoken with God's presence in mind? Have I been grateful for my trials as well as my consolations? Have I lived up to my commitment to trust in God's love completely?"[2] During one of her headaches, "adoration welled up through the pain.... She fell upward into brilliance, where all suffering was released.... The cloister bell, the voice of Christ. He spoke again: *I am.* She tried to obey but was frozen in beauty.... *Nothing exists apart from me.* Self had been an illusion, a dream. God dreaming" (17–18). We have indeed seen her welcoming her severe headaches as trials, and her troubled decision to go ahead with the operation is an act of supreme trust and faith, for she knows what she will lose: everything that has made life feel worthwhile. She may continue to express faith, but the mystic experiences made her *feel* a reality behind the faith, and *know* it in a fashion that faith alone had not supplied. Life after the operation is hollow: "The psalms read like the libretto of an opera delivered as a speech" (169).

The assault on readers' beliefs lies in the implications. Salzman raises the possibility that all mystic experiences derive from physiochemical events in the brain. Indeed, nonreligious and scientific seekers like Aldous Huxley have argued that such experience may result from tumors and seizures, trauma, the alteration of blood chemistry by special breathing practices, dervish whirling, or drugs such as peyote and LSD. Freud associated the mystic experience with the oceanic sensation of oneness that he attributed to early infancy. The wondrous and even life-changing nature of the experience is not denigrated by Huxley and others, but their interpretations challenge religious assumptions. Merely by mentioning, as Salzman delicately does, that Saint Teresa of Avila suffered epileptic brain malfunctions wipes out the long-standing mystic alternative to Scripture as guarantor of God and His love. As a matter of practical politics, the church has not denied Saint Teresa her place in a mystic tradition, but it does not welcome present-day sufferers of those same seizures as mystics.

The experience of the focal figure permits Salzman to upset religious readers with the notion that personal experience of God's love is just a matter of brain chemistry and offers no evidence for the existence of God. This attack is all the more effective for not seeming to come from hostility to religion; Salzman just appears to be ruefully curious. He mentions artists as well as religious figures who apparently underwent these physical symptoms and experienced ecstasy: Dostoevsky, van Gogh, possibly Tennyson and Proust, perhaps Socrates, and almost certainly Saint Paul and Saint Teresa of Avila (121). Mystic experience has given us great art, theology, philosophy, and fiction. The phenomenon is known in other religions, and similarly confirms their believers' sense of the divine. Salzman leaves wide open the question of what such experience means for readers, even if his nuns seem unshaken in their basic faith. They are prepared to live with hope and belief rather than vivid experiential certainty. For such a tonally mild book, the implications of the argument are very wide-reaching. If communion with God, Nirvana, ecstatic oneness with the universe, experience of The Light, or The Light seen in ordinary objects are all physiochemical accidents, then what other aspects of religious belief may be delusional?

Salzman's treatment of mystic experience as an epileptic phenomenon encourages readers to consider several options. Convinced believers may decide that God chooses to communicate through physiochemically abnormal conditions, and that the love is real. Alternatively, readers may decide that mysticism is worthless as confirmation of any religious reality, and that personal experience of divinity is insanity or at any rate just a chemical reaction. Or we might feel that everyone should take LSD or peyote in order to experience this ecstasy, as Aldous Huxley argues in his utopian novel *Island*. Salzman gives us the opportunity to mull over the nature of the most intense relationship to reality that is available to humans, but he does not tell us what to think. The nun's losing her ability to feel God's love makes the book disturbing to anyone prepared to take religion seriously. Those who have had mystic experience attest that it reveals the truest, most fundamental nature of reality, something that far transcends the dead material husks that are all that most of us can see.

We find a very different sort of assault on our readerly comfort in Chuck Palahniuk's *Fight Club*.[3] His unreliable narrator baffles us for more than half the book. The central character himself is surprised when he discovers that someone he considered a friend is actually a part of his own personality. This friend, Tyler Durden, spreads mayhem by blowing up offices and flats and killing the protagonist's boss. They inhabit the body alternately, as Tyler puts it, and that body is living two separate, active lives. The book

opens with Tyler apparently sticking a gun into the mouth of the protagonist, about to kill him, and only at the end do we learn that the protagonist
is doing this to himself, trying in this way to kill Tyler off.

The narrator will tend to upset middle-class readers. As a waiter, he
pees in soup being brought up in the elevator to an expensive restaurant,
and he and fellow waiters tell stories of desecrating food on its way to the
table. In the afterword, the authorial persona recounts how a London
waiter told him "Margaret Thatcher has eaten my cum" because the waiters enjoy polluting the food on its way to the table (215). Anyone who has
paid for an expensive meal starts to wonder whether he or she has been
thus victimized. That kind of upset to reader comfort is easy to deliver, and
it does disturb and anger any readers who have dined expensively.

Tyler Durden, the alter ego, is definitely a threat to readerly comfort.
He evidently comes close to blowing up the tallest building in the world
(only his use of an unreliable chemical in his explosive mix prevents success); he castrates men, and we watch such a scene; he apparently kills
some people. He founds fight clubs where men can prove their manhood
through physical violence and where they can take out their frustrations
at fathers, at blue-collar jobs, at the unrealizable dream of becoming
rich. Tyler's attitude toward culture is "wipe your ass with the *Mona
Lisa*" (141). He wants to "blast the world free of history" (124). The protagonist summarizes their joint attitude: "I wanted to destroy everything
beautiful I'd never have. Burn the Amazon rain forests. Pump chloro-
fluorocarbons straight up to gobble the ozone. Open the dump valves
on supertankers and uncap offshore oil wells. I wanted to kill all the
fish I couldn't afford to eat, and smother the French beaches I'd never
see" (123).

Because the narrator is unreliable, this revolutionary-terrorist aesthetic
may just be one manifestation of the protagonist's insanity, or the philosophy may motivate Tyler's followers. Because of his mental problems, we
cannot be sure about anything he says. Tyler's many monk-like acolytes,
for instance, may just be his hallucinations. Or they may be real, in which
case the fictional world is in trouble, because those followers happily throw
off previous obligations and rules and luxuriate in physically assaulting
others who still live by those rules.

Palahniuk renders law-abiding readers uneasy with his philosophy of
fighting. By offering spaces in which men can fight, he frees those men of

their fear. They learn they can lose a fistfight yet feel better about themselves by bearing the pain. Moreover, they find amusement in the way their
co-workers carefully avoid asking about black eyes, broken noses, stitches,
and other souvenirs of the fight. Even if they lost that particular fight,
they look dangerous to their fellow workers, and therefore gain respect
in their everyday lives. The protagonist speaks lyrically about bottoming
out, about having everything go wrong and learning to let go, about not
fighting back but ignoring the blows that fall. Such men learn to focus on
pain and give in to it when Tyler wetly kisses the backs of their hands and
pours on lye flakes, burning a kiss-shaped scar; the pain pushes them much
further into themselves than they have ever gone before. In a weird way,
this surrender echoes the surrender demanded of Salzman's nuns as they
strive to shed their individuality and submit to a greater power. The narrator uses mystic vocabulary to attract readers who would otherwise not be
drawn to the violence in his world. He tells of bottoming out through pain
and surrender, and finding thereafter total freedom from all the petty rules
and social constraints of which one may not even be aware. He lyrically
offers the sense of freedom from laws that is desired but also questioned in
texts that rely on horror. Readers who abide by the laws more or less willingly can feel threatened by characters who choose not to. Readers who
would like to break the rules may enjoy vicarious indulgence in Tyler's
trying to damage the world, which includes blowing up buildings and killing those inside.

One way of viewing the temptation is to see it as an invitation to go insane, as the narrator appears to be by conventional standards. Palahniuk's
may be a romanticized view of insanity (and of fighting and of social mayhem), but the very attractiveness testifies that something is lacking in our
society. A warrior experiences fear, challenge, practice in enduring pain,
and the adrenaline surge of a fight. These are now missing in most people's
lives, yet are something that myths, legends, and initiation rites suggest are
desirable and enabling. Palahniuk makes us rethink assumptions about
insanity and society, and if those are in need of redefinition, then so too
may be our sense of reality.

As the afterword makes plain, part of Palahniuk's impetus is blue-collar
anger at white-collar life. In the narrator's first exchange of blows with
Tyler, they both realize, "We'd gotten somewhere we'd never been and
like the cat and mouse in cartoons, we were still alive and wanted to see

how far we could take this thing and still be alive" (53). They exchange
more blows:

> Instead of Tyler, I felt finally I could get my hands on everything in the
> world that didn't work, my cleaning that came back with the collar but-
> tons broken, the bank that says I'm hundreds of dollars overdrawn. My job
> where my boss got on my computer and fiddled with my DOS execute com-
> mands. And Marla Singer, who stole the support groups from me. Nothing
> was solved when the fight was over, but nothing mattered. (53)

They don't fight to win; they fight to become different people, people who
cannot be upset by the problems in their lives.

The appeal of this experience reaches beyond a blue-collar audience.
Most Americans are dissatisfied and often bored with their lives. They feel
that something more ought to be possible, something better and more ful-
filling. Donald Barthelme muses on this concept in his *Snow White:* "What
does it look like, this *something better?* Don't tell me that it is an infant's
idea because I refuse to believe that. I know some sentient infants but they
are not that sentient. And then the great horde of persons sub-sentient who
nevertheless can conceive of *something better.*"[4] William S. Burroughs tried
to imagine a society that would minimize the repressions demanded by
living in groups, but his pirate communes in *Cities of the Red Night* were
rendered impossible once the industrial revolution enabled large city populations. Cities need highly controlled systems of supply to meet basic needs.
Control means regimentation and little flexibility for the individual. Palahniuk touches on dissatisfactions, but his solution of introducing mayhem in
hopes of a revolution would not improve matters for most of his readers.
For that reason, some readers will resist the argument, even if they see
the romantic attractions of his broader program. Admittedly, his limited
agenda in the fight club probably would supply satisfactions for some members of society. Palahniuk wants to change society radically, but his image
of what that change would be and how a better society might be achieved is
obscure. Nevertheless, by destabilizing our sense of what is real, he makes
us more open to his argument that we need drastic social change.

What do we gain from his undermining our proprieties? Those readers who get their physical challenge from gyms are reminded of people
who would prefer a less artificial (and pricey) source of physical challenge.

Carolyn Chute explores a related problem in her fiction set in rural Maine; men who can hunt, fish, and repair anything are rendered useless in the world of mega-conglomerates. These men have led the life of hunter-gatherer-frontiersmen and are used to fighting when the need arises. Their living pattern has defined human existence for much longer than urban life has done, and they were very good at it. Humanity owes its survival to men who could face such challenges; now we just toss them onto the trash heap.[5] Palahniuk's fight club aficionados are similarly men who need a physical immediacy that is discouraged in the world of office routines. One reason to tolerate Palahniuk's making us uneasy is to be reminded of a different kind of life and its satisfactions.

What do we gain from facing the fact that our personality can split and we may be doing complex things with no waking awareness of those actions? The novel, as one dust jacket blurb puts it, is "wonderfully unpleasant." The map of reality that we depend on may be inaccurate. By implication, we may be more responsible for some deplorable actions than we realize. We may think ourselves law-abiding, but some dark force within us is not. And yet... we also enjoy the thought of loosing mayhem on the world—and escaping. We can enjoy the humor of using human fat removed through liposuction to make expensive soap that will be sold back to those same humans who paid to get rid of their fat. We may feel drawn by the mystic promises of pain leading to revelation. Many contemporary readers lack intensity, let alone mystical intensity, in their lives, so are drawn by Palahniuk's messianic promise that we will feel meaning if we yield—to pain, to fighting, to Tyler Durden.

Use of the focal character to disturb and upset readers can be found in many Philip K. Dick novels. His hallmark procedure is to peel off putative layers of reality as though the world were an onion, and what we end up with is likely to be ambiguous at best, or yet more mystery.[6] *Ubik* famously destabilizes our sense of the fictional world through the confusing experiences of Joe Chip, a tester of psi powers for a firm that employs various kinds of psychics to ward off hostile telepathic invasions of industrial privacy.[7] Also present in this world of the 1990s (mildly futuristic, given its publication in 1969) is a way of preserving the dead and communicating with them, though each communication reduces their half-life until they really will be psionically dead. When a band of psychics from Joe's firm are attacked by a rival firm, the only victim seems to be Mr. Runciter, their boss. The realities start falling away, however. Joe and his friends think themselves to be alive, but their world mysteriously keeps regressing toward 1939, and they find themselves, for instance, with money from their own time that is not acceptable currency in the 1940s. Cigarettes bought fresh turn to dessicated flakes; ads in newspapers and drugstore medicines regress to nostrums of an earlier era. A swank car Joe drives regresses to a rattletrap before he can sell it (141). Is Runciter dead or on half-life? He keeps making his presence felt in Joe's world with messages—graffiti on walls, words on a slip of paper in a purchase. Alternatively, are Joe and his fellows dead, and is Runciter alive and trying to establish communication with them through these indirect means because of some glitch in the usual psionic means of contact? We follow Joe each reluctant step of the way until he comes to accept that Runciter is alive, and his head appearing on coins in Joe's world is something that Runciter is projecting into the half-life world from outside. Joe and his friends, therefore, are dead. Then we see Runciter draw out of his pocket some coins with Joe Chip's head on them (216). The book ends with our realization that the careful explanation Joe has reached, which does cover the facts as he has seen them, is probably not the correct one.

How much of an assault on reader comfort can be launched by anything that is read for fun? Speculative fiction, perhaps because it always offers an alternative to our normal reality, may not seem much of a real threat; we are inured to that destabilization, and indeed read to be taken away from our ordinary assumptions. Dick, however, is not offering us a comfortably attractive future world. If a speculative future is attractive in technological achievements (never mind for the moment that the characters we like are threatened by evils), we will cheerfully read on and not feel especially threatened. Dick's future is deliberately boring in many ways. His focal figure is a schlemiel so totally inept in personal and money matters that we only decide well into the book that he is smart as we watch him trying to piece together the chronologically regressing world. The more we believe in his insights and the more we come to trust his brains, the more destabilizing the dissolution of his reality. His ineptitudes eventually make us feel more helpless and more undermined. *Ubik* ends in an ontological abyss: no evidence decisively declares one or the other party dead or alive, and we lack information to put forward alternative explanations. Possibly both are dead, but in separate half-life worlds that cannot be fully interpenetrated.

What happens to the half-lifers "eaten" by the malignant Jory? Do the souls, or some of them, go on to rebirth, as one half-lifer believes is happening to her? We have been led a long way into the world of the dead, and Dick maliciously maroons us there.

These three novels illustrate different ways of making us uneasy through the focal character. Brain tumor, split personality, and a partial remission from death's finality all remind us of how unsupported some of our certainties may be, and how unreliable our mental processes are for figuring out what is happening. All three books, in very different ways, exhibit nightmarish qualities. That personal experience of God's love might be a delusion, or that someone might have a doppelganger self of whom that person is unaware, or that one may be dead and the victim of a defective communicating link to the living are all unsettling premises. Do these books teach us something, something that counterbalances their unpleasantness? Perhaps *Lying Awake,* if we accept the message of faith and trust, but otherwise not. Any assurance has to come from our own world, our own decisions about what to believe or do to make our lives more meaningful. A major attraction may be that if we engage fully with the fictional assault and defeat it in our own mind, we emerge feeling stronger than we were before reading. Perhaps on analogy with Palahniuk's fight club, we do not even have to defeat the attack on our comfort but just engage it actively, and in doing so we feel better about ourselves.

Textualizing Reality: *House of Leaves*

Using the focal character to upset us is not the only way of destabilizing our sense of reality. Textuality offers other tools for rendering the reader unsure, many of them employed by Mark Z. Danielewski in *House of Leaves.* By introducing different typefaces, columns, insets, colored lettering, and footnotes, Danielewski lays out three or more threads of narrative at a time. Some of the insets may be in mirror-image type. Sometimes the print runs diagonally on the page; sometimes it squeezes into a very small window, the rest of the page being blank. Many pages contain only a sentence or two surrounded by glaring white space. Quotations occur in a dozen languages. Within the world of the fiction, the reality of various authors or editors of the text is rendered problematic in the extreme. The central given is a house that is fractionally larger inside than out but leads to a vast inner world. That fraction-of-an-inch excess measurement is scarier in some fashion than the miles found once in the impossible space, but we engage with both at the textual level.

In a sense, one of the book's subjects is exactly the kind of attack on the reader being considered in this chapter. The Johnny Truant footnotes (which constitute half the text) document Johnny's becoming hooked by the spooky papers he decides to edit, his suffering on account of his obsession, and his insomnia—all because the papers drove him to doubt the consensus reality he has lived with. He warns us in his introduction that this book will someday do to us what it has done to him: "Out of the blue, beyond any cause you can trace, you'll suddenly realize things are not how you perceived them to be at all."[8] He goes on, "Then no matter where you are, in a crowded restaurant or on some desolate street or even in the comforts of your own home, you'll watch yourself dismantle every assurance you ever lived by" (xxiii). You will fight to avoid facing what you "truly are, the creature we all are, buried in the nameless black of a name. And then the nightmares will begin" (xxiii). Johnny's warnings to us not to proceed with our reading, of course, make us all the more eager to do so. We think ourselves safe from his obsessions. To judge from the fan discussion spools on the Internet, more than a few readers were seriously entranced, if not necessarily obsessed, by the book. They do not seem to have felt upset, though; they enjoyed this as a game rather than responding to it as an assault.

Danielewski's approach to reality is layered. At the heart is an account, supposedly filmed, of a house that proves to be larger inside than outside; indeed, the cavernous, labyrinthine interior seems to go on for hundreds of miles, and may be infinite. The spatial characteristics that turn this house into a nightmare become detectable only after it has been purchased by a Pulitzer Prize–winning photographer, Will Navidson. He films various attempts to plumb the depths of this impossible terrain. At one point, for instance, he has been heading downhill for hours, and tries to head back, only to find that whatever direction he goes in takes him downward. Doors appear in walls where none were before, and new kinds of terrain appear without warning. Everything about this space is impossible by the rules of material reality as we know it.

We are not, however, seeing the film made by Will Navidson. We read an account of it that was scribbled on hundreds of sheets of paper, envelopes, scraps of paper of any sort, by Zampanò, a blind man who could not have seen the film that he describes. Is he supposed just to have made it up, and is he therefore a (or the) novelist? Within this fictive world, however, his existence is debatable; he is dead, so we never see him. Johnny Truant has arranged all these papers and provided copious annotation. Johnny, however, deliberately undermines his own reliability as a narrator (16). Our confidence in his reliability is further weakened by the information that his mother, Pelafina, is institutionalized because she has apparently tried to kill her son. That trauma may have left him mind-damaged as well as badly scarred. When we have cleverly reached that explanation, however, Pelafina refers to Zampanò (in code), but by the logic of the plot she cannot know him, unless he is a fiction that she has created, along with all of his supposed writings. If that is the case, all that material has been falsely presented and contextualized by Johnny, consciously or insanely, or possibly even he himself and all the papers are his mother's invention. Other levels are provided by this text, such as invented comments from real critics and celebrities who were supposedly interviewed by Navidson's wife, Karen: Camille Paglia, Anne Rice, Harold Bloom, Douglas Hofstadter, Stephen King, Steve Wozniak, and Jacques Derrida, among others, supply their take on the unrealities of the house. We also get a pastiche account from colonial times of strange stairs appearing in the wilderness in this locale (413–14). This book destabilizes us epistemologically as well as ontologically.

How aggressive, though, is the attempt to undermine our personal sense of reality? Traditional haunted houses fall into the category of pleasantly shivery things to read about, not usually the material of nightmares, no matter how cleverly and originally handled—and this novel is both clever and original. True, a set of ghosts is something we absorb without uneasiness as a rule, in part because they are a literary trope. This "spatial rape" (as Will's brother, Tom, calls it [55]) is very unlike the effect of other haunted houses; we have no preexisting defenses. The endless space, always changing, is impossible by all the rules we know, yet Danielewski describes it so exactly that he gives it substance. Perhaps we are more caught because passages, walls, stairs, and shafts are not in and of themselves impossible, and hence they feel real in a way that C. S. Lewis's Narnia (accessed through a wardrobe) never does. The grubby plausibility of cellar stairs and darkness carries some power to disturb us.

More tactically important to tying us in knots is the complexity of the text. We must struggle to disentangle the confusing strands, struggle to follow up footnotes to footnotes and not lose our place in the text, and struggle to keep narrative possibilities straight. We are certainly drubbed into recognizing that nothing in a written text is "real," that all we have is just words in play, and yet the palpable representational detail of description of corridors and stairs keeps insisting on reality.

So for that matter does the emphasis on Navidson's filming his penetrations into this labyrinth. Without actually being able to see them, we find the descriptions of a film plausible. What can be filmed is something seen, and we tend to trust our sense of sight. Danielewski plays wonderfully with our sense of sight, and then pulls the rug out by reminding us that the person describing all these sights is blind, and makes no claim to have talked with the principals or visited their home. Zampanò's connection to any of this, other than as creative writer, is mysterious, if he exists. Is some connection implied between the huge claw marks grooving the floor by his corpse and the unknown beast heard in the house's interior? If he is not the creator, who is? We are forced to realize that the suspension of disbelief we ordinarily extend toward fiction is an act of our volition, and this text refuses to permit that suspension. Denying the usual comforts does damage to the cozy relationship that we generally enjoy with fiction.

What does Danielewski gain by arguing this? He certainly seems to enjoy making fun of our compulsion to explain the mysterious. In some ways the book undermines literary criticism and the hermeneutic urge. Proving anything about this story is impossible, at least in terms of literary interpretation. In David Lodge's *Changing Places* (1975), Professor Morris Zapp has written a multivolume study of Jane Austen that is supposed to exhaust all possible interpretations of her work. In a sense, Danielewski does the same for the Zampanò papers. Critics offer nothing not already suggested by the internal interpretations. What his initial setup does, though, is ensure that all but the dimmest readers will be dissatisfied with their attempts to explain his complex creation.

Presumably part of the fun for Danielewski is to anticipate as many interpretations as possible, leaving academic critics feeling belated and useless. He may also enjoy readers' attempts to rationalize and tame the text. He creates a text we can never "own" as we tend to feel that we own texts we have explained to our satisfaction. For an author, creating an untamable text that we nonetheless wish to read is presumably a challenge and a pleasure. Since he has done that without losing readers, he clearly found a workable balance between battering audience members and entertaining them. His secret is forcing us to acknowledge the textuality of the experience, but he avoids the extreme textual fragmentation that would leave us wandering, lost, among the words, and untethered to anything of substance. That gritty materiality of stairs and walls balances the textual games and keeps us assured by the elements that seem "real."

What do readers get from this intensified textuality? They get the entertainment of an intellectual game, of detective investigation, and each time they think they have solved a conundrum, they get intellectual satisfaction, a satisfaction that is probably only minimally reduced by the solution later proving incorrect. If we throw up our hands at the end, at least we have had a good run for our money. We may stand back and marvel at how easily we believe, in fictional terms, in an impossible world, but we are probably not driven to the nightmares of Johnny Truant as his reality crumbles about him. The assault does not penetrate deeply enough into our sense of personal reality to achieve that. We play, though, with that possibility, and will carry with us the traces of experiencing an impossible world.

Locating Reality within a Thousand-Page Novel: *Against the Day*

In *Against the Day,* Pynchon overtly proclaims Luddite and anarchist-labor politics. Far more explicitly than in any of his earlier novels except *Vineland,* Pynchon's characters rail openly and forcefully against capitalism, its effect on the country and on the people whose lives it consumes and destroys. His other main theme is religious; more than any of his other works, this novel has a Christian and even Catholic subtext of penance and life as pilgrimage. To make such arguments, why does he spend so many pages undercutting our sense of reality? How do those apparent goals square with what might be dismissed as obsessive ontological games-playing?

Trying to transcend everyday reality occurs frequently in *Against the Day,* a surprising gambit given that in *Gravity's Rainbow,* Pynchon links Rilke's romantic longing for transcendence with V-2 rockets and death. While Pynchon does not seem to think in *Against the Day* that one can escape our world through transcendence, he certainly encourages us to explore the multiple planes of existence that he insists lie beyond or above or below our normal level of operations. The many alternative realities go by the collective name of The Other Side in *Gravity's Rainbow,* and Pynchon exposes us to yet more such realities in *Vineland* and *Mason & Dixon.* Indeed, *Mason & Dixon* identifies the Enlightenment scientific project as the reason why we have closed out belief in other realities, so that novel frequently obtrudes other worlds on our awareness.

Against the Day produces so many kinds of alternative reality that I cannot possibly discuss them all, but will sketch the range of Pynchon's departures from consensus reality and analyze a few in more detail. One large group of departures stresses duality, and this group includes references to transcendence; lateral, counterfactual, and anti-worlds; bilocation; doubling, especially in connection with the visual doubling produced by Iceland spar (calcite); and, finally, instantaneous transits from one world to another. A second group suggests a sensory extension of reality through visions and voices. The other groups refer to fewer episodes but include impossible actions such as flying through the sand of the desert floor; experiences of light, mostly with mystic overtones; the ability of nonhuman entities to carry out human actions (read, talk); shifts of scale that include tiny humans and giant fleas; and then a variety of miscellaneous departures from normal reality ranging from hotels where your dreams are not your own, to giant angels, to film that can be developed so as to show what happened prior to the exposure of the film, thus making possible the solution of crimes by photographing the corpse. In addition to these, we get explicit references to Christ and penance, but also to rebirth, all of which assume something beyond the strictly material. Again, Pynchon does not seem to be pushing us to *go* to these other levels, but he wishes us to give up a narrow, materialist interpretation of existence. What, then, are the implications for his political and religious agenda? I want to look at these clusters of departures from ordinary reality and try to see what they suggest about Pynchon's ontology and about what he is trying to do to the ontological assumptions of his readers.

An emblematic episode stressing the different levels of reality takes place when the bisexual masochistic linguist-spy Cyprian joins an underground Bogomil convent in the Balkans a few months before the start of World War I.[9] In this sect, "the Manichæan aspect had grown ever stronger—the obligation of those who took refuge here to be haunted by the unyielding doubleness of everything. Part of the discipline for the postulant was to remain acutely conscious, at every moment of the day, of the nearly unbearable conditions of cosmic struggle between darkness and light proceeding, inescapably, behind the presented world" (957). Like Salzman's nuns, Cyprian will find all his actions meaningful if he succeeds in this contemplative discipline. Cyprian also hopes to escape his "tiresome gender questions" (958), and the nuns are evidently willing to take him as he is. His secular companions argue against his decision, partly because this location will obviously be overrun in the coming war. He sees himself as a sacrifice to primal night and refuses to think ahead to war. The members of the community see sleep as a way of returning to "the realms of the not-yet-created" (961). If you strip away the "heretical" nature of the Manichaean beliefs and Cyprian's gender, then this is a fairly conventional religious statement about higher reality. What Cyprian binds himself to do is very much what Pynchon does literarily: he remembers every minute the capitalist evil in the world and its oppressive effect on the poor, and tries to make us aware of this repressed part of our civilization.

Bilocation of various sorts is common in the novel, meaning, for instance, that people can be in two places at once or can transit instantly from one location to another. Pynchon's most elaborate version of this departure from consensus possibility involves an ocean liner, the *Stupendica,* which has another identity as the dreadnought *Emperor Maximilian,* and proves capable of becoming two ships going in different directions when some unknown signal calls the dreadnought forth from under the cruise ship exterior (516–24). The easy interpretation is to see how a luxury/consumerist society has buried mechanisms for war that can emerge and transform it at any time. Pynchon, however, denies such metaphoric readings elsewhere. In New York City, he shows us a "Turkish Corner" where you step through and find yourself "on the Asian desert, on top of a Bactrian camel, searching for a lost subterranean city" (431). An interlocutor derides this possibility: "After a brief visit to Chinatown to inhale some fumes, you mean." The answer: "Not exactly. Not as subjective as that.... Translation of the body, sort of lateral resurrection, if you like" (431). In other words, we are not supposed to write off such bilocations and simultaneous transits as imagination, hallucination, or metaphor, though we tend to, given our cultural inability to take such claims seriously. In that metaphoric vein, we would say that the ship's doubleness suggests that society has a tangible dual nature. The component involved with force, power, and oppression may sometimes be hidden under glossy, superficial enjoyment but is never absent.

Other worlds or layers of reality make themselves felt through the hearing of voices and through visions. One such attempt to link to a different reality is Kit Traverse's trying to produce a "low guttural tone" that would "transport him to 'where he should really be,' though he had no clear picture of where that was" (1080). This echoes both the sort of Star Gate favored in fantasy by Andre Norton (*Witch World*) that takes you to the world where you will feel truly at home, and C. S. Lewis talking about our longing for something beyond what we have, the desire for a "something better" that Lewis links to heaven.[10] Kit then muddles his rational mind by taking transportation in any direction to any stop, changing randomly, apparently not eating, and hallucinating. On the shore of Lake Baikal (or some mystic mirage thereof), he sees "on the far shore a city, crystalline, redemptive" that emits musical tones (1080). He then goes through a transparent doorway and finds himself in Paris and may, perhaps, meet up with his estranged wife (1082). For most of Pynchon's characters, redemption is a confused possibility, not understood except instinctively and indistinctly. Perhaps because Kit did marry legally, his redemption must come through that sacrament and obligation. Where he really should be seems in this instance to be with his wife, aware of the possibilities of redemption but working them out with her through penance in the world available to him.

One of Pynchon's stranger ways of suggesting other realities involves attributing advanced sentience to beings not normally thought to possess it. We have talking dogs who can read (Pugnax, 6 and passim; Ksenija, 1019) and a talking reindeer (785). A strange imputation of sentience includes a ball-lightning entity named Skip, who for some time follows Merle Rideout around and lights his cigars and fires, and provides light from a lantern until a nearby thunderstorm calls him back to his family. "You get sort of gathered back into it all, 's how it works, so it wouldn't be me anymore, really" (74), he says when Merle asks him to come back later.

Yet other techniques for challenging our ontological stability are Pynchon's use of scalar shifts—tiny people or huge fleas—and a variety of miscellaneous impossibilities that fit none of the previous patterns. Pynchon gives us tiny people, or at least humanoids seen moving about in the wallpaper by Lew Basnight (182), and giant talking sand fleas (440–41) capable of negotiating with their victims before biting them; these fleas are protected under law because of their sentience. The sand fleas cannot be dismissed as chemically induced hallucinations as can the small people; furthermore, they are met in a world in which the Chums of Chance must walk through sand in diving suits as if through water, in other words, in something impossible in the normal world. Other impossibilities that Pynchon enjoys are having the Chums of Chance speed through the Hollow Earth between the poles in their airship—admittedly a fringe theory of the time and so historically appropriate; the rise on the updraft to a counterworld; and the machine that makes photographs run back in time to show prior actions, or takes an old photo and extends it into its future to show what the person is doing at present.

How well do these and other assaults on our ontology succeed, or if true success is not Pynchon's aim, what is? Why so many attempts to disillusion us on so many fronts? My best guess is that Pynchon deplores our cultural adherence to the strictly material: if science cannot sense or explain something, then that something does not exist for us, and he wishes to make us consider alternative visions. Some of his alternate realities are historically appropriate; the Hollow Earth theory was entertained through the nineteenth century and even on the lunatic fringe into the twentieth, and it certainly figured in adventure novels, so Pynchon lets that fantasy sequence reflect the tastes of the period he writes about. His characters' walking and even sailing an airship under sand seems merely fantastic, along with the giant sentient sand fleas, and these adventures do not seem like especially motivated fantasy. When one meets fantasy that seems to be not motivated, or weakly so, one looks for metaphoric interpretations. While Pynchon denies metaphoric interpretation of bilocation, I doubt if he cares what we come up with as long as we engage with the fantasy. By doing so, we are giving up our absolute sense of reality and permitting another, at least for the space of time that we read. That goes for essentially all of the fantasy, some of it (the mystic) having pretty obvious religious meanings, but other parts having little—apparently—beyond a zany sense of humor and incongruity. Cumulatively, however, his argument seems to be that holes in our material explanation may exist, and by sheer quantity, he hopes to batter us into a more open frame of mind.

What do we get from reading all 1,085 pages, particularly given that the novel is so complicated that one must read it a minimum of two times? We may not feel that our ontology is truly shaken, but we have considered alternatives. We have pondered orienting toward the here and now rather than investing our lives in trying to control the future. That opens us to his political and religious messages, both of which assume the primacy of the here and now.

The political message is found in many places, but four instantiations stand out for their explicitness. First, Pynchon announces early of various industries—the Chicago Yards, Pullman, McCormick of reaper fame— "You could find this same structure of industrial Hells wrapped in public silence everyplace. There was always some Forty-seventh Street, always some legion of invisible on one side of the account book, set opposite a handful on the other who were getting very, if not incalculably, rich at their expense" (176). Second, in conjunction with a *Heart of Darkness* disquisition on Africa, one character remarks, "On the face of it, all mathematics leads, doesn't it, sooner or later, to some kind of human suffering" (541). Given that math is usually considered the most abstract of the sciences, the one whose theoretical heights seem least obviously applicable to everyday endeavor, this is a provocative statement. If even math is guilty, the other sciences can only be more so. Third, late in the book Pynchon issues a Luddite manifesto, this time against the railroad: "Who at some point hadn't come to hate the railroad? It penetrated, it broke apart cities and wild herds and watersheds, it created economic panics and armies of job-less men and women, and generations of hard, bleak city-dwellers with no principles who ruled with unchecked power, it took away everything indiscriminately, to be sold, to be slaughtered, to be led beyond the reach of love" (930). Finally, Jesse's school essay on "What It Means to Be an American" consists of a single sentence: *"It means do what they tell you and take what they give you and don't go on strike or their soldiers will shoot you down"* (1076). That paper gets an A+ from a teacher who had experience at the Coeur d'Alene mine strike of 1899.

What answers does Pynchon offer to the America he depicts? Yashmeen suggests secession—something also pushed by Native American author Gerald Vizenor, using as his template the sovereign nation status of some tribes. Yashmeen's sister-in-law, Stray, however, points out that "plain old personal meanness gets in the way" (1076) of any potentially utopian commune. Historically, what gets in the way of those who wish to secede from the United States is government guns: MOVE, Ruby Ridge, Waco, not to mention the Civil War. What Pynchon seems to offer on the political level is, fantastically, his agglomerating airship: "The ship by now has grown as large as a small city. There are neighborhoods, there are parks. There are slum conditions. It is so big that when people on the ground see it in the sky, they are struck with selective hysterical blindness and end up not seeing it at all" (1084). Children run the corridors. People not suited to air life go down to earth.

> Never sleeping, clamorous as a nonstop feast day, *Inconvenience,* once a ve-hicle of sky-pilgrimage, has transformed into its own destination, where any wish that can be made is at least addressed, if not always granted. For every wish to come true would mean that in the known Creation, good unsought and uncompensated would have evolved somehow, to become at least more accessible to us. No one aboard *Inconvenience* has yet observed any sign of this. (1085)

Despite the limitations, they are said to be heading for grace.

This amalgamation of various independent airship interests into a float-ing city operates relatively informally, and like the black market in *Gravity's Rainbow,* it seems as much a loose confederation of temporary arrange-ments as anything controlled by hierarchy. Given Pynchon's comments about penance and about pilgrimage, this air city is life as pilgrimage. It may transit or travel, but it is also a state to be in, a being, even if becoming is something on the horizon as a further possibility. Pynchon's handling of cities in this novel points toward the biblical line about our having no continuing city, but seeking one to come (Hebrews 13:14). The cities are on the horizon, across the lake; they are mostly mystic, lost, crystalline. Many of his mystic visions reveal such unreachable cities—unreachable from this plane, but perhaps to come. Whereas the mantra of *V.* was "Keep Cool but Care," Pynchon seems to downplay the cool now.[11] Caring remains cen-tral. The family unit in *Vineland* illustrated how caring can operate. The notions of penance and obligation show the family serving similar roles in *Against the Day.* The Traverse sons loop back to see the people they have begotten, been married to, hurt, loved. Other characters also try to recon-nect to old links. By caring, and by caring in the here and now, fixing what one can, one may "fly toward grace."

Ontological Lessons

Relatively rarely do people throw over their life assumptions about reality, whether physical, metaphysical, or moral, on the basis of reading a book. Augustine's "Tolle lege" experience is one such, and like Augustine, others have taken up and read the Bible for a new vision of their lives. *Uncle Tom's Cabin* is supposed to have changed values and political aims. A few such books do indeed change lives and the reader's sense of reality, but not many. Hence, destabilizing our ontology is a limited authorial exercise; as readers we are unsure how reality is supposed to be determined *within the text,* and must then decide what we make of that claim outside the text. Usually we carry over nothing but a few memories to our own lives, content to let the author have his or her way within the text and dismiss any differences from our own world picture as fantasy. An author has done well to provoke even modest uneasiness, because our assumptions about reality are usually pretty firm.

What ontologically troubling books do is try to stir some uneasiness and, like as not, offer us a challenge to our interpretive skills. The authors may wish us to accept the postmodern world of fragments, but we tend to want coherence, and we must make connections adeptly if we are to pull together a complex book that violates our assumptions, at least in the fashion that several of the texts discussed here do. Salzman's *Lying Awake* does not cause interpretive problems, and Palahniuk's *Fight Club* does so only modestly. Philip K. Dick, Mark Danielewski, and Thomas Pynchon push us to extremes. Danielewski and Pynchon cause problems in particular because their books are so long and so complex. What if, though, disturbing our complacent sense of reality were merely instrumental to shaking our confident assumption that we should be able to interpret what we read? Why do we as readers put up with this assault? Evidently, trying to make sense of the text gives us a sense of accomplishment, maybe even a sense of owning it if we like our interpretation. If we feel we understand, we consume the text. Doubtless part of what motivates such demanding authors is the determination that we shall *not* own and consume the text. Instead of making a novel submit to us, these authors try to make readers submit to the text.

CONCLUSION

Why Read Aggressive Fictions?

This book explores an aspect of recent fiction that criticism has ignored. Many of these novels were not designed to please readers, and the questions raised by that practice have not been recognized, let alone answered. Without claiming a unified field theory to explain fiction that attacks readers, I have sought answers to a number of these questions. How do in-your-face novels relate to pleasure and instruction, the traditional rewards of the reader-author contract? Or if authors abrogate that contract, what is taking its place? What means do some authors employ to compensate for their unpalatable material in the hope of retaining their audience? How can we learn to open ourselves to the experience and overcome our initial resistance? How does one best approach trying to read such fiction? To conclude, I want to consider a few more questions. Are writers of aggressive fiction employing an aesthetic designed to prevent readers from conquering or mastering a text by interpreting it? Are readers simply supposed to surrender to the experience of reading and delay any attempt to extract meaning, or even abandon all attempts to do so? Above all, why should we bother to read material that makes us uncomfortable or actively upsets or revolts us?

Frustrating the Reader Five Ways

Susan Sontag in "Against Interpretation" makes a comment about rapidity that seems relevant to *narrative speed:* "Ideally, it is possible to elude the interpreters in another way, by making works of art whose surface is so unified and clean, whose momentum is so rapid, whose address is so direct that the work can be... just what it is. Is this possible now? It does happen in films, I believe."[1] Mark Leyner may come close to achieving this purity in momentum, but when he raises the issue of people as sentient beings or robots, he implicitly invites us to consider on which side of the divide we fall. Sontag is right to wonder whether complete freedom from interpretation is possible for narrative forms.

Like the other tactics for distancing and alienating readers, speed produces contradictory effects. Insofar as it undermines rational structures for control, it makes us feel inferior yet also offers an exhilarating rush. If we relax and let it flow, then speed encourages passivity; its flashiness makes it a kind of spectator sport at which we watch the bravura performance rather than engage actively with characters. By refusing answers to any problems raised though, speed demands active thought and, ultimately, judgment. Speed challenges us, but what we do with the import of the text remains our own decision.

Complaint reduces our expectations of entertainment even further than speed does. Speed can be exhilarating, but complaint seldom offers pleasure or amusement, unless (as in Ozeki's case) complaint alternates with romance, or unless it introduces satire, as in *Portnoy's Complaint.* Mostly this form of attack makes us writhe or want to turn a cold shoulder to the pesky, repetitive, irritating voice that will not leave us alone. These writers demand that we both change our own lives and try to change the political structure of the country. Heightened emotionalism can alienate us, but vivid feelings can also draw us in. Acker's word-beings—characters who switch gender and name, or who derive from prior texts—are irritating, but their pain is very human, and we can connect, if we are willing, to their anguish, desires, and anger. If we do, we simulate emotionally the function of friend or relative; we listen. We may even feel good about ourselves because we have listened, much as we might for a friend. In reading such a novel, we practice a useful social interaction.

Complaint may also provide us with information. Reading Ozeki on meat or, in her second novel, on vegetable foods definitely supplies us with a great deal of instruction. Like Acker, though, Ozeki wants us to change our lives. Insofar as Ozeki and Acker want us to change society radically, we again can see a contradictory effect at work. Readers are supposed to keep the social fabric from tearing on the micro level of personal interactions, but should destroy the status quo on the macro level of politics. Such contradictory dynamics put pressure on readers to think and make choices.

The grotesque repels readers with elements that depart from safe norms: bodily deformity, sexual strangeness, cruelty, the unclean and taboo, the dissolution of form into rot or goo, and all kinds of the "unnatural." Novels presenting the grotesque drive home the point that our conventional ideas about meaning are inadequate. Meaning, after all, frequently comes from predictable form, both in plots and in physical shape; it relies on firm boundaries. The grotesque exists to break patterns, in particular the pattern of what it is to be human. When that pattern is no longer predictable, we have to make our own meaning, or learn how to live without. As in the case of speed, the grotesque encourages active thinking about our life assumptions. How do we make meaning-giving rules for our lives if God has died, as happens in Morrow's *Towing Jehovah*? What could possibly make life in the world of *Blood Meridian* desirable, and if life in the Southwest is less obviously violent now, is it any more ethical? Whereas in genre horror we join the mob to cast out the mutant, as Stephen King puts it, recent grotesque fiction often shows the norm to be as repellent as the mutant. When neither form nor mutation seems truly desirable, how do we make meaning for ourselves? How do we protect ourselves? What patterns matter?

Violent fiction also pushes us to think for ourselves. These authors deliberately place readers outside the laws, so if we do not welcome lawlessness, we have to decide which laws might be worth preserving. The conservative side of this fiction feeds the alligators in our unconscious so that the norm can continue; the radical side wants to smash that norm because of its excessive control. The characters themselves do not help us think our way through this clash of values; we learn no ethics from the boy in *Hogg* or from Patrick Bateman. Part of the aggressiveness of such fiction is its brutal insistence that we do our own thinking and make up our own minds about law, control, and the desires of the individual versus the comfort of society.

The fifth way of frustrating a reader, *ontological destabilization,* is either the easiest for a reader to shrug off or the most deeply disturbing. Some readers dismiss attempts to undermine "common sense" or religious statements about reality as a literary game or a clumsy challenge by unbelievers. Probably no one's view of reality is transformed by any single fictional narrative. We can, though, be pushed to question our beliefs or accept the possibility that other assumptions may offer a more satisfactory relationship to reality, even in terms, say, of offering a use-value if not a truth-value. Salzman's *Lying Awake,* by reducing mystic communion with God to a brain lesion, undercuts the alternative to Scripture, but he seems sympathetic to the usefulness of having a spiritual framework. Pynchon's *Against the Day* undercuts materialist assumptions about lived reality through his sheer plethora of alternatives. If any one of Pynchon's possibilities strikes us for a moment as desirable, he thus insinuates a "what if?" that can point our thinking in new directions.

All of these modes of aggression carry contradictions at their heart that cannot readily be resolved. They have radical and conservative strains. They all undermine our culture yet seem to uphold cultural values that exist in our theory if not always in our practice: fairness, the desirability of meaningful community, some legal protection, tolerance for difference. All show resistance to oppressive control, whether that control is exercised by the state on people or by readers on texts. Even more oppressive control, however, would be necessary to bring about and maintain the desired fairness and peaceful community. Utopia has never so far caused the powers of enforcement to wither away. Part of what makes these novels seem to attack us is their forcing contradictions on us and refusing to resolve them.

The Challenge of Hermeneutic Frustration

Because Susan Sontag called for an anti-hermeneutic approach to art, I might ask whether what we see in these user-unfriendly fictions makes sense in her terms. Is this art forcing us to suspend our interpretive impulses, and if so, why? She points out that "a great deal of today's art may be understood as motivated by a flight from interpretation. To avoid interpretation, art may become parody. Or it may become abstract. Or it may become ('merely') decorative. Or it may become non-art" (10). She calls transparence "the highest, most liberating value in art.... Transparence means experiencing the luminousness of the thing in itself" (13). Is this what is happening in the fiction discussed?

I would argue no, that what we see in these novels stems from a different impulse to block interpretation. What Sontag calls transparence, a luminousness or mystic intensity, does appear at moments. Evenson achieves it in the first sequence of *Dark Property;* Salzman does for readers attuned to religious life; Leyner comes close at times, as does McCarthy in moments of horror. Such pulsating passages paralyze our impulse to interpret, but only briefly. Avoiding intellectual issues is not easy in an art that describes human actions. Spatters of paint can form colorful and pleasing shapes, and random notes have been considered music. Art made from words chosen just for their sound, however, is usually small scale: a little goes a long way. Moreover, authors who wish to attack and shake the reader usually have an agenda they wish to communicate, and communication cannot divorce itself from interpretability. Acker does not articulate her emotions for their aesthetic beauty; she wants us to recognize iniquities and inequalities in American life. Vizenor shows his shaman laughing on a mesa top; he does this not just because it is an arresting image but because he has been sketching productive and nonproductive spiritual stances for dealing with a collapsing world. Coover constructs an elaborate tapestry of small-town interactions that will endlessly repeat themselves; insofar as we stand apart from his story, we are more inclined ultimately to judge than to appreciate sensually, as Sontag would have us do. Far from barring intellectual engagement, Danielewski invites it, even while going to great lengths to thwart our feeling successful in our endeavors.

I suggest that a different anti-hermeneutic aesthetic is at work here. Consider what happens during an initial reading and what happens during subsequent readings. During the first, the removal of connective tissue may force us to give up trying to interpret or extract meaning. After floundering, we helplessly open ourselves to the gush of disconnected or baffling material. This first reading (but only the first) is the anti-hermeneutic experience, or in Lyotard's terms, the postmodern experience. It ends when we finish reading, since then we have the option of standing back and puzzling out what it all might add up to. Only after trying to digest the whole may we be able to see some pattern. For the most experimental pieces, meaning will perhaps continue to elude us. The work may indeed be truly nonrepresentational, something aesthetic—word and image music rather than story, as in some of Burroughs's riffs. Or it may be a spelling game, as in Walter Abish's *Alphabetical Africa*. Or the author's point might just be that our rational schemata are all irrelevant constructions, and our reliance on them is unjustified.

For those works that fall somewhere in between traditional fiction and the avant-garde, however, we may start to see something at least fragmentarily interpretable. Leyner's *My Cousin, My Gastroenterologist* is about as confusing, nonlinear, and nonrational as any book discussed here, but a character's comments at the very end about people actually being robots does give us an idea to chew on. With Acker, we may never extract much plot, but we can try to figure out why characters change gender or species. Even if we grant that such literature is emotional expression rather than imitation of reality, we puzzle over such discrepancies between our experience of reality and what we find on the page. Only if we surrender to the experience and give up trying to parse it as we go along do we have the best chance of seeing it as a whole. A text's baffling our ordinary strategies for making sense prevents our rushing to judgment, even if it does not prevent eventual judgment. It reduces our assurance of being "right" and makes us reconsider our bases for extracting meaning.

That this kind of fiction can jam the mechanisms by which we process routine fictions is arguably the greatest reward for reading such novels—always supposing that we are willing to keep reading. When we enjoy traditional fiction, we and the author usually share basic cultural values. The fiction reinforces these, and rigs the ticks and tocks so that we find pleasurable release in an ending that basically upholds the cultural status quo. The degree of discomfiture caused by aggressive fiction can free us from our usual mental schemata by making them inoperable. This fiction liberates us from automatic responses. Instead of applying formulas, we must think and test our interpretive templates and try to construct new ones.

From Sontag's viewpoint, such fiction has failed. She wants fiction that "frees us from the itch to interpret" (11); in essence, she wants fiction to take us out of ourselves, reduce our intellectual involvement, and encourage sensuous engagement instead. What seems to happen with these fictions is more a delaying move to keep us from simply consuming the fiction and making it part of our mental library by means of interpretive pigeonholing or by a sense of intellectual conquest. Many of these novels succeed in leaving us unsure and therefore not successful as conquerors or consumers. They position us to rethink the assumptions that dictate our reading strategies.

In addition to short-circuiting our routine interpretive strategies, this fiction stands out for its *refusal to make the instruction easy.* Thus it offers one of the traditional rewards, instruction, but gives us that benefit without tidy verities to latch onto. It makes tough demands, and challenges us to try harder and not just passively accept answers. We are supposed to feel our way to our own conclusions. Instruction of the conventional sort can be simple pieties, mental comfort food that does not challenge us at all. If aggressive books can keep us reading, those that refuse us answers and instead push the questions and problems at us do us the great favor of opening new possibilities. Many of these books are not didactic in the usual sense. They show us plenty that is wrong, but they do little to structure our understanding of what is right. Many of these authors refuse to tell us what to think, and invite us to ponder ways in which we may cope with the horrors, doubts, and perplexities that confront the characters—and us—in a world that does not make much sense.

Traditional didactic fiction depends on solid values shared by author and reader. Many such values were destroyed for Americans by the Vietnam War. Younger citizens developed a highly critical view of their country, and even many of those who were not threatened by the draft lost faith in the government. Doubt, angst, and cynicism all undermine belief that life makes sense. While plenty of American novelists protest what they feel to be wrong, as I showed in *American Dream, American Nightmare,* the novelists being considered here mostly despair because they see no answers. The slow recovery from the financial meltdown that began in 2008 will only contribute to this lack of confidence in the culture. Protest literature grows from anger; many of these works grow more from cynicism, despair, and disgust over the people and cultures destroyed by capitalism and the implications of its global spread. Facile explanations do not appeal to these authors: they give us the problems and let us ponder and squirm. Wrongness is much clearer to them and to us than what might be right or what could be done. They provoke thought by making the reader work. What most of them share is the desire to make us question our interpretive formulas and our cultural values.

Aggressive fictions do not form a tidy subgenre. I could exclude some of the titles considered here in order to define a more unified phenomenon, but that would then leave out interesting and unusual forms of aggression. Given the variation between texts, I can offer no all-encompassing explanation of why we should want to read such works if we find them upsetting and off-putting. Three motives do stand out, though. One, as I have just tried to show, is as an investment in ourselves, in exercising our interpretive abilities after opening ourselves more widely and dangerously than usual. Another might be described as intensity of engagement, since riveting writing heightens our reading experience. The third is liberation from our own preconceptions and prejudices. This liberation can lead to greater ability to interact with what we find different.

Energy coruscates from most of these books. One could even divide them up into those operating on dark energy, those on light energy, and those on mixed energy. *Blood Meridian, Doctor Rat, Hogg, Dark Property, American Psycho,* and *Ubik* are all good examples of dark energy. They radiate various forms of nastiness and ugliness of behavior, or offer a threatening atmosphere that leaches away contentment with our assumptions about reality. A more positive, enlivening energy bombinates in *Towing Jehovah, My Cousin, My Gastroenterologist, Bearheart, Lying Awake,* and *House of Leaves.* The energies in Acker's novels tend to seem mixed: the amount of hurt projected would seem negative, but the main character simply cries it out and does not do damage to others, as we see energy being used in *Blood Meridian.* Palahniuk's energy seems mixed in *Invisible Monsters* because of his farcical element and the small compass in which it operates, a setting involving fewer than a dozen people, so even if the negative energy touches a few lives, the damage is limited. Pynchon's capitalist forces operate out of dark energy, but his own immense creative activity, as well as the actions of some characters, balance that with light energy of their own. Dunn similarly shows dark behavior driven by significant power, but also projects so much intensity of loving family life in her creation that we get mixed signals. These and other books discussed vibrate with this power, and being shocked awake, galvanized even, is not necessarily unpleasant in the long run. That power temporarily intensifies our reactions to everything—life outside and the book we are reading. While such energy, like luminescence, may encourage sensuous response, the energy amplifies our intellectual response as well.

Michael Kowalewski describes the kind of readers these fictions invite us to become: "The best readers of American fiction...are willing to surrender their perceptual equivalents of compass, watch, and gun (and maybe even the idea of a hunt) in entering the pages of a novel or a story. They are willing to be imaginatively lost before deciding it is better to be 'found.'" He goes on to say that such active readers will prefer an author's honest contradictions and confusions to "false clarifications."[2]

Finally, these books offer us temporary freedom from our preconceptions and prejudices. When our values and preconceptions are shaken, we must struggle to construct a mental framework for making sense of experience. Reading such challenging fiction pressures us to reconsider and perhaps radically revamp the values and organizational principles through which we view our world. These novels retain enough character, enough plotline, and just enough traditional kinds of meaning that readers who are motivated to broaden their horizons can benefit from reading them. Their bottom line is, "Are you willing to shed your preconceived values and *think*?"

NOTES

Introduction

1. Horace, *Ars Poetica,* ll. 343–44: "Omne tulit punctum qui miscuit utile dulci, lectorem delectando pariterque monendo." Horace, *Satires, Epistles, and Ars Poetica,* trans. H. Rushton Fairclough, Loeb Classical Library (New York: G. P. Putnam's Sons, 1926), 478.

2. Peter J. Rabinowitz, *Before Reading: Narrative Conventions and the Politics of Interpretation* (Ithaca: Cornell University Press, 1987), 20–36.

3. Susan L. Feagin, *Reading with Feeling: The Aesthetics of Appreciation* (Ithaca: Cornell University Press, 1996), 31–41.

4. Lisa Zunshine, *Why We Read Fiction: Theory of Mind and the Novel* (Columbus: Ohio State University Press, 2006).

5. Norman N. Holland, "Unity Identity Text Self," in *Reader-Response Criticism: From Formalism to Post-Structuralism,* ed. Jane P. Tompkins (Baltimore: Johns Hopkins University Press, 1980), 118–33; originally published in *PMLA* 90 (1975): 813–22.

6. Frank Kermode, *The Sense of an Ending: Studies in the Theory of Fiction* (1967; New York: Oxford University Press, 1970), 45–46.

7. Conclusion and resolution can be resisted by authors for various reasons. For a study of novels on the cold war that resist the satisfaction of closure because of its dangerous triumphalism or because it encourages false forgetting of the traumas, see Samuel Cohen, *After the End of History: American Fiction in the 1990s* (Iowa City: University of Iowa Press, 2009).

8. Leonard Cassuto, *The Inhuman Race: The Racial Grotesque in American Literature and Culture* (New York: Columbia University Press, 1997), 20–27.

9. Raymond Federman, *Critifiction: Postmodern Essays* (Albany: SUNY Press, 1993), 13–14.

10. Brian McHale, *Postmodernist Fiction* (New York: Methuen, 1987), 16.

11. Rabinowitz, *Before Reading*, 23, citing Barbara Foley, *Telling the Truth: The Theory and Practice of Documentary Fiction* (Ithaca: Cornell University Press, 1986), 43.

12. John Hawkes, interview with John J. Enck, *Wisconsin Studies in Contemporary Literature* 6 (1965): 141–55, quotation 149. For a brief analysis of Hawkes's theorizing of what he is doing, see Linda S. Kauffman, *Bad Girls and Sick Boys: Fantasies in Contemporary Art and Culture* (Berkeley: University of California Press, 1998), 193–201.

13. Ronald Sukenick, "The Death of the Novel," in *The Death of the Novel and Other Stories* (1969; Normal, IL: FC2, 2003), 41–102; quotation 41.

14. Federman, *Critifiction*, 26, 45.

15. McHale, *Postmodernist Fiction*, 9–11.

16. Alan Wilde, *Middle Grounds: Studies in Contemporary American Fiction* (Philadelphia: University of Pennsylvania Press, 1987), 49.

17. Gordon E. Slethaug, *Beautiful Chaos: Chaos Theory and Metachaotics in Recent American Fiction* (Albany: SUNY Press, 2000).

18. James Annesley, *Blank Fictions: Consumerism, Culture and the Contemporary American Novel* (New York: St. Martin's Press, 1998); Elizabeth Young and Graham Caveney, *Shopping in Space: Essays on America's Blank Generation Fiction* (1992; New York: Grove Press, 1994); John Johnston, *Information Multiplicity: American Fiction in the Age of Media Saturation* (Baltimore: Johns Hopkins University Press, 1998); and Fredric Jameson, *Postmodernism, or, The Cultural Logic of Late Capitalism* (Durham: Duke University Press, 1991).

19. Marcel Cornis-Pope, *Narrative Innovation and Cultural Rewriting in the Cold War Era and After* (New York: Palgrave, 2001); and Marc Chénetier, *Beyond Suspicion: New American Fiction since 1960*, trans. Elizabeth A. Houlding (Philadelphia: University of Pennsylvania Press, 1996).

20. Federman, *Critifiction*, 70.

21. Robert Alter, *Motives for Fiction* (Cambridge: Harvard University Press, 1984), 21. Bruce Fleming attacks the preciousness fostered by "literary studies," preferring that students learn to derive insights into living their own lives from novels about human interactions. See Bruce Fleming, *What Literary Studies Could Be, and What It Is* (Lanham, MD: University Press of America, 2008).

22. Jean-François Lyotard and Jean-Loup Thébaud, *Just Gaming*, trans. Wlad Godzich, (Minneapolis: University of Minnesota Press, 1985), 10.

1. Narrative Speed in Contemporary Fiction

1. Stephen Kern, *The Culture of Time and Space, 1880–1918* (Cambridge: Harvard University Press, 1983), 115.

2. For more analyses of how speed permeates modernist culture, see Klaus Benesch, "History on Wheels: A Hegelian Reading of 'Speed' in Contemporary American Literature and Culture," in *The Holodeck in the Garden: Science and Technology in Contemporary American Fiction*, ed. Peter Freese and Charles B. Harris (Normal, IL: Dalkey Archive Press, 2004), 212–24. Sara Danius discusses Proust's rhetoric of speed, and various ways he suggests speed, such as writing as if the automobile were stationary while scenery and buildings hurl themselves at it. While this creates narrative excitement, it need not sensibly quicken his narrative pace. See Sara Danius, "The Aesthetics of the Windshield: Proust and the Modernist Rhetoric of Speed," *Modernism/Modernity* 8.1 (2001): 99–126.

3. Shklovsky's translator Benjamin Sher prefers to call it "enstrangement" to make clear the nonstandard nature of the word *ostraniene* in Russian. Viktor Shklovsky, *Theory of Prose*, trans. Benjamin Sher (Elmwood Park, IL: Dalkey Archive Press, 1990), xviii–xix.

4. Gérard Genette, *Narrative Discourse,* trans. Jane E. Lewin (Oxford: Basil Blackwell, 1980), 92.

5. Gérard Genette, *Narrative Discourse Revisited,* trans. Jane E. Lewin (Ithaca: Cornell University Press, 1988), 34.

6. I discuss *John's Wife* instead of *Gerald's Party,* but for an analysis of the latter that recognizes its strange speed, see Jonathan Imber Shaw, "Cocktails with the Reader Victim: Style and Similitude in Robert Coover's *Gerald's Party,*" *Critique* 47.2 (2006): 131–46.

7. In "Speed, Rhythm, Movement: A Dialogue on K. Hume's Article 'Narrative Speed,'" *Narrative* 14.3 (2006): 349–55, Jan Baetens makes the telling point that in the 1950s and 1960s, the experimental writing of Robbe-Grillet stressed slowness. Baetens argues that "narrative innovation and radicalism are not based on speed (as we tend to believe today) or on slowness (as we used to believe some decades ago), but rather oppose the accepted mainstream narrative speed." Ibid., 354.

8. For a good discussion of contemporary compression of space-time based on its relationship to the economic shift from Fordism to flexible accumulation of capital, see David Harvey, *The Condition of Postmodernity: An Enquiry into the Origins of Cultural Change* (Oxford: Blackwell, 1990), esp. chap. 17, "Time-Space Compression and the Postmodern Condition," 284–307. Derrida analyzes cultural speed from a nuclear perspective; see Jacques Derrida, "No Apocalypse, Not Now (Full Speed Ahead, Seven Missiles, Seven Missives)," trans. Catherine Porter and Philip Lewis, *Diacritics* 14.2 (1984): 20–31. In "History on Wheels," 716–17, Benesch identifies a number of postmodern writers whose response to cultural speed is to suggest that we are becoming mired in or wrecking ourselves into stasis.

9. See Paul Virilio, *Speed and Politics: An Essay on Dromology,* trans. Mark Polizzotti, Foreign Agents Series (New York: Semiotext(e), 1986), 18, for one of many examples.

10. Ishmael Reed, *The Terrible Twos* (1982; New York: Atheneum, 1988), and *The Terrible Threes* (1989; New York: Atheneum, 1990).

11. Ishmael Reed, interview with John O'Brien in *The New Fiction: Interviews with Innovative American Writers,* ed. Joe David Bellamy (Urbana: University of Illinois Press, 1974), 130–41, quotation 131.

12. Robert Coover, *John's Wife* (New York: Simon and Schuster, 1996), 352.

13. Po Bronson, *Bombardiers* (New York: Penguin, 1995).

14. Ross, Reed, Coover, and James all enjoy their own dazzling performances and could be read as part of the American tradition traced by Richard Poirier in *The Performing Self* (New York: Oxford University Press, 1971).

15. Roland Barthes, "The Reality Effect" (1968), in *The Rustle of Language,* trans. Richard Howard (New York: Hill and Wang, 1986), 141–48, discussion 142–43.

16. John Gardner, *Grendel* (1971; New York: Ballantine, 1972), 55.

17. Fran Ross, *Oreo,* foreword by Harryette Mullen (1974; Boston: Northeastern University Press, 2000), 5.

18. Douglas Coupland, *Microserfs* (1995; New York: HarperPerennial, 1996), 12.

19. For Coover's determination to break bonds in fiction, see Kathryn Hume, "Robert Coover: The Metaphysics of Bondage," *Modern Language Review* 98 (2003): 827–41.

20. Amphetamines ("speed") were first synthesized in the 1880s, and were viewed as wonder drugs in the 1930s. They were heavily used, perfectly legally, throughout World War II and the Korean War to keep those giving orders and those operating machinery awake for long stints, a role they still play illegally for truck drivers. They later became popular for suppressing hunger and as enhancers of sports performance, and (under the name of Ritalin) are still used to quiet "overactive" children. See Philip Jenkins, *Synthetic Panics: The Symbolic Politics of Designer Drugs* (New York: New York University Press, 1999), 29–32. Marcus Boon studies writers known for writing under the influence of various drugs. Several famous authors openly touted amphetamines

for the concentration and energy these drugs gave them, allowing them to produce their material: Jack Kerouac, Jean-Paul Sartre, and Philip K. Dick were all amphetamine users, and exhibit the unedited gushes of words, and in Dick's case the paranoia, associated with serious use of speed. See Marcus Boon, *The Road of Excess: A History of Writers on Drugs* (Cambridge: Harvard University Press, 2002).

21. William Grimes, "The Ridiculous Vision of Mark Leyner," *New York Times Magazine,* September 13, 1992, 35, 51, 64, 65; comment on drugs 51.

22. Mark Leyner, *My Cousin, My Gastroenterologist* (1990; New York: Vintage, 1993).

23. Ronald A. T. Judy, "Irony and the Asymptotes of the Hyperbola," *Boundary 2* 25 (1998): 161–90, quotations 181.

24. Darius James, *Negrophobia: An Urban Parable* (New York: Citadel Press, 1992), 3.

25. Thomas Pynchon, *Gravity's Rainbow* (New York: Viking, 1973), 14–16.

26. William S. Burroughs, *The Ticket That Exploded* (1962; New York: Grove Weidenfeld, 1987), 18–20.

27. Mark Leyner, interview with Mark Leyner in *Some Other Frequency: Interviews with Innovative American Authors,* ed. Larry McCaffery (Philadelphia: University of Pennsylvania Press, 1996), 219–40, quotation 229.

28. Ibid., 220–21.

29. Ibid., 235.

30. Donald Barthelme, *The Dead Father* (1975; New York: Pocket, 1976), 50–51.

31. Saul Bellow, *The Dean's December* (London: Penguin, 1982), 285–86.

32. William G. Little says of Leyner, "Such hyperconsumption is redemptive because nothing is wasted; no leftovers remain. To consume everything is to assume absolute self-consciousness, to negate otherness by incorporating it into the self." William G. Little, "Figuring Out Mark Leyner: A Waste of Time," *Arizona Quarterly* 52.4 (1996): 135–63, quotation 141.

33. Grimes, "The Ridiculous Vision of Mark Leyner," 64.

34. Masochistic elements in reader response to literature have been explored by Marco Abel for violent literature and film. Criticism itself is seen as masochistic by Paul Mann. While reading literature that attacks the reader can be unpleasant, I hesitate to link it to what Abel and Mann call a masocritical approach, in part because no contract protects the reader except the power of closing the book. Moreover, the pleasure to be gained by undergoing the battery is exactly the issue in question here. The most plausible response I have seen so far is Susan Feagin's idea of taking pride in learning to appreciate a difficult text. If we appreciate something, having worked up to that position with effort, we do indeed achieve something pleasant. For how many readers this works is not clear, however. See Paul Mann, *Masocriticism* (Albany: SUNY Press, 1999), esp. the essay called "Masocriticism," 19–49; and Marco Abel, *Violent Affect: Literature, Cinema, and Critique after Representation* (Lincoln: University of Nebraska Press, 2007), esp. 15–28.

35. Randy Schroeder, "Inheriting Chaos: Burroughs, Pynchon, Sterling, Rucker," *Extrapolation* 43 (2002): 89–97, quotations 92 and 96.

36. Kathy Acker, *Empire of the Senseless* (New York: Grove Weidenfeld, 1988), 38.

2. Modalities of Complaint

1. Because women's voices are higher, this accusation is leveled more often by men at women than vice versa, but we will see some male protagonists who sometimes deserve the term "hysterical."

2. Susanne Günthner, "Complaint Stories: Constructing Emotional Reciprocity among Women," in *Communicating Gender in Context,* ed. Helga Kotthoff and Ruth Wodak (Amsterdam: John Benjamins Publishing Company, 1997), 179–218.

3. C. S. Lewis argues that both men and women are "feminine" (i.e., subordinate) in regard to the absolute masculine represented by God. See C. S. Lewis, *That Hideous Strength* (1946; New

York: Macmillan, 1965), 316. In *Mercy* (1990; New York, Four Walls Eight Windows, 1992), Andrea Dworkin makes this same observation in negative terms about men when commenting on circumcision that "the penis is sliced so they're girls to Him" (283).

4. John Peter, *Complaint and Satire in Early English Literature* (Oxford: Clarendon Press, 1956), 60–99.

5. John Kerrigan, ed., *Motives of Woe: Shakespeare and "Female Complaint"* (Oxford: Clarendon Press, 1991). See also Lawrence Lipking, *Abandoned Women and Poetic Tradition* (Chicago: University of Chicago Press, 1988).

6. Günthner ("Complaint Stories") makes the point that this transactional exchange is not found between men, since putting oneself in the victim position is too threatening to male self-esteem.

7. Roth fictionalizes the furor over *Portnoy's Complaint* in *Zuckerman Unbound*.

8. Philip Roth, *Portnoy's Complaint* (1969; London: Corgi, 1971), 15–17.

9. Murray G. H. Pittock, "The Complaint of Caledonia: Scottish Identity and the Female Voice," in *Archipelagic Identities: Literature and Identity in the Atlantic Archipelago, 1550–1800* (Aldershot: Ashgate, 2004) 141–52. Renaissance scholars have argued that even love plaints have a political level of meaning. See Arthur Marotti, "'Love Is Not Love': Elizabethan Sonnet Sequences and the Social Order," *ELH* 49.2 (1982): 396–428; also see Richard Helgerson, *Adulterous Alliances: Home, State, and History in Early Modern European Drama and Painting* (Chicago: University of Chicago Press, 2000).

10. My reading emphasizes the personal quest, but for an analysis more concerned with the metafictional and feminist-political elements of Acker's novel, see Linda S. Kauffman, *Bad Girls and Sick Boys: Fantasies in Contemporary Art and Culture* (Berkeley: University of California Press, 1998), 208–15.

11. Kathy Acker, *Don Quixote* (New York: Grove Press, 1986), 17.

12. That this is a persona became clear in interviews and obituaries, in which people insisted that the fun-loving, witty Kathy they knew bore no obvious relation to the lamenting, crying, hysterical-seeming persona. See, for instance, the obituary by Peter Guttridge in the *Independent,* December 2, 1997, where Acker is quoted as having said that except for her mother's suicide, all seeming autobiographical references are fictional. That may or may not be true, of course, but it puts in question the personal applications of stepfatherly sexual abuse, threats of lobotomy, and other harrowing material that certainly appears to be personal. She denies that her persona's sexual voraciousness is her own in Kathy Acker, "Devoured by Myths," an interview with Sylvère Lotringer in *Hannibal Lecter, My Father,* ed. Sylvère Lotringer (New York: Semiotext(e), 1991), 2, and *Eurydice in the Underworld* (London: Arcadia Books, 1997), 54. Lotringer asserts, "Well, I know for a fact that you're totally different from what you write" ("Devoured by Myths," 20).

13. Kathy Acker, *Pussy, King of the Pirates* (New York: Grove Press, 1996).

14. For contrast, consider the Egyptians, who did permit incest; for a fictional attempt to enter this very different mindset, see Norman Mailer, *Ancient Evenings* (1983; New York: Warner, 1984).

15. This is argued in greater detail in Kathryn Hume, "Voice in Kathy Acker's Fiction," *Contemporary Literature* 42.3 (2001): 485–513.

16. See Kathryn Hume, "Books of the Dead: Postmortem Politics in Novels by Mailer, Burroughs, Acker, and Pynchon," *Modern Philology* 97.3 (2000): 417–44.

17. William S. Burroughs, *Cities of the Red Night* (1981; New York: Owl Books, 1982), xv.

18. Thomas Pynchon, *Gravity's Rainbow* (New York: Viking, 1973), 539.

19. Robert Hughes, *Culture of Complaint: The Fraying of America* (New York: Oxford University Press, 1993), 10.

20. Peter, *Complaint and Satire,* 30–33.

21. Similarly, Acker has used first person to describe murders and sexually bizarre actions, and has thereby grossed out a supposedly sophisticated editor, who found all her critical faculties

bamboozled by that simple technique. See Acker's *On Our Backs* interview with Lisa Palac (May–June 1991): 19–20, 38–39, anecdote 19. In "Shakespeare's *A Lover's Complaint* and Early Modern Criminal Confession," *Shakespeare Quarterly* 53 (2002): 437–59, Katharine A. Craik notes that in Shakespeare's time, "imaginatively reconstructed confessions of female criminals flourished in ballad form.... Some dealt with murder, treason, and witchcraft; others with the breakdown in domestic order occasioned by crimes such as infanticide, adultery, or violence against husbands" (438). Dworkin's and Acker's use of first person gains yet more immediacy from their being women; most of the balladeers were presumably men.

22. Madison Smartt Bell, "Sustaining a Scream," *Chicago Tribune,* September 15, 1991. For hostile assessments of the novel, see Zoë Heller, "Nasties," *Times Literary Supplement,* October 5–11, 1990, 1072; and Martha Nussbaum's legalistic analysis of the concept of mercy within law (and of Dworkin's total lack of that quality) in "Equity and Mercy," *Philosophy and Public Affairs* 22.2 (1993): 83–125.

23. Dworkin, *Mercy,* 7.

24. Alice Walker, *The Color Purple* (1982; New York: Pocket Books, 1985), 4.

25. His *Reckless Eyeballing* is partly a satire on Walker's kind of successful feminist writer. Black male responses to both the book and the film were largely hostile. Reed evidently called both book and film "a Nazi conspiracy," according to Jacqueline Bobo, and the premiere of the film drew picketers for its portrayal of black men. "Other hostile views about the film were expressed by representatives of the NAACP, Black male columnists, and a law professor, Leroy Clark of Catholic University, who called it dangerous." See Jacqueline Bobo, "Black Women's Responses to *The Color Purple,*" http://www.ejumpcut.org/archive/onlinessays/JC33folder/ClPurpleBobo.html.

26. Frank Chin, *Donald Duk* (Minneapolis: Coffee House Press, 1991), 3.

27. William Kotzwinkle, *Doctor Rat* (New York: Alfred A. Knopf, 1976), 4.

28. Animal rights websites list such experiments as taking place, though without details and usually without documentation, so the value of the claims is unprovable. See http://www.animalsrighttolifewebsite.com/.

29. Ruth L. Ozeki, *My Year of Meats* (1998; New York, Penguin, 1999), 334.

30. A *New York Times Magazine* discussion of feedlots gives a very similar picture of hormone and antibiotic use; see Michael Pollan, "Power Steer," *New York Times Magazine,* March 31, 2002, http://www.nytimes.com/2002/03/31/magazine/power-steer.html. Pollan did a follow-up on an organic farm that gives animals natural and enjoyable lives but still produces meat; see "An Animal's Place," *New York Times Magazine,* November 10, 2002, http://www.nytimes.com/2002/11/10/magazine/10ANIMAL.html.

31. D. H. Monro, *Argument of Laughter* (Melbourne: Melbourne University Press, 1951). Superiority theories are discussed 83–146.

32. Kathy Acker, *Empire of the Senseless* (New York: Grove Weidenfeld, 1988), 12.

3. Conjugations of the Grotesque

1. William S. Burroughs, *The Place of Dead Roads* (1983; New York: Owl Books, 1995), 252.

2. At http://www.royalbcmuseum.bc.ca/Natural_History/Fish.aspx?id=294, the description reads as follows: "Males of some species may be parasitic on the female." A Wikipedia entry makes this merging even less a case of the female preying on the male: "When it is mature, the male's digestive system degenerates, making him incapable of feeding independently, which necessitates his quickly finding a female anglerfish to prevent his death. The sensitive olfactory organs help the male to detect the pheromones that signal the proximity of a female anglerfish. When he finds a female, he bites into her skin, and releases an enzyme that digests the skin of his mouth and her

body, fusing the pair down to the blood-vessel level. The male then atrophies into nothing more than a pair of gonads, which releases sperm in response to hormones in the female's bloodstream indicating egg release." http://en.wikipedia.org/wiki/Anglerfish. The reference cited for these facts is Theodore W. Pietsch, "Precocious Sexual Parasitism in the Deep Sea Ceratioid Anglerfish, Cryptopsaras couesi Gill," *Nature* 256 (July 3, 1975): 38–40.

3. Ewa Kuryluk, *Salome and Judas in the Cave of Sex: The Grotesque: Origins, Iconography, Techniques* (Evanston: Northwestern University Press, 1987); Istvan Csicsery-Ronay Jr., "On the Grotesque in Science Fiction," *Science Fiction Studies* 29.1 (2002): 71–99, quotation 71.

4. Wolfgang Kayser, *The Grotesque in Art and Literature* (1957), trans. Ulrich Weisstein (New York: McGraw-Hill, 1966), quotations 184–88 (in small capital letters in the original).

5. Critics who have explicitly explored ternary models are Geoffrey Galt Harpham, *On the Grotesque: Strategies of Contradiction in Art and Literature* (1982), 2nd ed. (Princeton: Princeton University Press, 2006); Sylvia Kelso, "Monster Marks: Sliding Significations of the Grotesque in Popular Fiction," in *Seriously Weird: Papers on the Grotesque,* ed. Alice Mills (New York: Peter Lang, 1999), 105–18; Wilson Yates, "An Introduction to the Grotesque: Theoretical and Theological Considerations," in *The Grotesque in Art and Literature: Theological Reflections,* ed. James Luther Adams and Wilson Yates (Grand Rapids: William B. Eerdmans, 1997), 1–68; and Csicsery-Ronay, "On the Grotesque in Science Fiction."

6. Margaret Miles, "Carnal Abominations: The Female Body as Grotesque," in Adams and Yates, *The Grotesque in Art and Literature,* 83–112.

7. Mark Dorrian, "On the Monstrous and the Grotesque," *Word & Image* 16.3 (2000): 310–17, quotation 314; Rosalind Krauss's more extended discussion of Bataille is found in *The Originality of the Avant-Garde and Other Modernist Myths* (Cambridge: MIT Press, 1985), 64.

8. Bernard McElroy, *Fiction of the Modern Grotesque* (London: Macmillan, 1989).

9. John Ruskin, "Grotesque Renaissance," chap. 3 of *The Stones of Venice* (1851–1853), vol. 9 of *The Complete Works of John Ruskin* (New York: Kelmscott Society, n.d.), 112–65; Philip Thomson, *The Grotesque* (London: Methuen, 1972).

10. Leonard Cassuto, *The Inhuman Race: The Racial Grotesque in American Literature and Culture* (New York: Columbia University Press, 1997), 20–27.

11. John R. Clark, *The Modern Satiric Grotesque and Its Traditions* (Lexington: University Press of Kentucky, 1991).

12. William Van O'Connor says that the grotesque flourishes when cultural values are in flux, changing from one paradigm to another. He understands twentieth-century American grotesque to emerge from the clash between the values of the eighteenth-century world and the world that has produced modern science, with its atomic bomb, among other things. See William Van O'Connor, *The Grotesque: An American Genre and Other Essays* (Carbondale: Southern Illinois University Press, 1962), 3–19.

13. Dunn uses "freaks," and I follow her usage. Less opprobrious terms that have been suggested are "prodigies" and "phenomena"; for a list of the many names tried, see Leslie Fiedler, *Freaks: Myths and Images of the Secret Self* (New York: Simon and Schuster, 1978), 13–17.

14. For these readings, see Katherine Weese, "Normalizing Freakery: Katherine Dunn's *Geek Love* and the Female Grotesque," *Critique* 41.4 (2000): 349–64; Michael Hardin, "Fundamentally Freaky: Collapsing the Freak/Norm Binary in *Geek Love,*" *Critique* 45.4 (2004): 337–46; Victoria Warren, "American Tall Tale/Tail: Katherine Dunn's *Geek Love* and the Paradox of American Individualism," *Critique* 45.4 (2004): 323–36; and Jack Slay Jr., "Delineations in Freakery: Freaks in the Fiction of Harry Crews and Katherine Dunn," in *Literature and the Grotesque,* ed. Michael J. Meyer (Amsterdam: Rodopi, 1995), 99–112.

15. Katherine Dunn, *Geek Love* (New York: Warner, 1990), 103. For the connection between compulsive orderliness and middle-class values, see Peter Stallybrass and Allon White, *The Politics and Poetics of Transgression* (Ithaca: Cornell University Press, 1986), esp. 125–48.

16. Mikhail Bakhtin, *Rabelais and His World* (1965), trans. Hélène Iswolsky (Cambridge: MIT Press, 1968), 25.

17. David Mitchell, "Modernist Freaks and Postmodern Geeks," in *The Disability Studies Reader,* ed. Lennard J. Davis (New York: Routledge, 1997), 348–64.

18. For a discussion of Arty's cult, see N. Katherine Hayles, "Postmodern Parataxis: Embodied Texts, Weightless Information," *American Literary History* 2.3 (1990): 394–421.

19. Chuck Palahniuk, *Invisible Monsters* (New York: Norton, 1999), quotation 57.

20. Dorrian, "On the Monstrous and the Grotesque," 310.

21. See Aretino's letter no. 53 to Messer Battista Zatti of Brescia, in *Aretino: Selected Letters,* trans. George Bull (Harmondsworth: Penguin, 1976), 156–57.

22. Robert Coover, *The Adventures of Lucky Pierre: Directors' Cut* (New York: Grove, 2002), 3–4.

23. See Kathryn Hume, "Robert Coover: The Metaphysics of Bondage," *Modern Language Review* 98 (2003): 827–41.

24. See Robert Coover, "A Theological Position," in *A Theological Position: Plays* (New York: E. P. Dutton, 1972), 166.

25. McElroy, *Fiction of the Modern Grotesque,* 5.

26. James Morrow, *Towing Jehovah* (New York: Harvest, 1994).

27. The giant in Joe Orton's *Head to Toe* is too little visualized to have any effect. Although it is supposedly "hundreds of miles high," someone can stand on the head and "contemplate a landscape of waving hair." Joe Orton, *Head to Toe* (1971; New York: Da Capo, 1998), 5. If the giant were only two hundred miles high, wavy hair would be about ten miles long and not visible as such to the human. Orton's conceit never develops; the landscape turns into something more like that in *Through the Looking-Glass.*

28. Donald Antrim, *Elect Mr. Robinson for a Better World* (1993; New York: Vintage, 2001).

29. Faced with similar reversions to the past in *Towing Jehovah,* the nun wonders whether the post-theistic future will contain "vigilante vengeance, public executions." Morrow, *Towing Jehovah,* 181.

30. Gerald Vizenor, *Bearheart: The Heirship Chronicle* (1978; Minneapolis: University of Minnesota Press, 1990), 95.

31. Gerald Vizenor and A. Robert Lee, *Postindian Conversations* (Lincoln: University of Nebraska Press, 1999), 101.

32. One version of this sexual celebration between monks and animals is recounted in Gerald Vizenor, *Hotline Healers: An Almost Browne Novel* (Hanover NH: Wesleyan University Press, 1997), 159–72. He repeats the story with variations elsewhere.

33. "Dog-lover" seems to have been a common and sometimes joking insult among the Blackfoot people; James Welch has two adolescent friends call each other "Dog-lover" and "Near woman" in *Fools Crow* (New York: Viking Penguin, 1986), 6.

34. Cormac McCarthy, *Blood Meridian, or The Evening Redness in the West* (1985; New York: Vintage, 1992).

35. The book sold in connection with the show is William H. Truettner, ed., *The West as America: Reinterpreting Images of the Frontier, 1820–1920* (Washington, DC: Smithsonian Institution Press, 1991).

36. Northrop Frye, *Anatomy of Criticism: Four Essays* (Princeton: Princeton University Press, 1957), esp. 223–39. Harold Bloom refuses to label the Judge, except to think in Gnostic terms and link him to the white whale rather than to Ahab, as other critics have done. Harold Bloom, *How to Read and Why* (New York: Scribner, 2000), 254–63. Emily J. Stinson labels him the tarot Fool in *"Blood Meridian's* Man of Many Masks: Judge Holden as Tarot's Fool," *Southwestern American Literature* 33.1 (2007) 9–21. Rick Wallach finds in him a strange biological neoteny, but also likens him to Shiva in "Judge Holden, *Blood Meridian's* Evil Archon," in *Sacred Violence: A Reader's*

Companion to Cormac McCarthy, ed. Wade Hall and Rick Wallach (El Paso: Texas Western Press, 1995), 125–36. George Guillemin convincingly links the Judge to Saturn and a monstrous child archetype associated with melancholia in " 'See the Child': The Melancholy Subtext of *Blood Meridian,*" in *Cormac McCarthy: New Directions,* ed. James D. Lilley (Albuquerque: University of New Mexico Press, 2002), 239–65.

37. Octavia E. Butler, *Dawn* (1987; New York: Warner, 1988).

38. Elizabeth Moon, *Moving Target* (London: Orbit, 2004), 93.

39. Jean-Paul Sartre, *Nausea,* trans. Lloyd Alexander (New York: New Directions, 1964), 159.

40. Vonda N. McIntyre, *Superluminal* (1983; New York: Pocket Books, 1984).

41. Anne McCaffrey and Mercedes Lackey, *The Ship Who Searched* (New York: Baen Books, 1992).

42. Ted Mooney, *Easy Travel to Other Planets* (1981; New York: Ballantine, 1983).

43. Rachel Ingalls, *Mrs. Caliban* (Boston: Harvard Common Press, 1983).

44. Marge Piercy, *He, She and It* (1991; New York: Fawcett Crest, 1993).

4. Violence

1. See http://en.wikipedia.org/wiki/Saw_(franchise).

2. Stephen King, *Danse Macabre* (New York: Everest House, 1981), 368.

3. See Richard Slotkin, *Regeneration through Violence: The Mythology of the American Frontier, 1600–1860* (Middletown: Wesleyan University Press, 1973), *The Fatal Environment: The Myth of the Frontier in the Age of Industrialization, 1800–1890* (New York: Macmillan, 1985), and *Gunfighter Nation: The Myth of the Frontier in Twentieth-Century America* (New York: Atheneum Press, 1992).

4. Martin Rubin, "The Grayness of Darkness: The Honeymoon Killers and Its Impact on Psychokiller Cinema," in *Mythologies of Violence in Postmodern Media,* ed. Christopher Sharrett (Detroit: Wayne State University Press, 1999), 41–64, esp. 55.

5. Amazon.com readers now turn in wildly favorable ratings for *American Psycho* (450 five-star reviews listed at this writing, many of them gushing), but *Hogg* still upsets readers, who produce few reviews, and most of those stress negative and disturbing elements, even when five star.

6. Analysts of horror make this assumption. Mark Pizzato argues that serial murderers act out suppressed rage that we all share, hence the box office appeal of killer films. Mark Pizzato, "Jeffrey Dahmer and Media Cannibalism: The Lure and Failure of Sacrifice," in Sharrett, *Mythologies of Violence,* 85–118, esp. 89. King (*Danse Macabre,* 175) talks about the alligators we all have hidden in our unconscious, and sees genre horror as a way of feeding the alligators so as to keep them from creeping out into our ordinary life.

7. In *Serial Killers: Death and Life in America's Wound Culture* (New York: Routledge, 1998), Mark Seltzer discusses alienation in our machinic society, our wound culture, and our body-machine-image complex as it creates and celebrates serial killers.

8. For a thoughtful analysis of contemporary fiction in terms of consumerism and late capitalism, see Elizabeth Young and Graham Caveney, *Shopping in Space: Essays on America's Blank Generation Fiction* (1992; New York: Grove Press, 1994). Another critic who links Bret Easton Ellis and Dennis Cooper to capitalism and consumerism is James Annesley in *Blank Fictions: Consumerism, Culture and the Contemporary American Novel* (New York: St. Martin's Press, 1998).

9. Carol Clover argues against the feminist mainstream on the serial-killer film when she points out that the final woman who stops the killer is masculinized in a variety of ways, and the killer is almost always somehow defective in his masculinity. She suggests that these films reflect some major shifts in cultural gender assumptions. See Carol Clover, *Men, Women, and Chain Saws: Gender in the Modern Horror Film* (Princeton: Princeton University Press, 1992). A more standard

feminist stance is put forward by Jane Caputi, who thinks that serial killers have become culture heroes who validate their superior masculinity by killing women. See Jane Caputi, "Small Ceremonies: Ritual in *Forrest Gump, Natural Born Killers, Seven,* and *Follow Me Home,*" in Sharrett, *Mythologies of Violence,* 147–74.

10. King, *Danse Macabre,* 37.

11. Brian Evenson, *Dark Property: An Affliction* (New York: Black Square, 2002), 10.

12. Evenson is Mormon by background, but his writing was seen as sufficiently unacceptable to the Latter-Day Saints that he left his teaching post at Brigham Young University. If this scene has particular Mormon overtones, I missed them, but the conservative nature of the clothing is rather like that of the Amish and Mennonites, and may just signify a conservative and past-oriented religious group rather than a specific faith.

13. Bellow, *The Dean's December* (London: Penguin, 1982), 272.

14. Carol Clover, for instance, notes that many American horror films manifest clashes between city and country values *(Men, Women, and Chain Saws),* and Elliot Leyton argues that class rather than sex is the driving issue for some serial killers in both film and real life. See Elliot Leyton, *Compulsive Killers: The Story of Modern Multiple Murder* (New York: New York University Press, 1986), 23–31.

15. Anthony Burgess's *A Clockwork Orange* and the Kubrick film similarly give us a new vocabulary; because the film (like the first American edition) ignores the original British ending, with its reinstatement of normal society, it upset viewers. They were left in the ugly world with no escape.

16. Elizabeth Young, "The Beast in the Jungle, the Figure in the Carpet: Bret Easton Ellis's *American Psycho,*" in Young and Caveney, *Shopping in Space,* 85–122, esp. 114–15.

17. Mark Storey, "'And as things fell apart': The Crisis of Postmodern Masculinity in Bret Easton Ellis's *American Psycho* and Dennis Cooper's *Frisk,*" *Critique* 47.1 (2005): 57–72, quotation 64. In *The Spaces of Violence* (Tuscaloosa: University of Alabama Press, 2006), James R. Giles points out that the homeless man murdered early on embodies the kind of failure that Bateman fears; Bateman tries to elicit from him admission of this degradation being his own fault, and cannot handle the argument that he was a blameless victim of being laid off (161–62).

18. Marco Abel criticizes the whole idea that violent images represent something and should be interpreted in light of their referent; instead he focuses on how these images affect readers. The only actual violence done by *American Psycho* is to readers' minds and stomachs; Patrick Bateman and his acts do not exist, so his violence does not exist; we can only look at its operation between text and reader. See Marco Abel, *Violent Affect: Literature, Cinema, and Critique after Representation* (Lincoln: University of Nebraska Press, 2007).

19. When a film actually does spawn a copycat crime, though, it may get blamed and the producers sued. *A Clockwork Orange, Magnum Force, Taxi Driver, First Blood, RoboCop 2,* and *Interview with the Vampire* are all cited as having spawned copycat crimes, including, in one instance, making victims drink Drano; http://www.ew.com/ew/article/0,295900,00.html. *Deer Hunter, Money Train, The Program, Child's Play, Natural Born Killers,* and *The Basketball Diaries* have also been blamed for subsequent crimes. See Robert H. Wicks, *Understanding Audiences: Learning to Use the Media Constructively* (Philadelphia: Lawrence Erlbaum, 2000), 122–23.

20. Julian Murphet, *Bret Easton Ellis's* American Psycho: *A Reader's Guide* (New York: Continuum, 2002), 17.

21. Bret Easton Ellis, *American Psycho* (New York: Vintage Contemporaries, 1991), 245–47.

22. Fredric Jameson, *Postmodernism, or, The Cultural Logic of Late Capitalism* (Durham: Duke University Press, 1991), 10.

23. Something like this is attempted by Michael Kowalewski in *Deadly Musings: Violence and Verbal Form in American Fiction* (Princeton: Princeton University Press, 1993); he concerns himself with "the ways in which it [violence] has been imagined or 'performed' in American fiction"

(8). He sees the violence on the page as separate from any in the material world, and studies it as deliberate authorial performance.

24. Samuel R. Delany, *Hogg* (1995) 2nd ed. (Normal, IL: FC2, 2004), 8.

25. Michael Hemmingson, "In the Scorpion Garden: Hogg," *Review of Contemporary Fiction* 16.3 (1996): 125–28, quotation 125.

26. Mary Douglas, *Purity and Danger: An Analysis of Concepts of Pollution and Taboo* (New York: Praeger, 1966).

27. Theodore Sturgeon, "If All Men Were Brothers, Would You Let One Marry Your Sister?" in *Dangerous Visions,* ed. Harlan Ellison (1967; London: Gollancz, 1987), 346–89.

28. A boy rape victim who is kidnapped by a carnival magician in Robertson Davies's *World of Wonders* (1975; New York: Penguin, 1976) says later in life that he can see how miserable his existence was then, but at the time he simply accepted what adults imposed (66). He further says that he was "not consciously unhappy. Unhappiness of the kind that is recognized and examined and brooded over is a spiritual luxury" (111).

29. Laura Chernaik, "The Importance of Precision: Samuel Delany's Pornographic Writing," *Philologie im Netz* 12 (2000): 13–28, quotation 19.

30. Samuel R. Delany, "The Scorpion Garden" (originally the preface to *Hogg*), in *The Straits of Messina* (Seattle: Serconia Press, 1989), 1–16, quotations 14, 1. In "The 'Scorpion Garden' Revisited: A Note on the Anti-Pornography of Samuel R. Delany," Delany writes a feminist comment on himself under the name of K. Leslie Steiner.

31. Thomas Pynchon, *Gravity's Rainbow* (New York: Viking, 1973), 729.

32. Dennis Cooper, *Frisk* (New York: Grove, 1991), 38.

33. Leora Lev argues that "Cooper's discourses of eroticism and violence, with their evocation of bodily orifices, fluids, and spasms, are a conduit for profound questions about the relation between death, desire, language, and alterity, and the nature of abjection and epiphany." Leora Lev, ed., *Enter at Your Own Risk: The Dangerous Art of Dennis Cooper* (Madison, NJ: Fairleigh Dickinson University Press, 2006), 15. She relates his work to French avant-garde and underground literature as well as to "the minimalist vernacular of contemporary teenagers" and a "queer slacker inarticulacy" (15).

34. Dennis Cooper, *Try* (1994; London: Serpent's Tail, 2004), 187.

35. Richard Grossman, *The Alphabet Man* (Boulder, CO: Fiction Collective Two, 1993).

36. Kathy Acker, *Blood and Guts in High School* (1978; New York: Evergreen, 1989).

37. "Cannibalism represents the ultimate in possessiveness, hence the logical end of human relations under capitalism." See Robin Wood, "An Introduction to the American Horror Film," in *American Nightmare: Essays on the Horror Film,* ed. Andrew Britton, Richard Lippe, Tony Williams, and Robin Wood (Toronto: Festival of Festivals, 1979), 21. Barry Keith Grant cites Wood and stresses the parallels between horror film and *American Psycho,* including the critique of consumerism, in "American Psycho/sis: The Pure Products of America Go Crazy," in Sharrett, *Mythologies of Violence in Postmodern Media,* 25. As Brian McHale puts it in an email message dated April 1, 2009, *American Psycho* and, he thinks, *Frisk* exhibit "the worldview of 'everything is mine to consume, if I want it' that drives consumer capitalism and that consumer capitalism in turn foments."

38. Dennis Cooper, an interview with Robert Glück, in Lev, *Enter at Your Own Risk,* 241–59, quotations 254.

39. See Abel, *Violent Affect;* Young, "The Beast in the Jungle"; and Naomi Mandel, " 'Right Here in Nowheres': *American Psycho* and Violence's Critique," in *Novels of the Contemporary Extreme,* ed. Alain-Philippe Durand and Naomi Mandel (London: Continuum, 2006), 9–19.

5. Attacking the Reader's Ontological Assumptions

1. Brian McHale, *Postmodernist Fiction* (New York: Methuen, 1987), 45.

2. Mark Salzman, *Lying Awake* (New York: Vintage, 2000), 17.

3. Chuck Palahniuk, *Fight Club* (1996; London: Vintage, 2005).

4. Donald Barthelme, *Snow White* (New York: Atheneum, 1972), 179.

5. See Carolyn Chute, *Merry Men* (New York: Harcourt Brace, 1994), esp. 684.

6. Not only does Dick follow patterns regarding the nature of reality, but also his underlying psychological patterns repeat certain traumas of his early life; see N. Katherine Hayles, *How We Became Posthuman: Virtual Bodies in Cybernetics, Literature, and Informatics* (Chicago: University of Chicago Press, 1999), 184–88, who notes the anxiety over boundaries between inside and outside as they play out in *Ubik*. Michael Bishop treats the book as deliberately evading all attempts to pin it down or interpret it; see "In Pursuit of *Ubik*," in *Philip K. Dick*, ed. Joseph D. Olander and Martin Harry Greenberg (New York: Taplinger, 1983), 137–47. For a very different approach, see Peter Fitting's reading of it as a deconstruction of bourgeois science fiction and of capitalism in "*Ubik*: The Deconstruction of Bourgeois SF," also in Olander and Greenberg, *Philip K. Dick*, 149–59.

7. Philip K. Dick, *Ubik* (1969; New York: Vintage, 1991).

8. As the title page puts it; Mark Z. Danielewski, *House of Leaves by Zampanò, with Introduction and Notes by Johnny Truant*, 2nd ed. (New York: Pantheon Books, 2000), xxii.

9. Thomas Pynchon, *Against the Day* (New York: Penguin Press, 2006).

10. C. S. Lewis, "The Weight of Glory," in *The Weight of Glory and Other Addresses* (1949; Grand Rapids: William B. Eerdmans Publishing Company, 1965), 1–15, esp. 3–4.

11. Thomas Pynchon, *V.* (1963; New York: Harper Perennial Modern Classics, 2005), 406.

6. Conclusion

1. Susan Sontag, "Against Interpretation," in *Against Interpretation and Other Essays* (New York: Delta, 1966), 3–14, quotation 11.

2. Michael Kowalewski, *Deadly Musings: Violence and Verbal Form in American Fiction* (Princeton: Princeton University Press, 1993), 249.

BIBLIOGRAPHY

Abel, Marco. *Violent Affect: Literature, Cinema, and Critique after Representation.* Lincoln: University of Nebraska Press, 2007.

Acker, Kathy. *Blood and Guts in High School.* 1978. New York: Evergreen, 1989.

———. "Devoured by Myths." Interview with Sylvère Lotringer. In *Hannibal Lecter, My Father,* edited by Sylvère Lotringer, 1–24. New York: Semiotext(e), 1991.

———. *Don Quixote.* New York: Grove Press, 1986.

———. *Empire of the Senseless.* New York: Grove Weidenfeld, 1988.

———. *Eurydice in the Underworld.* London: Arcadia Books, 1997.

———. "The On Our Backs Interview." Interview with Lisa Palac. *On Our Backs* (May–June 1991): 19–20, 38–39.

———. *Pussy, King of the Pirates.* New York: Grove Press, 1996.

Alter, Robert. *Motives for Fiction.* Cambridge: Harvard University Press, 1984.

Annesley, James. *Blank Fictions: Consumerism, Culture and the Contemporary American Novel.* New York: St. Martin's Press, 1998.

Antrim, Donald. *Elect Mr. Robinson for a Better World.* 1993. New York: Vintage, 2001.

Aretino, Pietro. *Aretino: Selected Letters.* Translated by George Bull. Harmondsworth: Penguin, 1976.

Baetens, Jan. "Speed, Rhythm, Movement: A Dialogue on K. Hume's Article 'Narrative Speed.'" *Narrative* 14.3 (2006): 349–55.

Bakhtin, Mikhail. *Rabelais and His World.* 1965. Translated by Hélène Iswolsky. Cambridge: MIT Press, 1968.

Barthelme, Donald. *The Dead Father.* 1975. New York: Pocket, 1976.

———. *Snow White.* New York: Atheneum, 1972.

Barthes, Roland. "The Reality Effect." In *The Rustle of Language,* translated by Richard Howard, 141–48. New York: Hill and Wang, 1986.

Bell, Madison Smartt. "Sustaining a Scream." *Chicago Tribune,* September 15, 1991.

Bellow, Saul. *The Dean's December.* London: Penguin, 1982.

Benesch, Klaus. "History on Wheels: A Hegelian Reading of 'Speed' in Contemporary American Literature and Culture." In *The Holodeck in the Garden: Science and Technology in Contemporary American Fiction,* edited by Peter Freese and Charles B. Harris, 212–24. Normal, IL: Dalkey Archive Press, 2004.

Bishop, Michael. "In Pursuit of *Ubik.*" In *Philip K. Dick,* edited by Joseph D. Olander and Martin Harry Greenberg, 137–47. New York: Taplinger, 1983.

Bloom, Harold. *How to Read and Why.* New York: Scribner, 2000.

Bobo, Jacqueline. "Black Women's Responses to *The Color Purple.*" http://www.ejumpcut.org/archive/onlinessays/JC33folder/ClPurpleBobo.html.

Boon, Marcus. *The Road of Excess: A History of Writers on Drugs.* Cambridge: Harvard University Press, 2002.

Bronson, Po. *Bombardiers.* New York: Penguin, 1995.

Burroughs, William S. *Cities of the Red Night.* 1981. New York: Owl Books, 1982.

———. *The Place of Dead Roads.* 1983. New York: Owl Books, 1995.

———. *The Ticket That Exploded.* 1962. New York: Grove Weidenfeld, 1987.

Butler, Octavia E. *Dawn.* 1987. New York: Warner, 1988.

Caputi, Jane. "Small Ceremonies: Ritual in *Forrest Gump, Natural Born Killers, Seven,* and *Follow Me Home.*" In *Mythologies of Violence in Postmodern Media,* edited by Christopher Sharrett, 147–74. Detroit: Wayne State University Press, 1999.

Cassuto, Leonard. *The Inhuman Race: The Racial Grotesque in American Literature and Culture.* New York: Columbia University Press, 1997.

Chénetier, Marc. *Beyond Suspicion: New American Fiction since 1960.* Translated by Elizabeth A. Houlding. Philadelphia: University of Pennsylvania Press, 1996.

Chernaik, Laura. "The Importance of Precision: Samuel Delany's Pornographic Writing." *Philologie im Netz* 12 (2000): 13–28.

Chin, Frank. *Donald Duk.* Minneapolis: Coffee House Press, 1991.

Chute, Carolyn. *Merry Men.* New York: Harcourt Brace, 1994.

Clark, John R. *The Modern Satiric Grotesque and Its Traditions.* Lexington: University Press of Kentucky, 1991.

Clover, Carol J. *Men, Women, and Chain Saws: Gender in the Modern Horror Film.* Princeton: Princeton University Press, 1992.

Cohen, Samuel. *After the End of History: American Fiction in the 1990s.* Iowa City: University of Iowa Press, 2009.

Cooper, Dennis. An interview with Robert Glück. In *Enter at Your Own Risk: The Dangerous Art of Dennis Cooper,* edited by Leora Lev, 241–59. Madison, NJ: Fairleigh Dickinson University Press, 2006.

———. *Frisk.* New York: Grove, 1991.

——. *Guide.* New York: Grove, 1997.

——. *Try.* 1994. London: Serpent's Tail, 2004.

Coover, Robert. *The Adventures of Lucky Pierre: Directors' Cut.* New York: Grove, 2002.

——. *John's Wife.* New York: Simon and Schuster, 1996.

——. "A Theological Position." In *A Theological Position: Plays,* 121–72. New York: E. P. Dutton, 1972.

Cornis-Pope, Marcel. *Narrative Innovation and Cultural Rewriting in the Cold War Era and After.* New York: Palgrave, 2001.

Coupland, Douglas. *Microserfs.* 1995. New York: HarperPerennial, 1996.

Craik, Katharine A. "Shakespeare's *A Lover's Complaint* and Early Modern Criminal Confession." *Shakespeare Quarterly* 53 (2002): 437–59.

Csicsery-Ronay, Istvan, Jr. "On the Grotesque in Science Fiction." *Science Fiction Studies* 29.1 (2002): 71–99.

Danielewski, Mark Z. *House of Leaves by Zampanò, with Introduction and Notes by Johnny Truant.* 2nd edition. New York: Pantheon Books, 2000.

Danius, Sara. "The Aesthetics of the Windshield: Proust and the Modernist Rhetoric of Speed." *Modernism/Modernity* 8.1 (2001): 99–126.

Davies, Robertson. *World of Wonders.* 1975. New York: Penguin, 1976.

Delany, Samuel R. *Hogg.* 1995. 2nd edition. Normal, IL: FC2, 2004.

——. *The Mad Man.* 1994. Revised and expanded edition. Np: Voyant Publishing, 2002.

——. "The Scorpion Garden." In *The Straits of Messina,* 1–16. Seattle: Serconia Press, 1989.

——. [under the pseudonym K. Leslie Steiner]. "The 'Scorpion Garden' Revisited: A Note on the Anti-Pornography of Samuel R. Delany." In *The Straits of Messina,* 17–35. Seattle: Serconia Press, 1989.

Derrida, Jacques. "No Apocalypse, Not Now (Full Speed Ahead, Seven Missiles, Seven Missives)." Translated by Catherine Porter and Philip Lewis. *Diacritics* 14.2 (1984): 20–31.

Dick, Philip K. *Blade Runner (Do Androids Dream of Electric Sheep?)* 1968. New York: Ballantine, 1982.

——. *Ubik.* 1969. New York: Vintage, 1991.

Dorrian, Mark. "On the Monstrous and the Grotesque." *Word & Image* 16.3 (2000): 310–17.

Douglas, Mary. *Purity and Danger: An Analysis of Concepts of Pollution and Taboo.* New York: Praeger, 1966.

Dunn, Katherine. *Geek Love.* New York: Warner, 1990.

Dworkin, Andrea. *Mercy.* 1990. New York: Four Walls Eight Windows, 1992.

Ellis, Bret Easton. *American Psycho.* New York: Vintage Contemporaries, 1991.

Evenson, Brian. *Dark Property: An Affliction.* New York: Black Square Editions, 2002.

Feagin, Susan L. *Reading with Feeling: The Aesthetics of Appreciation.* Ithaca: Cornell University Press, 1996.

Federman, Raymond. *Critifiction: Postmodern Essays.* Albany: SUNY Press, 1993.

Fiedler, Leslie. *Freaks: Myths and Images of the Secret Self.* New York: Simon and Schuster, 1978.

Fitting, Peter. "*Ubik:* The Deconstruction of Bourgeois SF." In *Philip K. Dick,* edited by Joseph D. Olander and Martin Harry Greenberg, 149–59. New York: Taplinger, 1983.

Fleming, Bruce. *What Literary Studies Could Be, and What It Is.* Lanham, MD: University Press of America, 2008.

Frye, Northrop. *Anatomy of Criticism: Four Essays.* Princeton: Princeton University Press, 1957.

Gardner, John. *Grendel.* 1971. New York: Ballantine, 1972.

Genette, Gérard. *Narrative Discourse.* Translated by Jane E. Lewin. Oxford: Basil Blackwell, 1980.

——. *Narrative Discourse Revisited.* Translated by Jane E. Lewin. Ithaca: Cornell University Press, 1988.

Giles, James R. *The Spaces of Violence.* Tuscaloosa: University of Alabama Press, 2006.

Grant, Barry Keith. "American Psycho/sis: The Pure Products of America Go Crazy." In *Mythologies of Violence in Postmodern Media,* edited by Christopher Sharrett, 23–40. Detroit: Wayne State University Press, 1999.

Grimes, William. "The Ridiculous Vision of Mark Leyner." *New York Times Magazine,* September 13, 1992, http://www.nytimes.com/1992/09/13/magazine/the-ridiculous-vision-of-mark-leyner.html.

Grossman, Richard. *The Alphabet Man.* Boulder, CO: Fiction Collective Two, 1993.

Guillemin, George. "'See the Child': The Melancholy Subtext of *Blood Meridian.*" In *Cormac McCarthy: New Directions,* edited by James D. Lilley, 239–65. Albuquerque: University of New Mexico Press, 2002.

Günthner, Susanne. "Complaint Stories: Constructing Emotional Reciprocity among Women." In *Communicating Gender in Context,* edited by Helga Kotthoff and Ruth Wodak, 179–218. Amsterdam: John Benjamins Publishing Company, 1997.

Guttridge, Peter. "Kathy Acker." *The Independent,* December 2, 1997.

Hardin, Michael. "Fundamentally Freaky: Collapsing the Freak/Norm Binary in Geek Love." *Critique* 45.4 (2004): 337–46.

Harpham, Geoffrey Galt. *On the Grotesque: Strategies of Contradiction in Art and Literature.* 1982. 2nd edition. Princeton: Princeton University Press, 2006.

Harvey, David. *The Condition of Postmodernity: An Enquiry into the Origins of Cultural Change.* Oxford: Blackwell Publishing, 1990.

Hawkes, John. "John Hawkes: An Interview," with John J. Enck. *Wisconsin Studies in Contemporary Literature* 6 (1965): 141–55.

Hayles, N. Katherine. *How We Became Posthuman: Virtual Bodies in Cybernetics, Literature, and Informatics.* Chicago: University of Chicago Press, 1999.

——. "Postmodern Parataxis: Embodied Texts, Weightless Information." *American Literary History* 2.3 (1990): 394–421.

Helgerson, Richard. *Adulterous Alliances: Home, State, and History in Early Modern European Drama and Painting.* Chicago: University of Chicago Press, 2000.

Heller, Zoë. "Nasties." *Times Literary Supplement,* October 5–11, 1990, 1072.

Hemmingson, Michael. "In the Scorpion Garden: Hogg." *Review of Contemporary Fiction* 16.3 (1996): 125–28.

Holland, Norman N. "Unity Identity Text Self." In *Reader-Response Criticism: From Formalism to Post-Structuralism,* edited by Jane P. Tompkins, 118–33. Baltimore: Johns Hopkins University Press, 1980.

Horace. *Satires, Epistles, and Ars Poetica.* Translated by H. Rushton Fairclough. Loeb Classical Library. New York: G. P. Putnam's Sons, 1926.

Hughes, Robert. *Culture of Complaint: The Fraying of America.* New York: Oxford University Press, 1993.

Hume, Kathryn. "Books of the Dead: Postmortem Politics in Novels by Mailer, Burroughs, Acker, and Pynchon." *Modern Philology* 97.3 (2000): 417–44.

———. "Narrative Speed in Contemporary Fiction." *Narrative* 13.2 (2005): 105–24.

———. "Robert Coover: The Metaphysics of Bondage." *Modern Language Review* 98 (2003): 827–41.

———. "Views from Above, Views from Below: The Perspectival Subtext in *Gravity's Rainbow.*" *American Literature* 60.4 (1988): 625–42.

———. "Voice in Kathy Acker's Fiction." *Contemporary Literature* 42.3 (2001): 485–513.

Hume, Kathryn, with Jan Baetens. "Speed, Rhythm, Movement: A Dialogue on K. Hume's Article 'Narrative Speed.'" *Narrative* 14.3 (2006): 349–55.

Ingalls, Rachel. *Mrs. Caliban.* Boston: Harvard Common Press, 1983.

James, Darius. *Negrophobia: An Urban Parable.* New York: Citadel Press, 1992.

Jameson, Fredric. *Postmodernism, or, The Cultural Logic of Late Capitalism.* Durham: Duke University Press, 1991.

Jenkins, Philip. *Synthetic Panics: The Symbolic Politics of Designer Drugs.* New York: New York University Press, 1999.

Johnston, John. *Information Multiplicity: American Fiction in the Age of Media Saturation.* Baltimore: Johns Hopkins University Press, 1998.

Judy, Ronald A. T. "Irony and the Asymptotes of the Hyperbola." *Boundary 2* 25 (1998): 161–90.

Kauffman, Linda S. *Bad Girls and Sick Boys: Fantasies in Contemporary Art and Culture.* Berkeley: University of California Press, 1998.

Kayser, Wolfgang. *The Grotesque in Art and Literature.* 1957. Translated by Ulrich Weisstein. New York: McGraw-Hill, 1966.

Kelso, Sylvia. "Monster Marks: Sliding Significations of the Grotesque in Popular Fiction." In *Seriously Weird: Papers on the Grotesque,* edited by Alice Mills, 105–18. New York: Peter Lang, 1999.

Kermode, Frank. *The Sense of an Ending: Studies in the Theory of Fiction.* 1967. New York: Oxford University Press, 1970.

Kern, Stephen. *The Culture of Time and Space, 1880–1918.* Cambridge: Harvard University Press, 1983.

Kerrigan, John, ed. *Motives of Woe: Shakespeare and "Female Complaint."* Oxford: Clarendon Press, 1991.

King, Stephen. *Danse Macabre.* New York: Everest House, 1981.

Kotzwinkle, William. *Doctor Rat.* New York: Alfred A. Knopf, 1976.

Kowalewski, Michael. *Deadly Musings: Violence and Verbal Form in American Fiction.* Princeton: Princeton University Press, 1993.

Krauss, Rosalind. *The Originality of the Avant-Garde and Other Modernist Myths.* Cambridge: MIT Press, 1985.

Kuryluk, Ewa. *Salome and Judas in the Cave of Sex: The Grotesque; Origins, Iconography, Techniques.* Evanston: Northwestern University Press, 1987.

Lentricchia, Frank, and Jody McAuliffe. *Crimes of Art + Terror.* Chicago: University of Chicago Press, 2003.

Lev, Leora, ed. *Enter at Your Own Risk: The Dangerous Art of Dennis Cooper.* Madison, NJ: Fairleigh Dickinson University Press, 2006.

Lewis, C. S. *That Hideous Strength.* 1946. New York: Macmillan, 1965.

——. "The Weight of Glory." In *The Weight of Glory and Other Addresses,* 1–15. 1949. Grand Rapids: William B. Eerdmans Publishing Company, 1965.

Leyner, Mark. "Maximum, Flat-out Drug Overkill: An Interview with Mark Leyner," with Larry McCaffery. In *Some Other Frequency: Interviews with Innovative American Authors,* edited by Larry McCaffery, 219–40. Philadelphia: University of Pennsylvania Press, 1996.

——. *My Cousin, My Gastroenterologist.* 1990. New York: Vintage, 1993.

Leyton, Elliot. *Compulsive Killers: The Story of Modern Multiple Murder.* New York: New York University Press, 1986.

Lipking, Lawrence. *Abandoned Women and Poetic Tradition.* Chicago: University of Chicago Press, 1988.

Little, William G. "Figuring Out Mark Leyner: A Waste of Time." *Arizona Quarterly* 52.4 (1996): 135–63.

Lyotard, Jean-François, and Jean-Loup Thébaud. *Just Gaming.* Translated by Wlad Godzich. Minneapolis: University of Minnesota Press, 1985.

Mailer, Norman. *Ancient Evenings.* 1983. New York: Warner, 1984.

Mandel, Naomi. "'Right Here in Nowheres': *American Psycho* and Violence's Critique." In *Novels of the Contemporary Extreme,* edited by Alain-Philippe Durand and Naomi Mandel, 9–19. London: Continuum, 2006. Mann, Paul. *Masocriticism.* Albany: SUNY Press, 1999.

Marotti, Arthur. "'Love Is Not Love': Elizabethan Sonnet Sequences and the Social Order," *ELH* 49.2 (1982): 396–428.

McCaffrey, Anne, and Mercedes Lackey. *The Ship Who Searched.* New York: Baen Books, 1992.

McCarthy, Cormac. *Blood Meridian, or The Evening Redness in the West.* 1985. New York: Vintage, 1992.

——. *The Road.* New York: Alfred A. Knopf, 2007.

McElroy, Bernard. *Fiction of the Modern Grotesque.* London: Macmillan, 1989.

McHale, Brian. *Postmodernist Fiction.* New York: Methuen, 1987.

McIntyre, Vonda N. *Superluminal.* 1983. New York: Pocket Books, 1984.

Miles, Margaret. "Carnal Abominations: The Female Body as Grotesque." In *The Grotesque in Art and Literature: Theological Reflections,* edited by James Luther Adams and Wilson Yates, 83–112. Grand Rapids: William B. Eerdmans, 1997.

Mitchell, David. "Modernist Freaks and Postmodern Geeks." In *The Disability Studies Reader,* edited by Lennard J. Davis, 348–64. New York: Routledge, 1997.

Monro, D. H. *Argument of Laughter.* Melbourne: Melbourne University Press, 1951.

Moon, Elizabeth. *Moving Target.* London: Orbit, 2004.

Mooney, Ted. *Easy Travel to Other Planets.* 1981. New York: Ballantine, 1983.

Morrow, James. *Towing Jehovah.* New York: Harvest, 1994.

Murphet, Julian. *Bret Easton Ellis's* American Psycho: *A Reader's Guide.* New York: Continuum, 2002.

Nussbaum, Martha. "Equity and Mercy." *Philosophy and Public Affairs* 22.2 (1993): 83–125.

O'Connor, William Van. *The Grotesque: An American Genre and Other Essays.* Carbondale: Southern Illinois University Press, 1962.

Orton, Joe. *Head to Toe.* 1971. New York: Da Capo, 1998.

Ozeki, Ruth L. *My Year of Meats.* 1998. New York, Penguin, 1999.

Palahniuk, Chuck. *Fight Club.* 1996. London: Vintage, 2005.

———. *Invisible Monsters.* New York: Norton, 1999.

Peter, John. *Complaint and Satire in Early English Literature.* Oxford: Clarendon Press, 1956.

Piercy, Marge. *He, She and It.* 1991. New York: Fawcett Crest, 1993.

Pietsch, Theodore W. "Precocious Sexual Parasitism in the Deep Sea Ceratioid Anglerfish, *Cryptopsaras couesi Gill.*" *Nature* 256, July 3, 1975, 38–40.

Pittock, Murray G. H. "The Complaint of Caledonia: Scottish Identity and the Female Voice." In *Archipelagic Identities: Literature and Identity in the Atlantic Archipelago, 1550–1800,* 141–52. Aldershot: Ashgate, 2004.

Pizzato, Mark. "Jeffrey Dahmer and Media Cannibalism: The Lure and Failure of Sacrifice." In *Mythologies of Violence in Postmodern Media,* edited by Christopher Sharrett, 85–115. Detroit: Wayne State University Press, 1999.

Poirier, Richard. *The Performing Self.* New York: Oxford University Press, 1971.

Pollan, Michael. "An Animal's Place." *New York Times Magazine,* November 10, 2002, http://www.nytimes.com/2002/11/10/magazine/10ANIMAL.html.

———. "Power Steer." *New York Times Magazine,* March 31, 2002, http://www.nytimes.com/2002/03/31/magazine/power-steer.html.

Pynchon, Thomas. *Against the Day.* New York: Penguin Press, 2006.

———. *Gravity's Rainbow.* New York: Viking, 1973.

———. *Mason & Dixon.* New York: Henry Holt, 1997.

———. *V.* 1963. New York: Harper Perennial Modern Classics, 2005.

Rabinowitz, Peter J. *Before Reading: Narrative Conventions and the Politics of Interpretation.* Ithaca: Cornell University Press, 1987.

Reed, Ishmael. "Ishmael Reed." Interview with John O'Brien. In *The New Fiction: Interviews with Innovative American Writers,* edited by Joe David Bellamy, 130–41. Urbana: University of Illinois Press, 1974.

———. *The Terrible Threes.* 1989. New York: Atheneum, 1990.

———. *The Terrible Twos.* 1982. New York: Atheneum, 1988.

Rosenblatt, Roger. "Snuff This Book! Will Bret Easton Ellis Get Away with Murder?" *New York Times Book Review,* December 16, 1990, 3, 16.

Ross, Fran. *Oreo.* 1974. Foreword by Harryette Mullen. Boston: Northeastern University Press, 2000.

Roth, Philip. *Portnoy's Complaint.* 1969. London: Corgi, 1971.

Rubin, Martin. "The Grayness of Darkness: *The Honeymoon Killers* and Its Impact on Psychokiller Cinema." In *Mythologies of Violence in Postmodern Media,* edited by Christopher Sharrett, 41–64. Detroit: Wayne State University Press, 1999.

Ruskin, John. "Grotesque Renaissance." Chapter 3 of *The Stones of Venice,* 112–65. 1851–1853. Volume 9 of *The Complete Works of John Ruskin.* New York: Kelmscott Society, n.d.

Salzman, Mark. *Lying Awake.* New York: Vintage, 2000.

Sartre, Jean-Paul. *Nausea.* Translated by Lloyd Alexander. New York: New Directions, 1964.

Schroeder, Randy. "Inheriting Chaos: Burroughs, Pynchon, Sterling, Rucker." *Extrapolation* 43 (2002): 89–97.

Seltzer, Mark. *Serial Killers: Death and Life in America's Wound Culture.* New York: Routledge, 1998.

Shaw, Jonathan Imber. "Cocktails with the Reader Victim: Style and Similitude in Robert Coover's *Gerald's Party.*" *Critique* 47.2 (2006): 131–46.

Sharrett, Christopher. *Mythologies of Violence in Postmodern Media.* Detroit: Wayne State University Press, 1999).

Shklovsky, Viktor. *Theory of Prose.* 1929. 2nd Moscow edition. Translated by Benjamin Sher. Elmwood Park, IL: Dalkey Archive Press, 1990.

Skipp, John, and Craig Spector, eds. *Book of the Dead.* New York: Bantam, 1989.

Slay, Jack, Jr. "Delineations in Freakery: Freaks in the Fiction of Harry Crews and Katherine Dunn." In *Literature and the Grotesque,* edited by Michael J. Meyer, 99–112. Amsterdam: Rodopi, 1995.

Slethaug, Gordon E. *Beautiful Chaos: Chaos Theory and Metachaotics in Recent American Fiction.* Albany: SUNY Press, 2000.

Slotkin, Richard. *The Fatal Environment: The Myth of the Frontier in the Age of Industrialization, 1800–1890.* New York: Macmillan, 1985.

——. *Gunfighter Nation: The Myth of the Frontier in Twentieth-Century America.* New York: Atheneum Press, 1992.

——. *Regeneration through Violence: The Mythology of the American Frontier, 1600–1860.* Middletown: Wesleyan University Press, 1973.

Sontag, Susan. *Against Interpretation and Other Essays.* New York: Delta, 1966.

Stallybrass, Peter, and Allon White. *The Politics and Poetics of Transgression.* Ithaca: Cornell University Press, 1986.

Stinson, Emily J. "*Blood Meridian*'s Man of Many Masks: Judge Holden as Tarot's Fool." *Southwestern American Literature* 33.1 (2007) 9–21.

Storey, Mark. "'And as things fell apart': The Crisis of Postmodern Masculinity in Bret Easton Ellis's *American Psycho* and Dennis Cooper's *Frisk.*" *Critique* 47.1 (2005): 57–72.

Sturgeon, Theodore. "If All Men Were Brothers, Would You Let One Marry Your Sister?" In *Dangerous Visions,* edited by Harlan Ellison, 346–89. London: Gollancz, 1987.

Sukenick, Ronald. "The Death of the Novel." 1969. In *The Death of the Novel and Other Stories,* 41–102. Normal, IL: FC2, 2003.

Thomson, Philip. *The Grotesque.* London: Methuen, 1972.

Truettner, William H., ed. *The West as America: Reinterpreting Images of the Frontier, 1820–1920.* Washington, DC: Smithsonian Institution Press, 1991.

Virilio, Paul. *Speed and Politics: An Essay on Dromology.* Translated by Mark Polizzotti. Foreign Agents Series. New York: Semiotext(e), 1986.

Vizenor, Gerald. *Bearheart: The Heirship Chronicles.* 1978. Minneapolis: University of Minnesota Press, 1990.

———. *Hotline Healers: An Almost Browne Novel.* Hanover, NH: Wesleyan University Press, 1997.

Vizenor, Gerald, and A. Robert Lee. *Postindian Conversations.* Lincoln: University of Nebraska Press, 1999.

Walker, Alice. *The Color Purple.* 1982. New York: Pocket Books, 1985.

Wallach, Rick. "Judge Holden, *Blood Meridian*'s Evil Archon." In *Sacred Violence: A Reader's Companion to Cormac McCarthy,* edited by Wade Hall and Rick Wallach, 125–36. El Paso: Texas Western Press, 1995.

Warren, Victoria. "American Tall Tale/Tail: Katherine Dunn's *Geek Love* and the Paradox of American Individualism." *Critique* 45.4 (2004): 323–36.

Weese, Katherine. "Normalizing Freakery: Katherine Dunn's *Geek Love* and the Female Grotesque." *Critique* 41.4 (2000): 349–64.

Welch, James. *Fools Crow.* New York: Viking Penguin, 1986.

Wicks, Robert H. *Understanding Audiences: Learning to Use the Media Constructively.* Philadelphia: Lawrence Erlbaum, 2000.

Wilde, Alan. *Middle Grounds: Studies in Contemporary American Fiction.* Philadelphia: University of Pennsylvania Press, 1987.

Wood, Robin. "An Introduction to the American Horror Film." In *American Nightmare: Essays on the Horror Film,* edited by Andrew Britton, Richard Lippe, Tony Williams, and Robin Wood, 7–28. Toronto: Festival of Festivals, 1979.

Yates, Wilson. "An Introduction to the Grotesque: Theoretical and Theological Considerations." In *The Grotesque in Art and Literature: Theological Reflections,* edited by James Luther Adams and Wilson Yates, 1–68. Grand Rapids: William B. Eerdmans, 1997.

Young, Elizabeth. "The Beast in the Jungle, the Figure in the Carpet: Bret Easton Ellis's *American Psycho.*" In Elizabeth Young and Graham Caveney, *Shopping in Space: Essays on America's Blank Generation Fiction,* 85–122. 1992. New York: Grove Press, 1994.

Young, Elizabeth, and Graham Caveney. *Shopping in Space: Essays on America's Blank Generation Fiction.* 1992. New York: Grove Press, 1994.

Zunshine, Lisa. *Why We Read Fiction: Theory of Mind and the Novel.* Columbus: Ohio State University Press, 2006.

INDEX